CHINA'S CHRISTIAN MILLIONS

TONY LAMBERT

MONARCH
BOOKS

First published in the UK in 1999 by Monarch Books
(a publishing imprint of Lion Hudson plc),
Mayfield House, 256 Banbury Road, Oxford, OX2 7DH.
Tel: +44 (0) 1865 302750   Fax: +44 (0) 1865 302757
Email: monarch@lionhudson.com
www.lionhudson.com

Reprinted 2000.
This edition 2006.

ISBN-13: 978-1-85424-748-3(UK)
ISBN-10: 1-85424-748-4 (UK)
ISBN-13: 978-0-8254-6115-6 (USA)
ISBN-10: 0-8254-6115-4 (USA)

Distributed by:
UK: Marston Book Services Ltd, PO Box 269,
Abingdon, Oxon OX14 4YN.
USA: Kregel Publications, PO Box 2607,
Grand Rapids, Michigan 49501.

Most photos taken by the author.

British Library Cataloguing Data
A catalogue record for this book is available
from the British Library.

Printed in Great Britain.

Contents

English-speaking OMF centres

Australia: PO Box 849, Epping, NSW 1710
Tel: 02 9868 4777   email: au@omf.net   www.au.omf.org

Canada: 5155 Spectrum Way, Building 21, Mississauga, ONT L4W 5A1
Toll free: 1 888 657 8010 email: omfcanada@omf.ca   www.ca.omf.org

Hong Kong: PO Box 70505, Kowloon Central PO, Hong Kong
Tel: 852 2398 1823   email: hk@omf.net   www.omf.org.hk

Malaysia: 3A Jalan Nipah, off Jalan Ampang, 55000, Kuala Lumpur
Tel: 603 4257 4263   email: my@omf.net   www.my.omf.org

New Zealand: PO Box 10159, Dominion Road, Balmoral, Auckland, 1030
Tel: 09 630 5778   email: omfnz@omf.net   www.nz.omf.org

Philippines: QCCPO Box 1997-1159, 1100 Quezon City, M.M.
Tel: 632 951 0782 email: ph-hc@omf.net   www.omf.org

Singapore: 2 Cluny Road, Singapore 259570
Tel: 65 6475 4592   email: sno@omf.net   www.sg.omf.org

Southern Africa: PO Box 3080, Pinegowrie, 2123
Tel: 2711 781 0946   email: za@omf.net   www.za.omf.org

UK: Station Approach, Borough Green, Sevenoaks, Kent TN15 8BG
Tel: 01732 887299   email: omf@omf.org.uk   www.omf.org.uk

USA: 10 West Dry Creek Circle, Littleton, CO 80120-4413
Toll free: 1 800 422 5330   email: omfus@omf.org   www.us.omf.org

OMF International Headquarters:
2 Cluny Road, Singapore 259570
Tel: 65 6319 4550
email: ihq@omf.net
www.omf.org

Foreword

God has chosen China, the most populous nation on earth, as a canvas on which to portray his power and love in our generation. It is a huge and amazing portrait. As Tony Lambert observes, "There is no need to sensationalise or exaggerate – the truth speaks for itself." It does indeed. Those who serve that extraordinary Church are constantly brought face to face with the evidence of the Lord Jesus and his work in our times.

It is the more extraordinary when one considers the background to these events. In the 1970s some scholars of the Church were convinced that it had perished under successive waves of persecution and abuse. Others attempted to rewrite their supposed "gospel" in Marxist terms, as though some new kingdom of God were to be revealed through Chairman Mao's now discredited "new man". But the reality is that God has used the weakness of men and women to reveal his power.

In the first chapter, when commenting on an area where 18 per cent of the population names the Name of Christ, Tony sums it up like this: "Who could have imagined in their wildest dreams that the seed originally sown by a one-legged Scotsman and a paralysed Chinese boy would over a century later bear such fruit?" Even as a Scotsman, I have to give the glory to God and not to my one-legged fellow Scot! But what joy that brings: God has done great things in this mighty nation of China in our day and age.

And yet so few believers in the West, and even in the churches of other Asian nations, seem either to know what God has done in China or, even worse, to care whether or not they know. God has done something special in that land in recent years. We need to learn from it, and to serve his Church there.

Tony's book is a much-needed analysis of these events and with that, an inspiration to understand and embrace them. It covers all of China's provinces, and includes God's work in the official and the unofficial church. It thus offers us clear and factual evidence of this most extraordinary activity of God.

For many years I have respected Tony Lambert for his courage, his scholarship and his zeal for the Lord. His courage because he stands on the truth of what the Lord shows him, and does not bend to more popular winds. His scholarship, because he can read Party documents (and other material) in their original characters, something that very few – including myself as a fluent Mandarin speaker – can do. His love for the Lord, because this is not a book about theory; it is a book about the Lord whom Tony loves, and about what he is saying and doing in our day.

Tony has researched his subject carefully and widely. Some of his positions might not be universally embraced – for example, where there is uncertainty about the number of believers, he has cautiously taken a lower figure than some sources suggest. But even where people might disagree with him, none who know him would ever question the depth and compelling quality of what he writes.

I hope that this book is widely read, so that the silent story of China's Church, masked behind official statements, might be more clearly heard. I pray that it will create a wider interest in this great and special land. The most populous nation on earth and, arguably, the fastest-growing Church on earth, must receive more prayer and attention from the Church worldwide. I hope, too, that many in the West, who sincerely pray for revival in their own land, would research this excellent manual to see what revival has meant in China today.

"There is no need to sensationalise or exaggerate – the truth speaks for itself." It does, but only when it is heard and received. I pray that this might be the role of this book.

Ross Paterson
Singapore
May 1999

From the General Director of OMF International

China's Christian Millions by Tony Lambert is the fruit of three decades of research, reflection and writing. It is a work of love, reflecting the author's commitment to Christ and to the Chinese people.

On the eve of the Cultural Revolution, Tony Lambert was beginning his study of the Chinese language at the School of Oriental and African Studies in London. There in 1965, as a new Christian, he was already reaching out to share the gospel with people from China. But *China's Christian Millions* is not his story; it is rather a penetrating account of God's sovereign work in China, "reviving his Church, deepening the spiritual life of his people and thrusting them out in sacrificial service and evangelism".

China's Christian Millions begins with a moving overview of the current situation – both in the State-approved church as well as in the house church movement. Here the reader discovers that the amazing revival taking place in China is not limited to one or the other. While at the close of the Cultural Revolution in 1978, there was not one single official church open, today there are over 13,000 as well as 35,000 registered meeting points and countless unregistered house churches. Officials now acknowledge that the Church has grown twelve-fold in the space of twenty years. Church leaders told a visiting US delegation recently that 6.5 new churches and meeting points are being established every day throughout China! Tony Lambert reports how Zhejiang Province alone has seen an average annual growth rate of more than 60,000 new believers over the past thirteen years.

The pattern of growth in the house church movement has been even more dramatic. The province of Henan has been described as a "Jesus Nest" by some officials. In one place revival began as a result of a Communist cadre's wife being healed through the prayers of caring Christians when all medical help had been exhausted. Meetings then started in the homes of these party officials. The number of believers just grew. When the missionaries made their reluctant exodus in the early 1950s there were only 120,000 Christians in the province of Henan. Today there are more than 5 million believers meeting in house churches in the rural areas.

In *China's Christian Millions*, Tony Lambert shares moving testimonies of Chinese Christians and their families. It is like the Book of Acts all over again. In Beijing you will meet Professor Wu, the seminary professor who kept the study of the Greek New Testament alive in China and Dr Feng, the nuclear physicist, who taught a Bible class for university students after the main service every Sunday. There is Pastor Lamb who emerged from more than twenty years of hard labour to start a house church in his home that sees 2,000 meeting for worship and Bible study every week. Then you will read the story of the Miao minority Christian pastor, Wang Zhiming, who was commemorated at a service in Westminster Abbey as one of ten Christian martyrs of the twentieth century.

Although there are severe restrictions on the church engaging in children's and youth ministries, one begins to see how vitally important Christian education in the home has been. As in the case of Timothy, the Apostle Paul's co-worker, many believers in China today also trace their spiritual roots to the sincere faith of parents and grandparents.

Along with the explosive evangelism through personal witness and powerful testimony, the impact of gospel radio in evangelism, in discipling new believers and in leadership training has been profound. Had the book been longer, we might have read more about this as about the overseas Chinese, and the influence of Christian professionals from a host of countries.

We are indebted to Tony Lambert for the helpful analysis he provides of factors which have contributed to the revival that is taking place in China. They include:

God's Sovereignty. As he raised up Cyrus in Old Testament times and the Roman Empire in New Testament times to fulfil his purposes, so God has used political leaders in China to prepare for the spread of the gospel. Think of the unification of the country and language; the building of modern road, railway and telecommunication systems; and consider the attack on traditional religion, superstition and idolatry, as well as the attack on Confucianism, which is the traditional ideological foundation of China's intellectuals and civil servants.

China's Christian Millions describes how even the catastrophic political events have played their part in the process of preparation. Consider how Christians who were sent to the countryside in the 1950s and 1960s for hard labour took the gospel with them, and how, following Deng Xiaoping's Programme of economic reform, labourers from remote inland areas have found employment and found Christ in coastal areas with vibrant Christian churches, and have then carried their new-found faith back to their own unevangelised people. Tony Lambert speaks of the Cultural Revolution as "the defining moment which destroyed the utopian illusion of a whole generation and in its devastation of Chinese society and culture prepared the ground for the gospel". What a picture of our sovereign Lord at work!

God's Word. 180 years ago the first translation of the entire Bible in the Chinese language was completed by Robert Morrison. Thus the Protestant Church entered China with a clear affirmation of the Reformation's declaration that the Word of God is the rule for faith and life. The completion of the Union Version in 1919 gave the Chinese Church a Bible in the spoken language from which Christians have been nourished throughout ninety turbulent years of their nation's history. "In China," Tony Lambert writes, "we are confronted with an exciting phenomenon – a grass-roots Church that is orthodox, evangelical and eager to hear and obey God's Word." Though still very inadequate, it is amazing to learn that in March this year the Amity Press in Nanjing celebrated the printing of twenty million Bibles over the past thirteen years!

The Work of the Holy Spirit. Neither the individual nor society can save itself. The bankruptcy of ideology and inadequacy of idealism, the depravity of human nature and corruption of political process have created a spiritual hunger in China the likes of which has never been seen before. It was the Spirit of the Lord who led the prophet Ezekiel to the valley full of dry bones and showed him how by his power they would be reassembled, revived and rallied into a vast army. In no time in Church history have we seen a greater fulfilment of this vision than in China today. The author makes clear that not everything that claims to be Spirit-prompted is. Some leaders have led their followers into heresies or disastrous aberrations of the truth. However, they represent only a fanatic fringe while the larger picture of the Church reveals an authentic, powerful demonstration of the Holy Spirit at work in and through God's people.

Christians who take their faith seriously. This fact is expressed by men and women who are serious about repentance, serious about the cross of Christ and walking in obedience to God's will, serious about worship in spirit and in truth, serious about prayer in its multifaceted dimensions of praise, thanksgiving, confession, intercession and petition, serious enough about their faith to accept suffering and death rather than abandon it, and serious about faith that is holistic, incarnational and full of the love of Jesus. Over and over again, Tony Lambert describes how it is the love of individual Christians that has overcome hostility, prejudice, anger and indifference.

China's Christian Millions will stir you to praise God for what he has been doing and to pray for what he will yet do. It will challenge you to consider dimensions of the unfinished task of evangelism in China and the world and the part the Lord wants you to have. But, above all, it will humble you as you review your own spiritual life and ponder what God can do with a life totally committed to him.

David Pickard
OMF International Headquarters, Singapore
June 1999

A glossary of useful abbreviations

CCC China Christian Council. Founded in 1980 as a twin organisation to the TSPM (see below). The TSPM and CCC are colloquially known as the "two committees" (*lianghui*), and in practice the TSPM controls the CCC. Top leadership positions of both organisations in many cities are held by the same person. The CCC is responsible for reopening churches and seminaries, printing Bibles and Christian literature and the more overtly spiritual side of State-supervised religion in China.

CCP Chinese Communist Party. Founded in 1921, it took control of all Mainland China (except Taiwan) in 1949 after a bitter civil war. In 1999, it celebrated its 50th anniversary of taking power. There are about 60 million CCP members in China.

NPC National People's Congress. China's "parliament". It has limited powers, largely rubber-stamping Party decisions, but in recent years has become more vocal.

PLA People's Liberation Army. It numbers about 3 million (down from 4.7 million in the early eighties).

PRC People's Republic of China. Officially established on 1 October 1949 by Mao Zedong from the rostrum overlooking Tiananmen Square in Beijing.

RAB Religious Affairs Bureau. An organ of the government for control of all religious affairs, especially the five recognised religions: Buddhism, Daoism, Islam, Protestantism and Catholicism. Now known as 'SARA' - 'State Administration for Religious Affairs'

RMB Renminbi (lit: "People's Currency"). In early 2006 approx. 14RMB = £1 and 8RMB = 1US$. Many rural people earn less than 100RMB per month.

TSPM Three-Self Patriotic Movement. An organ founded in the early fifties by "patriotic" and – theologically – mainly liberal Christians with the encouragement of the Party. It supervised the destruction of all independent denominations by 1958. It became moribund during the Cultural Revolution (1966–1976) but was reinstituted at Party behest in 1979. Today it is responsible for relaying Party religious policies to Christians at the local level, and reporting back to the Party.

UFWD United Front Work Department. An organ of the CCP which supervises the rallying of non-Communists in every area of life, including religion, to support CCP policies.

MEDIA

AFP Agence France Presse
ANS Amity News Service
NCNA New China News Agency
TF *Tianfeng* ("Heavenly Wind"). The monthly (and only) Christian magazine published nationally in China by the TSPM/CCC.

1

Transformations

Beijing in 2006. A city constantly reinventing itself. New ring roads snake round the inexorably advancing suburbs. The once ubiquitous cyclists are in danger of becoming an extinct species – the highways are clogged with traffic spewing gases into a leaden, polluted sky. Wangfujing is a fashionable pedestrian precinct with vast shopping malls where Starbucks and McDonald's stand next to chic foreign designer boutiques. The endless tourists gawp while Western businessmen hurry by in earnest conversation with Chinese counterparts. The mobile phone seems an apt symbol of this restless, self-confident, materialistic society, already bracing itself to welcome the world to its gleaming luxury hotels when in 2008 Beijing hosts the Olympics.

Beijing in 1976. A very different, drab, sad world of run-down back lanes with ancient courtyard homes (Thirty years later largely torn down by frenzied development). In Wangfujing a sea of people in khaki green or blue Mao jackets jostle outside the one frowzy department store. In corners of courtyards, piles of half-rotten cabbage are piled alongside coal-dust briquettes to see the impoverished populace through the bitter winters. The endless phalanxes of cyclists pedal wearily past the huge red and white billboards of Mao Thought – "Take Class Struggle as the Key Link". Indeed, life is a constant struggle – just to survive. Eggs, meat and fresh vegetables are in short supply. Vicious political struggle at the top makes people wary. Zhou Enlai, the last hope of the moderates, has died of cancer. Brief riots in Tiananmen Square have been bloodily suppressed. The Gang of Four, including Mao's unpopular wife, are riding high. The Chairman himself is rumoured to be dying. Better to keep one's head down, and hope against hope for better times...

1976–2006 – in a brief three decades China has totally transformed itself. The economic reforms begun by Deng Xiaoping in 1979 have made China an economic superpower. For more than a decade the annual growth rate has been 9 per cent – while Japan has been stagnant and Europe has aimed at 2 per cent. China has become the "workshop of the world", pouring forth from the factories of Shanghai and Shenzhen an endless variety of goods – firstly cheap textiles but now increasingly computers and electronics. In 2005 when Beijing revalued the RMB against the dollar (it is the dollar that is the weak currency) the world markets trembled. Washington blocked the Chinese takeover of an American company. Earlier, Spanish leather workers faced with the closure of their uncompetitive company rioted and burned down a Chinese shoe factory. Europe and America are simply unable to compete with a seemingly endless supply of Chinese cheap labour, fuelled by the mass migration of peasants to the cities in search of work.

In China itself the private sector roars ahead while old State-controlled firms rust into obsolescence. The new urban middle class fuels a growing consumerism. In the old Mao days a bicycle was everyone's dream. Now, foreign cars, expensive clothes and cosmetics are the must-have trinkets. Over 100 million Chinese are linked to the Internet and it goes without saying that virtually everyone in the cities has a mobile phone. In June 2005, peasants in Hebei protesting against the illegal confiscation of their village land for redevelopment filmed the pitched battle they fought against corrupt officials and developers on video and circulated it worldwide to the media.

The Communist Party remains dominant politically and Mao's portrait still hangs over the entrance to the Forbidden City. The one-Party Leninist State is about the only part of the Maoist heritage to which the Party fiercely clings. To maintain power it has cleverly reinvented itself. After the 1989 Democracy Movement, the Party saw the rise of the new entrepreneurs and middle class as a potentially threatening new power base. So it has opened the doors of Party membership to budding capitalists, slyly co-opting the very class that might have grown to oppose it. The fig leaf of "socialism with Chinese characteristics" covers a raw capitalism under which almost anything goes.

The Party struggles to ride the tiger of high-speed economic development. Alongside genuine improvement of the standard of living for the majority of the population, it has its downside. Some 200 million peasants are in the process of leaving permanent impoverishment in the countryside for a better life in the cities. When Mao took power 90 per cent of the Chinese people were rural; by 2020 (if not before) the ratio of rural to city dwellers will be 50 per cent to 50 per cent. The greatest mass migration from countryside to town in human history is under way. It dwarfs the British Industrial Revolution by ten to one. The latter took over a century – the Chinese version is squeezed into just 30 years. The authorities admitted that in 2004 there were over 70,000 protests – some of them violent – across the country. Ordinary people are incensed by official corruption and the greed of developers who land-grab, even demolishing entire villages.

The fallout from all this is growing social disorder. The gap between rich and poor, far from being narrowed, is becoming wider. The government is seriously concerned and from time to time launches anti-corruption campaigns. They seem largely ineffectual. Can a Party that has remained in power for over half a century and ruthlessly suppressed all opposition genuinely reform itself? It seems doubtful.

A new Five-Year Plan for 2006–2010 was approved in October 2005, focusing on improving people's livelihoods, not just breakneck growth, and on ensuring the benefits of growth are divided more equally. The government has already poured money into developing infrastructure in the poor western areas such as Xinjiang and Tibet. However, unrest simmers just beneath the surface. In the cities, many migrant peasants turn to begging, crime or prostitution in their desperation. Urban workers thrown out of inefficent State-run industries stand on street corners with pathetic pieces of cardboard stating "carpenter" or "labourer", desperately seeking work. And those lucky enough to find work on booming construction sites often are cheated of their wages. A world recession or an economic downturn in China itself could lead to serious political and social instability.

Economic insecurity is mirrored by increasing moral and spiritual confusion. The old Confucian moral order was largely swept away by Mao, and then the collapse of Maoism itself left a yawning moral void. The divorce rate is soaring and it is common for young people to sleep together before marriage. AIDS is on the increase, as is drug-taking, not just in the Golden Triangle in the south-west but across the country.

People are looking for answers and seem willing to try anything. In 1999 the government was rocked to its core when 10,000 Falun Gong devotees demonstrated in central Beijing. Seemingly coming out of nowhere, and blocking the top Party leadership compound, Falun Gong was seen as the greatest rival to the Party, far surpassing any democratic stirrings that have been nipped in the bud. The movement, which had infiltrated senior Party circles, was quickly outlawed and ruthlessly suppressed. Falun Gong cleverly used modern technology such as videos and DVDs to spread its syncretist message – a mishmash of Buddhism, Daoism and New Age with a benign exterior of physical exercises and a darker, demonic core. A whole array of other cults has sprung up, many of them pseudo-Christian. The most dangerous is currently Eastern Lightning, which preaches a Chinese, female Messiah and uses gangster methods to win and keep converts.

But genuine spiritual transformation is to be had. In fact, the spectacular growth of the Christian gospel is transforming China spiritually, and on a massive scale. In 1976 there were no churches open (apart from two for foreign diplomats and visitors). In 2006 there are over 50,000 registered Protestant churches and "meeting-points" – as well as a vast number of unregistered house churches. In 1949 when the Communists took power there were only 700,000 Protestants – today there are officially 17–20 million – over twentyfold growth. (The real figure which includes the house-church believers may well be over 60 million.) This means China is well on the way to having the largest evangelical Christian community of any country in the world, already rivalling that in the United States in terms of numbers.

In 1976 the church was a tiny, often frightened and persecuted minority. Today, Christians are open about their faith and vibrant in their evangelism. There has been a sea change in China in attitudes towards the faith. Thirty years ago many still believed the Maoist propaganda that Christianity was no more than a "tool of Western imperialism" and no self-respecting young person would have dreamed of darkening the doorstep of a church – even if any had been open. Today, public perceptions are very different. Ordinary people, themselves not believers, generally regard Christians as good people and Christianity as a "good thing". The loving witness of individual Christians – and increasingly of corporate action in social-service projects – has had a profound impact.

Remnants of Maoist attitudes still linger in some Party circles and, ironically, in the higher echelons of the Protestant Three Self Patriotic Movement (TSPM) itself. In 2003 Luo Guanzong, a former TSPM leader, published a long book on the "History of How Imperialism Used Christianity to Invade China". Such fossilised ideology is openly laughed to scorn by serious academics in Chinese universities. In fact, there are so many intellectuals seriously researching the influence of Christianity on Western culture and history that they have been dubbed "Culture Christians". Institutes for Religious Studies have sprung up in many universities and theology is openly studied and debated by students at Beijing University and many others. Seminars are eagerly attended by not just the "Culture Christians" but many committed Christian students from both the TSPM and house churches. Today, most universities and colleges have some form of Christian meeting for students or faculty, albeit low-key, as religious meetings are still officially banned on campus.

In 2004–2005, as I visited packed TSPM churches in Beijing, Shanghai, Hangzhou, Urumqi, Chongqing and elsewhere, it was hard to believe I was in the same country I had first lived in thirty years ago. Then, I had found churches either derelict and boarded up or turned into factories or warehouses. Today, Christians poured into huge churches for several services on Sunday, often having to squeeze into overflow halls fitted with CCTV. Many already large urban churches have had to tear down their original premises to erect much larger edifices of five or six storeys. The church in Urumqi, the capital of the Uygur region of Xinjiang, is a good example. When I first visited in 1985 about 100 Christians were meeting in a poorly-lit shack. Returning 20 years later I discovered 3,000 meeting on Sundays in four halls on four different storeys of a large, modern church building.

The Christian revival in China is hard for jaded, post-Christian Europeans to fathom or even accept. Certainly it is time that academia in the West seriously studied the phenomenon of Christian continuity and growth from before 1949 right through till the present day, rather than relegating Christianity in China to a 19th-century or early 20th-century missionary pigeonhole.

The visibility of the Christian church in China with its large congregations of thousands testifies to a deeper, spiritual transformation in changed lives. This was very apparent to me on a visit to a Beijing house church in late 2005. The young professional couple who invited me to their pleasant apartment had no qualms about inviting me to their home, as would have been the case years ago (and even now in some more tightly controlled areas). Indeed, I found that three other foreigners had been invited, along with about fifteen local believers.

The Chinese Christians shared their testimonies of how they had come to faith in Christ. One was a young professor of physics at a leading university. In stark contrast, a woman and her daughter were migrant workers who had been begging on the streets. Christians had come across them and given them food and money, and helped her find a job. As a result they had both believed in Jesus Christ. A little boy of nine or ten shyly told us how he, too, was a Christian. A middle-aged man shared his vision with passion to get proper Bible and cross-cultural training to go out and spread the gospel to remote minority tribal peoples in SW China. Looking at their shining faces I saw a microcosm of the church in China – eager, vibrant, positive and confident in God.

Christian faith in China has triumphed in the face of adversity. Although the savage, relentless persecution of the 1950s and the Cultural Revolution days (1966–76) is long gone, for some in the house churches and occasionally even those sheltering under the broad umbrella of the TSPM State church, arbitrary repression leading to arrest and even imprisonment is by no means past. Recently, in one city, a house-church leader told me how his elder brother had been sentenced to three years "re-education through labour". He was released only in 2004. It was still too dangerous to visit him directly. The older "patriarchs" of the house churches are still suspicious of government intentions, and virtually unanimous in rejecting the option of registering their meetings. This has again been dangled before them in new Religious Regulations promulgated in March 2005. By the end of the year my enquiries revealed that no house churches had registered. They fear being drawn under TSPM control. The only exceptions were one or two younger, educated leaders in Beijing who were considering registration (while remaining clear of the TSPM) as an avenue that might provide legal cover for the house churches to take part more openly in social-service projects at the neighbourhood level.

In the cities I visited in 2003–05 house churches were generally functioning half in the open with a new boldness in evangelism. It seems unlikely that in the remaining time of the run-up to the Olympics the government would risk alienating international opinion by any large-scale crackdown. But China is a large place, and religious policy is implemented according to local conditions and often at the whim of local cadres. In November 2005 reports came out of a house-church pastor in Henan who was arrested while the police were searching for his son. The son bravely turned himself in to secure his father's release, but both were held under arrest. House-church historian Zhang Yinan was released at the same time, but cautioned by police as to what he could and could not say in future. Christian businessman Tong Qimiao was tortured by government agents and ended up in hospital with a broken chest bone. He was warned by them not to publicise the attack, but he plans to sue. His boldness is shared by other believers who are now not prepared to meekly suffer unjust persecution, but are willing to speak out and seek the limited legal redress open to them. This is a major difference in the situation from even ten years ago, when few persecuted Christians were prepared to speak out. Now, many detailed cases are freely circulated on the Internet.

At the heart of church growth and revival in China is personal transformation by the living Christ through the power of the Holy Spirit. At root, the church, whether house church or TSPM-related, is firmly biblical. The authority of the Bible is taken for granted as a divinely given axiom. Bishop Ding of the TSPM has bemoaned the fact that the vast majority even within the State-supervised church are evangelical or even – to use a pejorative term – "fundamentalist". Destructive critical theology, which has devastated the Western church, is still largely unknown, or kept at bay, at the grass-roots level. It is true that since the infamous Jinan Conference in Shandong in 1998 Bishop Ding has headed a "theological construction" movement within the TSPM seminaries, the thinly disguised aim of which has been to cut the church's conservative evangelical moorings and guide it down a theological cul de sac. Ding's "new theology" is a turgid blend of Marxism, liberal Christianity and process theology. His cleverly cloaked denials of the sovereignty and holiness of God, the centrality of the atonement, the uniqueness of Christ and the importance of justification by faith are surprisingly close to dangerous trends such as the new "openness theology" threatening Western evangelicalism. It is ironic that the best theologically educated pastors and students within the TSPM churches are precisely those who have seen this new theology as bogus. Some Christian academics at Nanjing Seminary have paid for their outspoken opposition by being dismissed, as have a number of students and graduates. Few within China have been fooled. Indeed, many are grateful the controversy has come out into the open and that Ding and the top political TSPM leadership are finally revealed in their true colours. They find it hard to credit that some evangelical seminaries and leaders overseas still take it all at face value. They are spearheading a new movement of educated young church leaders bridging both the TSPM churches and the house churches, and seeking to develop an authentic evangelical and biblical theology which can deal with the pressing problems facing them in modern Chinese society. In many areas of China, pastors within the TSPM churches pay lip service to the new movement – which they view as a throwback to the political movements of the Mao era – but in reality carry on with the urgent work of pastoring and preaching the authentic gospel of Christ.

The sheer tenacity of the Chinese Church in holding to, and holding forth, the certainties of Christian faith are a challenge and a rebuke to a Western church ground down by secularism and a loss of nerve. The Chinese Church may lack academic sophistication (although a new, younger generation is showing a refreshing ability to wrestle with relevant theological and social issues). There can be no doubt about its robust faith in the Bible and in the centrality of the atonement, which is the basis for a deep spiritual experience open to the supernatural working of God.

A good example of this was when I unexpectedly came across a group of some 200 Wenzhou Christians holding their own fellowship meeting 1,000 miles away from home in a large TSPM church in Chongqing. While a group of young mothers sat with babies on their laps at the back of the church, the rest of the congregation had fallen to its knees in prayer. Two men led from the front. Their prayers centred on the efficacy of the shed blood of Jesus Christ for the full forgiveness of sins. The congregation all prayed simultaneously and loudly, many weeping and agonising in prayer. Unlike at some Western conferences, where emotions are worked up artificially from the front, I felt deeply humbled in the presence of raw, genuine emotion. Here were working people facing many family and social pressures. The cross of Christ was being lifted up as the only final answer to sin and self. Many were openly repenting and rededicating themselves to God.

It has been my steadily growing conviction over more than twenty years that we in the West need to learn from what God has done and is doing in China. In an era of superficial spirituality and spurious movements that have falsely claimed revival, it is vital that we learn lessons from God's people who have experienced genuine renewal. The vast growth of the last thirty years did not suddenly spring out of nowhere. The ways of God are mysterious – "behind a frowning providence He hides a smiling face". Revival is rarely instant, still less can it be manufactured or called down by man. The gracious purposes of God for China have been fulfilled over many decades, even centuries. Seeds sown a century or more ago are only now bearing fruit. God is Lord of history and works through history. Spiritual principles have been at work – of seed-time, patient watering and harvest, and of a bitter winter of suffering before the bursting out of spring.

2

Seeds of revival

The year was 1868. The port of Wenzhou on China's south-eastern coast had escaped the ravages of the pseudo-Christian Taiping Rebellion which had devastated southern and central China over the previous decade. The Taipings, who had read a few Christian tracts and created a weird mish-mash of Old Testament religion and native Chinese folk belief, had smashed every Buddhist and Taoist temple in their path. But Wenzhou had been spared. As a result, when George Stott of the China Inland Mission first set foot in the city in 1868, the place was full of temples and idols. Like the apostle Paul nearly two millennia earlier, his heart was stirred within him.

But preaching the gospel was no easy matter. China had only recently opened up its coastal ports to Western missionaries as a result of the "unequal treaties" which had been forced upon her by Great Britain and other European powers following the iniquitous Opium Wars. Chinese officialdom was edgy and hostile and often stirred up the local populace to riot and attack missionaries. However, eventually George Stott secured a foothold, renting a modest room which he turned into a school room to attract local boys. There he taught the "three Rs" and, of course, the Bible.

Gradually, opposition was broken down. George Stott was no threat. A quiet, polite Scotsman, he dressed in a Chinese gown and slippers to blend in as best he could. Moreover, he had only one leg. His wooden peg doubtless attracted merriment and curiosity from the local lads. Some began to show genuine spiritual interest.

A few years passed. Some new believers were baptised and a small church was formed. One of the young Chinese boys who believed was himself handicapped. Paralysed down his left side he could walk only with some difficulty; however this did not quench his hunger for God, nor dampen the clear call to preach which he eventually felt. He became the first native Chinese evangelist in Wenzhou. The gospel spread, and a decade later the China Inland Mission built a large church capable of seating several hundred in the centre of the city. Unlike some of the gothic cathedrals placed insensitively by some western missions in other Chinese cities, this church was built in Chinese style. Its low, graceful Chinese roof seemed to say that, after all, the true gospel was no threat to China and the message of Jesus could make itself authentically heard in Chinese dress.

Decades passed. In 1911 the Manchu dynasty collapsed and was replaced by a Republic. High patriotic hopes were dashed as the country soon fell apart among avaricious war-lords. It was not unknown for the downtrodden peasants to have to pay taxes a century in advance. The age-long miseries of famine and flood were capped by the Japanese invasion in the 1930s. Millions moved west in a tidal wave of refugees to escape their cruelties. The war ended in 1945 only to be quickly succeeded by a drawn-out civil war between the Nationalist government forces of Chiang Kai-shek and the disciplined peasant troops of the Chinese Communists, led by Mao Zedong.

In 1949 when Mao finally triumphed and declared the "People's Republic", the church in Wenzhou had survived more than seven decades of tribulation. Several thousand Christians still worshipped in the city and in the surrounding smaller towns and rural villages. But greater testing was to follow. By 1952 foreign missionaries all had to leave. The Chinese Church had to stand alone. A series of intense political campaigns squeezed the Church into submission. Pastors were politically "re-educated" and many sent to labour camps as "rightists" and "counter-revolutionaries". By 1958 most churches were closed. In 1966 Mao unleashed the fanatical Red Guards. The last few churches in Wenzhou were closed down, as happened across China. Wenzhou was declared an "atheistic zone" and intensive efforts were undertaken to wipe away the very thought of God from the minds of the people, and especially the young.

For more than two decades (1958–79) the church in Wenzhou disappeared into deep darkness. Overseas, many academics and even missionary researchers agreed with the words of one American professor who, in 1973, stated: "The evangelicals' few Chinese converts were swallowed up by history, leaving scarcely a visible trace."

But he was wrong.

The church now: an explosion of gospel witness

In the summer of 1997 and again in 2004 I visited Wenzhou. The city has taken full advantage of the economic reform programmes initiated by Deng Xiaoping since the early 1980s. Unlike many Chinese cities, it is clean and neat, evidence of civic pride. Wenzhou is famous for its entrepreneurs who have helped raise living standards to among the highest in China, comparable with Shanghai or Canton. The peasants in the surrounding rural areas are also among the most prosperous in the entire country, building two or three storey villas, often decorated with ornamental tiles showing traditional Chinese landscapes. But I had come mainly to see what evidence there was of the survival of the church.

The former CIM church was still in the centre of the old city, overlooking a busy street market where farmers sold every conceivable kind of fresh meat, fish and vegetables. A Bible verse (John 3:16) inscribed on the wall, was a witness to the teeming passers-by, as was a large red cross gracing the traditional Chinese roof. I walked inside a rather dilapidated courtyard to attend the Sunday morning service to find over a thousand Chinese crowded into the main worship hall. The hymns were rousingly sung, a sermon lasting nearly an hour (common in China today) was preached, and then several hundred Christians remained behind for a communion service.

The pastor, quite a young man, invited me to stay for lunch. He told me the church had been reopened in 1979 after the debacle of the Cultural Revolution. Today, in the entire Wenzhou Municipality which has six million inhabitants, there are more than 600,000 evangelical Protestants – ten per cent of the population! Wenzhou, which only three decades ago was an "atheistic zone" is now popularly known among Chinese Christians as the "Jerusalem of China".

Today, greater Wenzhou has over 2,000 church buildings officially open for worship. In addition there are over 2,000 registered "meeting-points" which are more simple venues for worship, often in rural areas, but also usually attended by hundreds of people. Then there are also many unregistered house churches which meet more clandestinely. In less than two decades there has been a positive explosion of gospel witness across the entire region.

The packed congregation at the former CIM church was proof of the continuing, growing evangelism in the heart of the city. In fact, there are so many new believers that the church, now over a century old, is bursting at the seams. There are plans to knock it down and erect a much bigger, modern building to accommodate the thousands of believers. A pity, in that a historic monument of the early mission days will disappear. But no doubt George Stott and his Chinese helpers would heartily approve.

A church every kilometre

It is in the rural areas that the revival is most apparent. I hired a taxi and travelled outside the city for some fifty miles, to visit two large towns, passing through many villages and townships on the way. After a ferry crossing we found ourselves in the main township of Yongjia, a satellite county which is part of the Greater Wenzhou Municipality. On a small hill a gigantic church towered above the other modern blocks of flats, offices and shops. Large Chinese characters over the entrance gate proclaimed "the Gate of Salvation" – the name of the church. I was greeted by a friendly, elderly hunchbacked man who was one of the elders of the church. He showed the interior of the church with pews and a gallery to seat 1,000 people. The church was beautifully built in marble-like stone. Proudly he told me that not a penny had been given by the government towards the cost, which had been "very expensive". It had all come from the free-will donations of the local farmers and workers. The church was at least 150 feet high with a huge red cross raised on its Italianate-style cupola. "Look across the valley," the elder said. I did so, to see an even more enormous church rearing out of the rice-fields only half-a-mile away. He beamed: "Here, every kilometre or so we have built a new church!"

This was no exaggeration. Over the next four hours driving through the region I must have seen more than a dozen churches, and doubtless missed as many more, in every village and hamlet we passed through. Nearly all appeared to have been erected in the past decade. Just as remarkable was the open Christian witness of many of the local inhabitants who had pasted Bible verses and crosses over their doors. Some modern blocks of flats had "Emmanuel" engraved in large Chinese characters on their fancy tiled facades.

The elder told me that Yongjia County with a total population of 730,000 has a registered evangelical Christian (adult) population of 130,000 souls. This does not include children under eighteen, nor, presumably, many unregistered house church believers.

The implications are staggering – here in the lush, southern Chinese countryside on the outskirts of a modern, port city, 18 per cent of the population are officially recognised to be Bible-believing Christians!

One may ponder further – where in Britain, or for that matter the whole of Western Europe, is there such a high percentage of evangelical Christians in a comparable large concentration of population? Nowhere, to my knowledge.

God's miracle

Who could have imagined in their wildest dreams that the seed originally sown by a one-legged Scotsman and a paralysed Chinese boy would over a century later bear such fruit? Here was evidence that God has done something special in China in recent years. In the West we have talked about revival and some of us have prayed and yearned for revival. But in China the evidence of widespread revival was apparent, even in the cold statistics. God, in an area which twenty years ago was an "atheistic zone" with not a single church open, had worked a miracle of saving grace, raising up a glorious Church.

But why Wenzhou? Why China? This book is an attempt to answer these questions. I hope to give you an overview of the scale of the revival across China since the Cultural Revolution thirty years ago. Based on interviews with Christians in twenty-five of China's thirty provinces drawn from a wide spectrum of both registered and unregistered churches, I will give you direct evidence of the scale of the spiritual awakening. I will even quote what the Communist Party itself has admitted on occasion about the growth of the Church. Then I plan to give some reasons why God has been pleased to work in this amazing way, sharing what Chinese believers themselves have told me. We may close with some sobering truths that the Church in the West needs to learn from our Chinese brothers and sisters. There is no need to sensationalise or exaggerate – the truth speaks for itself.

3

Church growth explosion

Fifteen years ago I was passing through the great city of Lanzhou, capital of the arid northwestern province of Gansu. It was Sunday morning, so I went to the large church that has been reopened for worship in Zhangye Road. I entered through a gateway over which a large red cross was prominently displayed. A banner proclaimed that a special baptism service was being held that very day. The old church had been built by the China Inland Mission and was packed out with people sitting in the balcony as well as in the main part.

Thousands of baptisms

An old lady whom I later discovered was a pillar of the church greeted me and ushered me to the front, where the former baptismal pool had been opened, and filled with water. I asked if I could take photos and was assured this was no problem. Two elderly pastors appeared and walked down the steps into the water and the service began. First the men were baptised, and then the women. It was exhausting work for the pastors, both of whom looked well over seventy. So many people! Young and old they emerged smiling from the waters of baptism. Eventually, as lunch-time neared, I whispered to my companion: "How many are being baptised altogether today?"

"Oh, two hundred and fifty," she replied!

A year or two later I was in Kunming in the steamy, sub-tropical province of Yunnan in southwest China. I attended morning worship at the former CIM church in Wucheng Road. This time I came late, and had to sit upstairs right at the back of a balcony overlooking a packed church. From this vantage point I was to witness about one hundred converts being baptised at the front. In 1997 this historic church was demolished as part of a modernisation programme, and a much larger church is planned for the same site.

Such scenes are common throughout China in many of the registered churches. Unregistered churches also hold baptismal services more clandestinely, often for small numbers of people, but sometimes on a very large scale as well. In 1995 a house church leader in Shanghai reported that he had been invited that summer to take part in a mass baptism in central China where the house church revival is greatest. The believers had poured concrete to build a new baptismal pool in a farm courtyard. The service did not start until 4.00 am while it was pitch dark, so large numbers of Christians could congregate with the minimum risk of discovery. He himself stood up to his waist in the water for six hours continually baptising the new converts. The entire process lasted nine hours until it was past noon. By that time 1,100 new believers had been baptised!

Samuel Lamb's ministry in south China

Lin Xiangao (Samuel Lamb) is a well-known house church leader in the centre of Guangzhou in south China. He preaches to large, unregistered congregations of nearly 3,000 people each week. He has been left relatively free to preach the gospel by the authorities, but has suffered periodic harassment. In February 1990 about fifty police entered the house and confiscated several thousand Bibles and Christian books and tapes, and took him away for interrogation overnight. He is quite fearless and has nothing to hide, so publishes mimeographed booklets of his testimony which give details of the number of people who have come to Christ since he started the house church in 1980.

In 1980 the first baptism was held and four people were baptised. In the next few years over one thousand were baptised. Since the confiscation in 1990 Pastor Lamb has kept detailed records as follows:

TABLE OF BAPTISMS AT PASTOR LAMB'S CHURCH

1991: 265 in six baptismal services
1992: 273 at six services
1993: 357 at seven services
1994: 332 people baptised at six services
1995: 382 people at six meetings
1996: 468 people at six services
1997: 351 people at five services
1998: 428 people at six services
1999: 394 people at six services
2000: 306 people at six baptisms
2001: 346 people at six services.

Pastor Lamb himself writes:

Praise God for his abundant love. King David said it was good for him to be afflicted. In 1955 at our Sunday worship the congregation did not exceed 400 people. After I was released from jail in 1978, it increased from four to over 900 (in three meetings every week). Ever since the confiscation in 1990 until now (1998) it has already passed beyond 1,600 people (in four weekly meetings). The more we are persecuted the more people come to our church. Many times there are not enough seats. Five people are squeezed into pews meant for four and still many people are standing in the street.

People are drawn by the powerful preaching of the gospel by him and his co-workers. He notes, almost in passing:

On 17 December 1992 at the gospel preaching meeting led by my co-worker, there were more than 400 people in attendance. Many were converted.

Huge numbers of converts

Large numbers attracted by the preaching of the gospel, and then converted and baptised, is surely evidence of a powerful movement of the Spirit of God. It would be untrue to suggest that revival is sweeping the entire country, but in many areas the growth of the Church has been staggering, with huge numbers of converts in recent years. It is the biblical gospel centring on the need for repentance from sin, combined with faith in the atoning work of Christ, which is the means of this revival. In a church in Changsha, in Hunan (Mao's home province) I politely gate-crashed a mid-week afternoon catechism class for some ninety new converts in one of the city's large churches. The young pastor gave an excellent basic Bible study on the doctrine of the new birth:

"Why must you be born again? How can you be born again? What are the signs of the new birth? How can you *know* you are born again?" All over China, it is evangelical truth based on the Bible which is an ever-new fountain feeding the streams of renewal and revival.

There is plenty of evidence from official sources of the explosive growth of the Chinese Church. For instance, in 1995 the magazine *Religion* (Zongjiao) which is a publication largely written by government researchers, contained a detailed article on the growth of the church in the northern province of Shaanxi.

> In the early 1950s there were about 30,000 Protestant Christians in the province, but by 1990 they had increased to 125,000, and are continuing to increase at present. Baoji City had about 1,500 Christians in 1950, but now they have grown to 26,000, a 21-fold increase. Tongchuan City on the eve of the Cultural Revolution [1965] had only about 300 Christians; today they have increased to 11,000.

The same writer also noted that in three counties, sixteen Communist Party members and sixty-three leading village cadres had become Christians, which "had had a big influence on the local people". Such admissions have become increasingly common. I should add that by 1997 the total number of Protestants in Shaanxi had increased to 350,000, according to

TSPM figures. In other words, the registered Christian community had nearly tripled in just seven years.

In north China I was once invited to attend the 8.00 am Sunday service at a large city church. The young pastor kindly invited me to stay the previous night. I was woken before 6.00 am by the sound of people entering the church courtyard. By 6.15 am hymn singing could clearly be heard. Puzzled, I asked the pastor: "I thought you said the service started at eight o'clock. Why are all these people here so early?" He smilingly replied, "They come two hours early to ensure they get a seat, and spend the two hours in prayer and worship, preparing for the service." These people who were workers and peasants came to church through the cold north China winter on foot, by draughty public bus, or on bicycles. The church was packed with about one thousand people. The worship was reverent but vibrant, as they sang the hymns with gusto. The preaching lasted about an hour. At the close of the proceedings it was difficult to get out of the door because another eight hundred people were beginning to push into the building for the second service at ten o'clock!

We went for a walk in the park, and I asked the pastor: "How many people are in your congregation?"

"About six or seven thousand."

"And how many people have been converted so far this year?" (It was November 1995.)

"About 1,100 have been converted, baptised and added to our church this year."

In this city, many house meetings had sprung up, and because the gospel was truly being preached at the State-registered church which had resisted political pressures, many independent house church Christians were returning to worship there. There was a great sense of unity.

At another large State church I visited in Anhui, more than a thousand people were crammed into the building. Every side-hall, room, nook and cranny was also filled to overflowing. It was pouring with rain, but dozens of people who could not gain entry into the building were standing quietly under their umbrellas in the church courtyard listening to the preacher's message relayed over a loudspeaker.

People standing in torrential rain for over an hour. People coming in all weathers two hours early to worship God. This, I believe, is more convincing evidence of revival in China than any sensational stories of miracles – although many could be related. Indeed, it is *the* great miracle – on the verge of the 21st century. In a country where Maoism did its utmost to extinguish the very name of God from the consciousness of the people, closed all the churches and indoctrinated several generations in atheistic materialism, the greatest ingathering the Church has seen since Pentecost has been taking place over the past two decades or more.

4

Renewal in the Three-self churches

It was Easter Sunday, 2005. My wife and I were standing in the courtyard of the Gangwashi church in central Beijing. We had just missed the early morning service, and hundreds of people were streaming out of the main church and various side halls where they had watched the service on CCTV. "Let's go for a quick coffee!" I suggested to Frances, as there were still 45 minutes until the next service began. "I don't think that's such a good idea!" she replied. Already, over on the other side of the courtyard a long queue was forming. We joined it, and managed to get seats right at the back of the main hall. The sermon was good, and then we had the joy of witnessing about 30 people being baptised – nearly all of them young. This scene was no doubt being played out in many other churches all over the country. In China over the last twenty years it has been common at Easter and Christmas for 20... or 50... or 100... or even more new converts to be baptised in the large city churches. Yet we should remember that it was not always so.

In early 1979 there were still no churches officially open anywhere in China. However, Deng Xiaoping had come to power and was busy reversing the extreme policies of Mao. As part of his new "open door" policy he decided to return to the limited religious freedom of the early 1950s. The various "patriotic" religious organisations for the five officially-recognised religions (Buddhism, Daoism, Islam, Catholicism and Protestantism) were reactivated, and religious activities again tolerated.

In April 1979 the first church was reopened in Ningbo, Zhejiang Province and by Easter a church had been opened in Beijing. I attended worship there for a few weeks just after the initial reopening. The atmosphere was taut with emotion.

Elderly believers prayed quietly and intensely. "Zhu! Ah, Zhu!" (Lord, oh, Lord!) they whispered, heads bowed. When they went forward to receive the Lord's supper, many had tears streaming down their faces. I realised that they had been deprived of the opportunity of worshipping God publicly for at least thirteen years, since the outbreak of the Cultural Revolution in 1966 when all the churches had been closed. In fact, many had probably not gone to church for twenty years since the Three Self Patriotic Movement (TSPM) closed most of the churches in 1958 under the pretence of "reunification".

Half a million baptisms each year

Since 1979, churches have been reopened with government permission throughout China. By 2001, according to Deng Fucun, the vice-president of the TSPM, there were 16,000 registered Protestant churches open, as well as 32,000 registered meeting-points. Many new churches have been built over the last two decades. Every day six churches are either reopened or newly set up somewhere in China. This is a considerable achievement, and a testimony to the reality of the revival of Christianity in a country where it had been written off as totally extinct only thirty years ago.

In 2004 the TSPM issued a figure of 17 million Protestants in China. This is an extremely low figure, based on baptised or registered adult members of TSPM-supervised churches and meeting-points. It does not include children under the age of eighteen, or the millions of believers who meet in unregistered house churches. However, even if this figure is accepted as the reality, one must bear in mind that as recently as 1980 the TSPM were claiming there were only one million Protestants. Today the TSPM and the government are openly admitting that the Church has grown twelve-fold in the space of twenty years. In the UK, the total number of church members of all denominations ranging from Roman Catholic and Church of England to Pentecostals and Mormons is six million. China, by official admission, already has triple that number of Protestants who are overwhelmingly evangelical and Bible-believing. In fact, in recent years more than half a million people per year have been baptised and received into the TSPM church – and this figure does not take account of vast numbers who have been converted through unregistered house churches.

Reopening a church, let alone building a new one, is no easy task in China. Each church opened reflects the prayer, patience, faith and determination of local Christians often faced with an indifferent, even hostile, bureaucracy. There are huge discrepancies in the numbers of places of worship officially permitted in different parts of the country. Wenzhou, which is a small corner of Zhejiang Province, has seven million people, of whom 10 per cent (700,000) are officially registered as Protestant Christians. Officialdom here has been relatively benign and no fewer than 2,000 registered churches and a further 2,000 meeting-points exist to serve this thriving Christian community. However, Sichuan Province with an enormous population of over 83 million had only 250,000 registered Protestants in 2001 and only 119 churches open in 1996. Shanghai Municipality, which has a population of over 17 million (more than double that of Wenzhou), and a thriving Christian community of at least 187,000 in 2005, only had a total of 165 registered churches and meeting-points open in 2002. Yet before 1949 there were over 200 churches open in the city.

Uneven implementation of policy

In some areas the church is allowed to grow and put up new buildings with a minimum of fuss. In others, local cadres, whose outlook is still governed by Maoist hostility to all religion, obstruct the growth of the church and refuse planning permission. In such cases there is little the believers can do, as appeals to distant central government are usually useless. Even in cases where the church building is finally permitted, much tortuous negotiation is often needed. One elder in north-east China stated that he had to meet local village officials several hundred times, regional officials a hundred times, and county officials at least ten times. Only after three years of such patient negotiation was the church finally built!

In some cases, local officials take a very hostile attitude to the Christian faith. In parts of Yunnan and Inner Mongolia, for example, local cadres have refused to sanction any new church buildings whatsoever. Their flimsy excuse for refusing permission, and also for persecuting the Christians, has been that there never were any missionaries in that particular area in the past, nor any Christian community, so by definition there "cannot" be any Christians in the region now. Their reaction to the spread of the gospel by itinerant house church evangelists to their region is one of total suppression.

Despite such attitudes, and continuing persecution in many areas, the overall situation for the Church in China has shown real improvement since the death of Mao. No one should be in any doubt about the nature of the Chinese government's control of religious affairs and of the registered churches through the Three-Self Patriotic Movement. Its constitution clearly states that its main reason for existence is to pass down the Party's policies and ensure that they are implemented by believers at the local level. No one who has sat with pastors and believers in both the registered and unregistered churches over the last twenty years can ignore the evidence that there is still a high degree of political control operating behind the scenes. Certain pastors are avoided by believers as known collaborators, and as those who betrayed their brethren in the dark days of the 1950s and 1960s. The rift between the TSPM and the unregistered house churches is a fact of life based on years of bitter experience of betrayal and persecution.

And yet… there is a qualitative difference between the situation in most of the registered TSPM churches now, compared with what it was in the 1950s and early 1960s. Then sermons were drearily political and the churches empty of all save a faithful remnant of the elderly and a *coterie* of politically-motivated church leaders whose liberal theology shaded into total and abject collaboration with the Party. Today churches are packed with eager believers clasping their Bibles and hymnbooks and drinking in hour-long sermons. Mostly the preaching is evangelical with the very barest lip-service paid to politics. The churches attract sacrificial service by a whole array of unpaid *yigong* (volunteer workers) both young and old, who preach, visit the sick, counsel, pray and evangelise.

Acting with courage and caution

Many are on fire for God, taking calculated risks for the sake of the gospel as they go right up to (and sometimes beyond) the borders of what is permitted. Many in private are as critical of the political control element in the TSPM as the house church leaders. Yet they have chosen to work within the system. In a very Chinese way, it may be said that they are subverting the system which has been set up to subvert the church. The power of the Holy Spirit enables them to work patiently from within, alongside "colleagues" whose motivation may be totally ideological and political.

In such an environment there are constant dangers which lead Chinese Christians to a total reliance on the Holy Spirit. Intense spiritual warfare is being fought, often quietly and under the noses of the Party cadres and their informers. One pastor in south China told me he baptised many people openly in the church. But then, with a smile, he added he also went out at night and "baptised people in streams and ponds".

In Fuzhou an elder has a foot in both camps (the TSPM and the house churches). He was often invited to preach in the big registered church, and seized the opportunity to preach a series on the Second Coming – a subject strongly discouraged by the more political elements in the TSPM. One day, after he had just finished his sermon, one of the TSPM cadres approached him and angrily denounced him for "preaching against Deng

Xiaoping's 'Four Modernisations Policy' "(!) Calmly, he opened his Bible and told the man that so long as the teaching was in God's Word he would continue to preach it. The TSPM leader angrily stalked off and no more was said about it. It was one more small victory for the cause of Christ. More recently, in East China, I met with a graduate from the prestigious Nanjing Theological Seminary. He lives on the TSPM church compound. He told me that, although highly qualified, he was forbidden to preach by the local pastors who were politically motivated. Then, smiling, he said quietly: "All my effective ministry is with the house churches."

Such interviews with men and women of God who are working under the umbrella of the TSPM are enough to dispel the falsity of blanket-statements, still made by some Christians overseas, that anyone working within the TSPM official churches is necessarily compromised or a Party agent. It is true that in the higher echelons of the movement there are still many leaders who have a very dark reputation. Bishop Ting himself who was, until 1997, the leader of both the TSPM and the China Christian Council, is on record as having complained that the government is too involved in interfering in church affairs and that "we have even seen Communist Party members taken out of the Religious Affairs Bureau and put into the churches as atheistic church leaders".[1] Probably every church has one or two opportunists who act as informers to the authorities.

In some cases pressures may have been brought to bear so that pastors and elders collaborate unwillingly. However, the vast majority of those who attend the so-called TSPM churches appear to be devoted Christians or sincere enquirers. The theology undergirding the registered churches is traditional evangelical teaching (with some exceptions). One has only to compare the pages of the one officially-permitted Christian magazine, *Tianfeng*, as it was published in the 1950s and in the 1990s, to see that the Church has become overwhelmingly evangelical, despite all the efforts of the authorities and the TSPM to steer it into liberal theology. In the 1950s there were turgid articles denouncing Wang Mingdao and American imperialism. Today, although there is the odd article relaying Party policy, most of the magazine is taken up with devotional and spiritual matters.

Social and political opportunities

There is a tension at work within the TSPM system which may in the long run actually benefit the Church. Some of the established leadership seek to teach old-style liberal theology in the seminaries and to channel believers' enthusiasm into social service away from direct evangelism. Some leaders are on record as saying the Church is growing too fast and there is no need to evangelise China's massive population. They clearly adhere to a vague universalism and incarnational Christianity which is uncomfortable with a biblical emphasis on the universality of sin and the centrality of Christ and his atoning blood.

However, the Church at grass roots seems solidly evangelical and happy to use every opportunity offered by the TSPM and the government for social service as an avenue for gospel witness. All over China, Christians are busy setting up medical clinics and advice centres, and repairing roads and bridges. In 1998 when the worst floods in fifty years devastated many areas, affecting up to 200 million people, the churches responded magnificently, raising over four million RMB and donating large quantities of blankets, foodstuffs and medicines for the flood victims.

Such practical demonstrations of Christian love have broken down much prejudice. No longer is it said, as in the old days, "One more Christian – one less Chinese!"

Christians are seen as moral examples and model citizens whose self-sacrificing care often shines out in painful contrast to venal officials who mouth empty slogans about "serving the People". Whereas in the days of Mao, Christians were a despised and suspect minority, viewed as a subversive force linked with foreign imperialism, today there seems much evidence that in the eyes of the general populace, both peasants and intellectuals, Christians are often respected and seen as a force for good in society. Many Christian families have received government awards as model households, and individual Christians have received awards in the workplace.

If Christians in the Three-Self and China Christian Council (CCC) churches can maintain a holistic witness, combining robust evangelical theology with practical social service, they may be poised to make major contributions to Chinese society in the twenty-first century. Many young people studying at the seminaries care deeply for their country and see the gospel as the answer to China's many problems when sensitively applied. This became apparent in 1989 during the student demonstrations in Beijing and many other cities. The house church Christians largely stood aside, as it would have been suicidal for them to take part in any political activity. Also, their theology strongly discourages political and social activism. Ironically, it was Christian TSPM seminary students in Nanjing and Beijing who took to the streets, seizing the opportunity not only to denounce corruption and to call for greater political and religious freedom, but to witness to their faith. In Tiananmen Square at the height of the movement, a small band carried a banner proclaiming "God is Love" and singing hymns, attracting much interest from students and citizens alike.

Political and social activism are dangerous in China today, but as evangelicals have found in the West, biblical standards must be worked out and applied to the problems of modern societies if the Church is not to remain in a ghetto or pushed to the margins of society as an irrelevancy. China is facing many major social problems which need dealing with from a thoroughly biblical position, as in our own Western society. Young intellectuals within the TSPM churches and seminaries are in a key position. If they can avoid drifting into the sterile liberalism which has devastated so many churches and denominations in the West, they will be spiritually and intellectually equipped to provide biblically-based leadership for the Chinese

Church in the next century. Some of the teaching at the seminaries, particularly at Nanjing, is hostile to evangelical theology, and there have been cases of graduates denying the
authority of Scripture and the historicity of the resurrection.
However, many graduates emerge with their evangelical convictions strengthened.

The seminaries – a varied picture

In 2005 there were twelve seminaries and twelve Bible schools
and training centres officially open in China under TSPM/CCC
supervision.

These can be divided into three categories :

1) *National Level:* The Nanjing Union Theological Seminary is
the only one in this category.

2) *Regional:* Five seminaries fall into this category as they all
invite students from several provinces: North-eastern, South-
central, Eastern, Sichuan and Yanjing (Beijing). Yanjing, for
example, has students from across north China as far away
as Xinjiang.

3) *Provincial:* Six seminaries – Shandong, Zhejiang, Anhui,
Fujian, Guangdong and Yunnan; and twelve Bible schools
and training centres: Shaanxi, Jiangxi, Hunan, Henan, Inner
Mongolia, Jiangsu, Hebei (two centres: one at Shijiazhuang
and one at Handan), Gansu, Guizhou, Qinghai and
Heilongjiang.

Competition for places is keen – in the Jinan seminary in
Shandong, about fifty applicants are turned away for every
available place, and this is quite typical. Academic standards
and living conditions vary.

Nanjing and Shanghai are well endowed with money and
facilities. Churches in Shanghai hold a "theological Sunday"
once a year at which the huge congregations (including many

"upwardly mobile" business people) generously donate large sums. A new campus has been built for the seminary. Nanjing, in particular, has received large numbers of theological books from donors worldwide and has a respectable graduate programme.

In contrast, some of the provincial seminaries exist on a shoestring. Their libraries may contain only a couple of thousand books, many of them out-of-date, with a few precious reference volumes carefully kept under lock and key. At one such seminary I visited, the library room did not look in use. The volumes were locked in ancient cupboards and monsoon rains drove through the open windows onto the tables and floor. In another, the premises were nearly a century old and, looking up, one could glimpse the sky through cracks in the roof.

Dormitories are spartan, with a dozen students sharing bunkbeds in a small room. Those from the countryside arrive with a change of clothes, a toothbrush and a Bible – and much enthusiasm. The teachers at these schools are often elderly pastors who have little time or energy to spare from ministering to their huge urban congregations to spend time in careful lecture preparation. Sometimes political pressures also hamper the production of young, godly leaders. In one provincial seminary, a young graduate from Nanjing seminary is forbidden to preach in the church and only allowed to lecture on a volunteer basis because of his staunch evangelical convictions. In another, two graduates left the TSPM system and joined the house churches. Political pressures can ensure that bright young men and women on fire for God are effectively sidelined. After all, the Party religious policy clearly states that the goal of the State-controlled seminaries is to train "people who love the Fatherland, accept the leadership of the Party and the government, resolutely follow the socialist road and have religious learning" – in that order.[2]

Professor Wu's legacy

Fortunately, the system has been able to quench neither the

desire of godly pastors to pass on biblical learning and precious spiritual experience, nor the insatiable hunger of the young people who fill the seminaries. Men such as Professor Wu in Beijing died in harness striving to make up for the lost decades of the 1950s, 1960s and 1970s. Professor Wu had been sent for many years to a labour camp in Heilongjiang, China's Siberia, where temperatures can drop to minus 40 degrees Celsius for many years. He survived, and was released when Deng Xiaoping came to power. After returning to Beijing he was invited to join the seminary to teach Greek. After praying for definite guidance he accepted, despite the doubts of some of his house-church friends. In 1987 he wrote:

> My whole library was lost during the Cultural Revolution. We have no text-books. Every teacher has to write his own text-book. I compiled a grammar of New Testament Greek and translated a book into Chinese for an intermediate Greek course. Now I have just finished the draft of I Thessalonians. This is a commentary based on the Greek text for those who have finished the Greek course in the seminary and begun to study the Greek New Testament. Since we can't find a place here to print a book in Greek, the photocopying is very expensive. Pray for me that I may be spared for some years more to write more books.

God answered Professor Wu's prayer and for nearly a further decade he gave himself to preparing materials to help young seminary students read the New Testament in the original language. Without his heroic labours, the study of New Testament Greek in China would probably have died. As a result of his work, a whole new, young generation is able to go ahead in New Testament studies. The Professor acted as a spiritual mentor to many of his students and actively funded a poor, but promising, country girl who was the daughter of a garbage-collector who would never otherwise have been able to afford to attend seminary. His recent death has left a gap in theological training which will not easily be filled. His life is representative of many unsung pastors and church leaders whose sacrificial labours are the lifeblood of the Chinese revival.

Too few in training

Across China, at present (2006) there are only about 2,000 students in full-time State-registered theological training. Since the 1980s a few thousand have graduated. About one-third of these have since been ordained to full-time ministry, according to the Rev Su Deci, the General Secretary of the China Christian Council. Usually they have to work at least two years in a congregation, and some times even five, before being ordained. This gives them practical experience, but also creates a bottleneck in the provision of trained leadership. Considering the explosive growth of the church to probably over 50 million souls this is but a drop in the bucket. Fortunately, there are other ways of getting at least some rudimentary training. Many thousands who fail to gain entrance can get some part-time Bible-training as *yigong* (part-time workers), usually during the summer months or the agricultural slack season. Nanjing Seminary runs a successful Bible correspondence course for thousands more.

However, the lack of trained pastors and teachers has reached crisis proportions. Yunnan with over 800,000 believers had just 80 pastors by mid-2005 – a ratio of one pastor for every 10,000 believers! In inland Henan the ratio is about 1:45,000! Even allowing for a whole army of elders, *chuandaoren* (preachers) and *yigong* in every province, the situation is very far from ideal. It leaves congregations open to every wind of doctrine from enthusiastic, but extremist, elements in their midst and also makes them vulnerable to the ministrations of cultic evangelists who travel from village to village. In the long term, only an easing of the government stranglehold on theological education, and a massive increase in funding will enable the registered churches to provide the theological education which is so desperately needed, both in quantity and quality, to ensure the Church can pastor the vast numbers of new believers.

Bibles and Christian Literature

By the end of 2004 the Amity Press in Nanjing had printed a total of 38,711,502 Bibles and New Testaments. This considerable achievement has been made possible with the help of the United Bible Societies who have provided modern printing presses and paper, and technical aid. By 2005 there were seventy urban distribution points across China (set up by the China Christian Council) where believers can buy or order Bibles. Forty vans were in service by May 2004 to take Bibles to different places in China. Prices of Bibles are low – the most popular (printed in the "simplified script" which is used everywhere in mainland China as opposed to the "traditional script" still used in Taiwan and Hong Kong) costs only 12RMB. Pocket Bibles are even cheaper at 6.50RMB!

In general, it is not usually difficult for Christians in Chinese cities to buy or order Bibles. Even unregistered house church believers can often buy Bibles themselves or through friends from the CCC outlets in small quantities. From my personal observations over the last decade and more, most Christians in both registered and unregistered congregations have their own Bible which they take to meetings and use for personal study. The situation has completely changed from that of the 1970s when Bibles were scarce and were often laboriously hand-copied.

Supply can't keep up

However, the situation in the rural areas of China where 70 per cent of the population, and probably a similar percentage of Christians, live, is rather different. Many rural Christians are

Table of Bibles printed 1980–2005 within China

1. 1980–87   By presses in Shanghai, Fujian and Jiangsu
All types of Bible	3,000,000

2. 1987–1996   By the Amity Press at Nanjing
Bibles and New Testaments in Simplified Script	11,907,210
Bibles in Old Script (Using "Shangdi" for God)	372,812
Bibles in Old Script (Using "Shen" for God)	314,994
Reference Bibles	409,801
Large Print Bibles (for the elderly)	70,158
The Four Gospels	29,604
Minority Bibles:	
Yi	19,653
Korean	189,487
Miao	30,260
Lisu	75,272
Jingpo	20,027
Dai	2,093
Lahu	9,898
(Total Minority Bibles: 346,690)	

Sub-total of All Bibles/New Testaments Printed 1980–96(end):
                                                   17,180,920

(Source: Shuxun [Book News], No. 2, 20 December 1996, Shanghai)

3. 1997–2005 By the Amity Press at Nanjing
Total Number of Bibles and New Testaments
1997	2,221,721
1998	2,844,228
1999	2,974,943
2000	2,951,703
2001	2,502,318
2002	2,474,281
2003	4,271,573
2004	5,435,656
2005	(Projected) 5,245,375

NOTE: These figures also include some Bibles for export. For example, in 2003 only 2.86 million Bibles were for the mainland, the rest were for export; in 2004 of the 5.4 million Bibles printed, 3.4 million were for distribution in China, 2 million for export. Only in recent years has the export trade grown; the vast majority of Bibles have been distributed within China.

unable to afford to travel long distances to the city depots and even if they do, Bibles may be sold out, having been snapped up by the urban believers. In addition, many house church believers live in these country districts and have little or no contact with the TSPM church.

The evidence, although patchy, suggests that in some areas there is still a shortage of Scriptures, particularly where villages have experienced revival and a great growth of new converts. A few years ago I met house-church leaders who told me that in some villages in Shandong there was only one Bible to fifty or one hundred Christians. On a separate occasion, I was very moved when told that poor, rural believers in north-east China had donated 100RMB to a Christian literature agency in Hong Kong to send them Bibles. The reality of the situation seems to be that neither the supply of Bibles printed within China nor that of Bibles taken in from overseas can quite keep up with an ever-growing demand, especially in the rural areas.

With regard to commentaries, concordances, devotional books, etc. there is no doubt that the Chinese Church has an insatiable demand for all kinds of Christian literature, which is not being met by the CCC. In 2000, the TSPM at its 50th anniversary celebrations announced that it had published 90 different titles of devotional books and commentaries, totalling over one million copies. Though commendable, this is a drop in the ocean. It is no wonder that some 50 privately-run Christian bookshops have sprung up in cities all over China in the last five years or so, or that secular publishing houses in China increasingly are printing Christian titles. Small print runs (usually 4,000–10,000 copies) of interesting books by Martin Luther and C.S. Lewis, as well as a welter of "soft" Christian titles on childcare and marriage by modern authors such as Dr Dobson, seem to escape censorship and attract an avid readership.

The dearth of Christian books is somewhat counteracted by the circulation of Christian DVDs and the fact that educated, urban Christians are able to download much material.

However, on many visits I have made in recent years, TSPM pastors, house-church leaders and theological students are immensely grateful for every Bible commentary or book given them. Quite frequently they produce a list of books they would like to be brought to them on the next visit! Over the last three decades an immense number of books have been taken in from Hong Kong and other places – certainly millions. But this has not assuaged the growing demand. This is unsurprising in view of the tens of thousands of new converts added to the church each year in just one province. Believers in rural areas are particularly prevented by poverty and poor communications from obtaining Christian literature.

5

The house church movement

Dr Su is a sprightly old lady in her seventies who dresses in a neat, black trouser suit. We sat drinking tea in her shady court-yard one warm evening and she quietly began to unfold her life story. As a child of eight, she first heard the gospel from an American missionary, and believed in Christ. Her schooling was disrupted by the Japanese invasion and occupation. She glossed over the horrors and cruelties of that dark period. After the surrender of the Japanese in 1945 she married, but her life was again torn apart by the Civil War. Her husband escaped to Taiwan with Generalissimo Chiang Kai-shek, leaving her to bring up three small children. She never heard from him again as a curtain of separation descended, cutting off the belea-guered Nationalists in Taiwan from their compatriots on the now Communist-controlled Mainland for nearly forty years.

Schooled by suffering

Her sufferings deepened under the Communists. Accused of being an imperialist spy because of her conversion through an American missionary, she was imprisoned for six years and endured the degradation and numbing brutality of labour camp. She was chained so severely that the iron bit deep into her flesh. "But I felt no pain. The Lord supported me," she said quietly. "During those years I prayed continually."

After her release, she started attending a newly-opened TSPM church but rapidly became disillusioned with the degree of State interference and control. So she founded a house church in 1983 which has continued to this day and was instrumental in pioneering other house churches across a wide area of south-ern China. One group I visited in early 1998 had between two and three hundred members. A year later numbers had increased to 900. On occasion Dr Su will pay a pastoral visit to her far-flung flock, gamely riding pillion on a motorbike which takes her along rutted, dusty tracks to remote village house churches in the hills.

The details of Dr Su's story are unique and yet similar experiences were endured by many Christians throughout Mainland China from the early 1950s until the late 1970s. The house churches were born in suffering and have been led by a generation of men and women who were schooled by suffering. Their faith is characterised by complete reliance on the Word of God and they have learnt to walk close to Christ.

House churches have a long history in China. Before the Revolution many small groups of Christians used to meet together in the home for worship especially in areas where there were few believers and no regularised church buildings. Certain indigenous churches which sprang up in the 1920s and 1930s, such as the "Little Flock" founded by Watchman Nee, stressed the importance of close fellowship in small group meetings. After the Communist victory in 1949 they were better placed to survive under the new conditions than the more formal mainline denominations.

Even during the 1950s some groups of evangelical Christians began to meet in their homes as the mainstream churches were taken over by the TSPM and pulpits became increasingly politicised. I remember meeting a Little Flock elder in Hong Kong who assured me that his church in Fujian had first joined the TSPM but withdrew as early as 1952 or 1953; after this they met as an independent house church, and had continued to do so without any interruptions over the years. By the late 1950s the TSPM in its documents and published articles often attacked Christians who were meeting secretly in house churches as politically unreliable. Political campaigns were whipped up against the few Christian leaders who had taken a public stand against the TSPM such as Watchman Nee and Wang Mingdao, both of whom were arrested and sent to prison. Nee died a martyr's death in a labour camp in 1972 but Wang re-emerged in 1980 as a living testimony and encouragement to the many evangelical Christians throughout China who viewed the TSPM with suspicion and were not prepared to compromise.

Because of lack of information and misunderstanding by Western Christians, as well as deliberate disinformation put out by the TSPM and Chinese authorities, even some Western evangelicals came to regard the house churches as dubious and extremist sects who deliberately provoke the authorities into bringing down persecution onto their own heads. However, the heart of the house church movement takes a conscious stand on the authority of Scripture and has worked out a biblical view of church–State relations. Put simply, Christ is the Head of the Church, and while every Chinese house-church Christian sees it as his duty to be a good citizen, he is not prepared to accept State control of Christ's Church through its organ, the TSPM. The house churches seek to worship and evangelise according to the precepts of Scripture, not the various restrictions laid down by the government's Religious Affairs Bureau. If clashes or contradictions arise, then they are prepared to say, like the apostle Peter before the Sanhedrin, "We must obey God rather than men." (Acts 5:29)

What is a house church?

The word is vague and the definition unclear. In the UK the term has connotations with charismatic groups that have split from mainline denominations and even from conservative evangelical churches. In China house churches are overwhelmingly biblical; they are simply groups of evangelical Christians meeting independently in homes, farm-courtyards and fields. There is a strong wing who are charismatic or Pentecostal, but they are not in the majority. In Chinese, the term *jiating jiaohui* is used to mean "house church", often by Christians themselves in their letters; it refers to any independent group meeting in the home. The term *juhuidian* means "meeting point" and it can refer to large churches, registered or unregistered, which meet in various premises, and occasionally even have their own church building. These are to be distinguished from *libaitang* or *jiaotang* (church buildings), which are churches with their own buildings and formal structure registered with the government and the TSPM.

In many areas of China where the Church is strong, the situation can be quite complicated. There are large and small registered TSPM churches. There are also many "meeting points": some have registered with the authorities, others await registration. Some have been refused registration and been formally disbanded. (They usually disperse and spring up again meeting at a different location.) Others refuse to apply for registration. They are therefore illegal and may be suppressed; but sometimes the local authorities turn a blind eye. Such churches are labelled by the authorities as "spontaneous private meetings"; they are called 'house churches' by the believers themselves.

The size of house churches can vary considerably. In most cities they are small – often under twenty people, because larger numbers attract hostile attention from the authorities. (Samuel Lamb's house church of over one thousand in Guangzhou is exceptional.) However, in rural areas they may be very large, numbering hundreds of people. Many house churches function as independent churches. Others consider themselves part of a large, organised network stretching across many provinces, or even the entire country.

"Christianity Fever"

For years the authorities and the TSPM sought to deny the very existence of the house churches as an independent force. However, in late 1988 an internal report prepared by the New China News Agency revealed that in Henan alone the Religious Affairs Bureau had uncovered the existence of more than 2,600 "privately-established meeting-points" (house churches). In Henan also they estimated there were more than 500 "self-appointed preachers" (house church evangelists). Earlier, in Anhui province, local authorities had arrested an elderly preacher formerly associated with the China Inland Mission for wide-scale evangelistic activities. The indictment against him read:

> Apart from engaging in counter-revolutionary propaganda, he also networked across more than ten cities and counties setting up illegal meetings, and baptising more than 3,000 new converts.

Among the four hundred "reactionary books" they confiscated were listed "the Old and New Testaments and the Bible handbook".[1] Such internal reports reveal that the house church movement is very extensive and is often perceived by the authorities as a threat to be suppressed. So widespread is the revival of unofficial Christianity that they have even coined a special term for it: *jidujiao-re* or "Christianity Fever"!

Growth and fragility

Since the late 1970s and early 1980s the house church movement has grown, matured – and splintered. Older house church believers often consider themselves to belong to former denominations or missions in which they were brought up and converted as late as the early 1950s before all such groupings were abolished. Denominational teaching has left deep traces whether conscious or subconscious. In recent years several "streams" – or new denominations – have emerged, coalescing around certain doctrines and/or strong leadership. The input from abroad in the form of gospel radio broadcasts and Christian literature has also had a major impact, helping to crystallise such new groupings within China, and, sadly in some cases, exacerbate divisions.

All the traditional denominations and groupings were abolished when the TSPM forcibly "unified" the churches in 1958. In the providence of God, this has been one of the good things to emerge from the decades of persecution in China. However, there is mounting evidence that the present unity of the churches united under the TSPM and China Christian Council is only paper-thin. Leaders, such as Bishop Ting, have often expressed their concern that the old denominational divisions would re-emerge, given half a chance. Many overseas churches and missions are poised to donate large sums of money to Chinese churches. But sometimes there are conditions attached: that old denominational affiliations be openly re-established. So far the TSPM and CCC have resisted such blandishments. But there are signs that in the near future, as China continues to open up and aid from overseas is accepted and even touted for by the TSPM churches, the dyke preserving the unity and independence of the State churches from foreign control will give way, and many Chinese churches could come under overseas economic control. This would be disastrous, whether from the States, South Korea or Singapore. The house churches are equally vulnerable to such temptations.

On a more positive note, the strong teaching of many conservative evangelical missions and churches laid a firm foundation for the Church in China; this is often referred to by believers with gratitude. Indeed, older Christians sometimes still tell the startled visitor that they are "CIM" or "Baptist" even though these groupings officially disappeared by the mid-1950s. This precious biblical heritage in its various forms has provided strong theological underpinnings for the house church movement. That movement at its central core remains firmly evangelical and conservative (even fundamentalist) in theology to this day. Liberal theology is taught in many TSPM seminaries (alongside evangelical teaching) but has little influence as yet at the grass roots.

Charismatic and Pentecostal groups are growing rapidly in some areas such as Henan, and some extremist groups have caused serious divisions, denouncing other believers (even those who suffered for their faith) as "dead orthodox". However, the clear-cut divisions and denominational boundaries which we are used to in the West do not apply in China. What is one to make of such house church leaders as Pastor Lamb (Lin Xiangao) who is strongly evangelical and pre-millennial in his theology, practices exorcism and prays for healing of the sick, but does not allow speaking in tongues or prophecy at his meetings? The furnace of persecution and the melting pot of different Christians drawn together by the love of Christ have made many of the old labels redundant.

This having been said, some of the older denominations are still alive in China. In the southwest, many tribal churches, mostly linked to the TSPM/CCC, still consider themselves to be "CIM". And in Henan there is a large grouping of conservative Lutherans who meet independently of the TSPM, according to a recent house church statement issued in August 1998. Baptists were also mentioned.

However, in general the old denominations have disappeared, leaving only traces in theology and ritual as is apparent when worshipping at some TSPM churches which still retain an Anglican or Methodist flavour. It is the older, indigenous churches which have survived much better, probably as we have suggested, because they were better able to adapt to the rigorous climate in New China.

The major indigenous churches, all founded after World War I, include the True Jesus Church, the Jesus Family and the Little Flock. Unlike the Western denominations these groupings have preserved their own strong identity and ethos. Even where they have joined the TSPM, they hold their own services in registered churches separately from other Christians. Many, however, prefer to meet quite independently as house churches.

The True Jesus Church

The True Jesus Church was founded in 1917 by Paul Wei who was inspired by the Pentecostal movement. This group practices faith-healing, speaking in tongues, baptism by immersion, foot-washing and the Saturday Sabbath. By 1949 they claimed 120,000 members, meeting in 700 churches. Although banned in 1958 they have experienced rapid growth and have spread nationwide, although they are strongest in Jiangsu, Hunan and Fujian provinces. Some estimates put their numbers today at over one million. They strongly emphasise daily prayer, both private and corporate, and engage in vigorous evangelism.

The story of Mrs Ma from Shaanxi Province is a case in point. Her husband repeatedly beat her, and when she fell ill from four separate diseases blamed this on her foreign religion. She moved to her mother's home where believers prayed for her. Within three days she recovered, returned home, and became an itinerant evangelist. One day after coming home from preaching, her husband tied her to a cart and paraded her through the village, but friendly neighbours intervened. She has since led 150 of her fellow villagers to Christ.

The Jesus Family

The Jesus Family was founded by Jian Tianying in 1921 in Shandong Province. Jian was a remarkable man, converted from Confucianism by the Methodists. After this happened, he brought home his wife whom he had previously divorced, in obedience to Scripture – a very humiliating reversal in a traditional, patriarchal society. In 1921 he sold all his possessions, gave them to the poor and started a Christian commune in the village of Mazhuang. From his reading of the life of Hudson Taylor[2], the founder of the China Inland Mission, he first received a call to preach the gospel. However, he determined to break free of foreign control and from the beginning the new society was totally independent and self-supporting.

At Mazhuang the Christian community practised communal farming and silk-weaving, and also set up carpentry, printing and book binding departments as well as schools and kindergartens. The structure of each *jia* or "Family" was pyramidal with agriculture as the base and communal worship in a chapel at the apex.

The Jesus Family composed many hymns one of which expresses their ethos very well:

> Love is the organising principle of the Jesus Family. This is a heavenly conception. Since we are fathers and sons by grace and brothers in the Spirit, leadership is weak but body-life is very strong. All are one in Christ whether old or young, male or female, dull or gifted.

Jesus Family evangelists crossed north China, taking their meagre possessions with them in traditional wheelbarrows and living frugally in tents. New converts were encouraged to start house church meetings in their homes which became the nuclei of new "Families". Leaders had to sell their land and property and give the proceeds to the poor as a prerequisite of leadership, and were afterwards counted "least", taking joy in doing the most menial tasks such as collecting manure. By 1941 there were 141 "Families" in north China with some 6,000 members.

After 1949 the Jesus Family enthusiastically backed the new Three Self Patriotic Movement, naively believing that their unique Christian brand of Communism would be warmly welcomed by the authorities. In fact, they were rigorously suppressed as their profound Christian ethic based on love was in stark contrast to Marxist class warfare. Never numerous, their example appears to have had a major influence on present-day house church movements in north China with their stress on poverty, "tent-making" itinerant evangelism and close fellowship in the love of Christ.

Since the Cultural Revolution the Jesus Family has re-emerged as a separate grouping, but has had understandable difficulties in re-establishing Christian communities. In July 1987, Christians in Anhui sought to set up a "Family", but the house was burnt down by local authorities and they were bound with ropes and arrested. In 1985 or 1986 a "Jesus Family" was re-established in the village of Duoyigou in Shandong by Zheng Yunsu who had been imprisoned for his faith during the Cultural Revolution. By 1992 the group had grown to 3,000 converts of whom sixty lived together raising rabbits and mending shoes. The police, however, moved in, demolishing their church with a bulldozer and smashing the rabbit-hutches. The leaders were paraded in an open truck through the streets, with their "crime" publicised as being members of the Jesus Family. Zheng was sentenced to twelve years in prison and his three sons were sent to hard labour in the coal mines for between five and nine years. Twenty other leaders received sentences of three years "re-education through labour".

Despite persecution, the Jesus Family exists today as an influential stream of the house church movement. In the Spring of 1990 about one hundred national leaders managed to hold a conference for five days in a north Chinese village, despite police harassment. It is ironic that the Jesus Family has been dismissed by the TSPM and the authorities as a feudal relic totally out of place in new, socialist China. However, with unemployment rising in both town and countryside, the Jesus Family's uncompromising, radical Christianity is proving attractive to millions of impoverished peasants and workers, and provides a strong gospel counter-current to the tidal wave of materialism engulfing the country.

Watchman Nee and the Little Flock

Watchman Nee is still, perhaps, the evangelical Chinese Christian leader best known overseas, largely because of his prolific sermons, which have had a wide influence.

Ni Tuosheng, as he is known in China, was born in 1903 into a Methodist family. (His grandfather was the first Chinese Methodist pastor in the country.) He early came under the influence of two missionary ladies who had broken away from the mainline denominations. Nee was further influenced by the examples of Hudson Taylor, of George Muller who founded an orphanage in Bristol living by faith, and of certain Roman Catholic mystical writers such as Madame Guyon and Brother Lawrence. He began preaching at the age of twenty with other young co-workers and founded an indigenous movement. Its ecclesiology emphasised the importance of the local church.

The first such assembly was founded in Fuzhou in 1923. By 1950 about two hundred others had been established across China, and numbers had soared to 70,000 making the Little Flock one of the largest denominations (although it still fiercely denied being one). The Little Flock tended to attract intelligent young people with their stress on returning to the teaching of the New Testament through in-depth Bible study. For a time Nee was also influenced by the Strict (later Exclusive) Brethren movement, but he eventually broke away, finding their doctrines too narrow. However, the stamp of the Brethren remained in his radical denunciation of all denominationalism and insistence that there could only be one "local church" in any one locality. This radicalism alienated more mainline evangelicals but had great appeal to many young Chinese dissatisfied with traditional churches still largely controlled by foreigners.

For a time Nee came under a cloud and was even denounced by his fellow workers for going into business and setting up a pharmaceutical factory. In 1948 he finally admitted his mistake, and dedicated his factory entirely to the fellowship. Others followed suit and there was a great surge in sacrificial giving leading to vigorous evangelistic outreach on the very eve of the Communist takeover in 1949. Many "migrated" in groups of entire families to bring the gospel to unevangelised areas. In 1952 Nee was arrested and accused of being a capitalist because of previously owning a factory, and of committing various sexual improprieties. He was sentenced to fifteen years in prison. In 1956 the government launched a major offensive against the "Little Flock". Many of its leaders were also jailed, and on 15 April the movement was forced to accept control by the Three Self Patriotic Movement and, in effect, dissolved.

Watchman Nee died in a labour camp aged 69 on 1 June 1972. However, the Little Flock survived the persecutions of the 1950s and the Cultural Revolution. Their focus on the Scriptures, on close fellowship in small group meetings and their freedom from foreign control stood them in good stead. By the late 1970s many house churches in the Little Flock tradition were again flourishing in many cities, and their influence was strong in countryside areas, too.

In Fuzhou, the original home of the movement, the Little Flock remain strong today. In nearby Fuqing County as early as 1981 it was reported there were 70,000 Christians of whom 30,000 adhered to the Little Flock. By 1987 a local pastor reported growth to 100,000 Christians with corresponding growth among the Little Flock.

In northern Zhejiang Province, Xiaoshan County is home to large numbers of Little Flock Christians who remain adamantly opposed to joining the TSPM. In 1984 the Shanghai Academy of Social Sciences conducted an investigation of Christianity in Xiaoshan. They concluded that more than 95 per cent of the 63,000 Christians in Xiaoshan belonged to the Little Flock; that they were all opposed to joining the "Three Self" so met independently; but that they showed every sign of being patriotic citizens in every other respect. Two years later numbers had grown to 80,000 of whom 75 per cent were still outside TSPM control.[3] In 1998 local Christians reported numbers had grown to 100,000 (some even to 300,000).

The staggering growth of the Little Flock in Xiaoshan can be traced back to a small group of Christian families "migrating" from Shandong Province to the area in 1949–1950. During the Cultural Revolution great persecution came upon them, but in the late 1970s this was followed by a great spiritual awakening. House churches sprang up everywhere. Since 1994 when registration of all meetings was first enforced by the authorities they have been engaged in a constant spiritual battle. Many meeting places have been demolished, then rebuilt, only to be demolished and rebuilt again! Because of the large number of Christians the authorities have more recently taken a more conciliatory line. On 24 December 1996 the local *Xiaoshan Daily* reported that 174 meeting places had been officially registered. Unusually, they appear to have allowed house churches to register directly with the government without having to join the TSPM.

The direct headship of Christ over each local assembly is a truth upheld strongly by the Little Flock. Some have said they will never register nor accept government and TSPM interference in spiritual matters even if their buildings are demolished; others resolutely oppose joining the TSPM which they consider to be apostate, but are willing to register with the local authorities. Such debates are common in house church circles far beyond Little Flock assemblies. It appears that the Little Flock have had a widespread influence. Their emphasis on the headship of Christ, on fellowship, and on eschatology and separation from the world are generally accepted by many Chinese Christians, especially those who meet in independent house churches.

The new house church "streams"

Since the 1970s several very large house-church groupings have developed in Henan, Anhui and Wenzhou. These churches were started by charismatic figures who engaged in vigorous evangelism and usually had experience of being in and out of prison or labour camp for their pains. The vast majority of the believers are rural and many are only semi-literate. Over the last 20 years these groups have sent out teams all over China and have developed national networks. Each of these groups claims several millions of followers. It is difficult to find independent corroboration, and many overseas reports are exaggerated. For instance, the top leader of the China Gospel Fellowship is on record in 2004 as claiming 2.3 million believ-

The New House-church Streams		
Name of group	Original base	Leading figures
FANGCHENG	Henan	Zhang Rongliang
BORN-AGAIN (Weepers, Total Scope)	Henan	Deborah & Peter Xu
CHINA GOSPEL FELLOWSHIP	Tanghe, Henan	Shen Xiaoming
LIXIN	Lixin, Anhui	
YINGSHANG	Yingshang, Anhui	
WENZHOU	Zhejiang	Miao Zitong

ers, but in America that figure has been inflated to over 5 million. In 2002 Zhang Rongliang told Open Doors that his Fangcheng church comprised a loosely-knit underground flock of 10 million believers. In 2005 I saw some evidence that in some provinces Fangcheng had well over 100,000 believers in each. Claims that these six "streams" total 75 million or even over 100 million believers are still quite unsubstantiated, although undoubtedly they are large.

These churches are highly effective in their rural and small-town setting, but now face a crisis. The vast migration of some 200 million rural farmers to the cities in search of work is rapidly draining many villages of all their young people – including the Christians. In some villages it is reliably reported that 90% or more of the young believers (including many key or potential leaders) have already left, leaving behind mainly elderly women and children. In the light of this grim reality, the rural churches are struggling to cope. Calls to turn away from "worldliness" have fallen on deaf ears, as economic factors kick in. By driving a taxi in the city a young man can earn ten times the pittance he earned on the farm.

In the cities, rural farmers are sucked into factories and live in dormitories, working long hours in poor conditions. They struggle to survive as committed Christians. Many have written out to gospel radio stations in Hong Kong, bewailing their plight and asking for help. A few fortunate ones find work in factories owned by Christians (often joint ventures set up by Christians from Taiwan, Hong Kong or South Korea), where they can get spiritual nurture and training. It is clearly irresponsible for people overseas to encourage an army of rural evangelists to go to the Middle East, when they struggle to survive as Christians just by moving to the cities inside China. The main focus in China for the church and overseas agencies must be the winning of the cities and their huge, new migrant population to Christ.

A united appeal

Throughout the 1990s pressures have grown on independent house churches to register and to join the TSPM. By late 1996 leaders of several of the largest groupings were conscious that disunity was threatening the witness of the house churches. Their voice was fragmented and was not being heard overseas where increasingly sophisticated disinformation was being spread by the TSPM, leading even many evangelical denominations and para-church organisations to distance themselves from the house churches. The authorities within China were placing them under great pressure with meetings disbanded, leaders arrested and believers fined. This repression has often been justified as part of the general crackdown on criminal elements and extreme cults.

On 22 August 1998 leaders of ten major house church groupings issued a public statement calling on the Chinese government to cease persecution, and to open a dialogue with house church leaders. Entitled "A United Appeal by the Various Branches of the Chinese House Church", it was signed by representatives of eight major groups who remain outside TSPM control: Presbyterians, Charismatic Church, Local Church, Way of Life Church (also known as the Full-Scope Church), Little Flock Church, Pentecostal Church, and Lutherans and Baptists who are outside of TSPM. The seven-point appeal was as follows:

1) We call on the government to admit to God's great power and to study seriously today's new trends in the development of Christianity. If it were not the work of God, why have so many churches and Christians been raised up in China? Therefore, the judicial system and the United Front should readjust their policies on religion lest they violate God's will to their own detriment.

2) We call on the authorities to release unconditionally all house church Christians presently in labour-reform camps.

3) There are approximately 10 million believers in the Three Self Church but 80 million believers in the house church which represents the main stream of Christianity in China. The Three Self Church is only a branch. In many spiritual matters it has serious deviations.

4) We call on the central leadership of the Party to begin a dialogue with house church representatives to achieve better mutual understanding, to seek reconciliation, to reduce confrontation, and to engage in positive interaction.

5) We call on the government to spell out the definition of a "cult". This should be according to internationally recognised standards and not just according to whether or not people join the "Three-Self".

6) We call on the authorities to end their attacks on the house churches. History has proven that attacks on Christians who fervently preach the gospel only bring harm to China and its government. The legal system should end its practice of arresting and imprisoning house church preachers and believers, confining them in labour camps, or imposing fines as a punishment.

7) The Chinese house church is the channel through which God's blessings come to China. The persecution of God's children has blocked this channel of blessing. Support of the house churches will certainly bring God's blessing. We hope the government will respond positively to this united appeal.

This remarkable document in many ways marks the coming of age of the house church movement. Under pressure of continued persecution, leaders of the major groupings have come together and sunk their theological differences to issue an appeal to the Chinese government to recognise the reality of the existence of a huge body of Christians outside the aegis of the State-controlled "patriotic" religious affairs apparatus.

The statement shows a confidence in the sovereignty and providence of God as the controller of human history. Maturity is shown in the absence of any denunciation of either the government or the TSPM. The latter may have "serious deviations" from the faith, but the TSPM-controlled churches are recognised as a legitimate "branch" of Christ's Church in China. This shows a degree of moderation sometimes lacking in some other house church circles which refuse to recognise the TSPM churches as genuine churches at all, or to acknowledge (in the face of all the evidence) any believer who worships in a government-sanctioned church as a brother or sister in Christ.

Labelling can have severe consequences

One of the major pressures faced by unregistered evangelical house churches is the tendency of the authorities and the TSPM to label any group outside the registered churches as a cult. Once a group or person receives such a label (or "hat" in Chinese) it is virtually impossible to remove it. The results can be catastrophic – arrest, fines and even imprisonment. Thus the concern of the major house church networks to protest their orthodoxy.

A very good example of such labelling occurred in December 1997. The local government of Xinyang County in Henan issued a document headed "Cracking Down on the Cult Organisation of the China Evangelical Fellowship Henan/Hebei Mission". The document states that "the China Evangelical Fellowship is a cult organisation secretly developed by Shen Xianfeng and his followers". They falsely accuse the present society as a "kingdom of the devil, and an age of darkness" attempting to "form another nation and build up God's kingdom". It declares the Fellowship dissolved, and orders "the president, associate-president, bishops, associate bishops, elders, associate elders and teachers etc to report immediately to the local Public Security Bureau and hand over name lists... "[4]

From this document one certainly gains the impression of a large, well-organised house church network. But is it a cult? The leader himself, Shen Xianfeng issued a statement soon after his arrest on 6 November 1997 which casts severe doubt on the government decree. He writes:

Along with another brother I was arrested on the night of 6 November 1997 on my way to a house church meeting and sent to the Public Security Bureau of Xinyang County in Henan. I was interrogated there all night before being transferred to a detention centre the next morning. While with-holding the news of my arrest, the PSB phoned one of our sisters in Christ and said: "We are doctors. There are two persons by the name of Shen and Hao injured in a car accident. Notify the families immediately and bring money to the hospital." But when they arrived, what awaited them were handcuffs and detention.

They were robbed of all their money and forced to kneel on the ground. After interrogations, the PSB knew the location where the believers gathered. Immediately they surrounded the meeting-place and took away all the winter blankets and clothing. Thirteen brothers were arrested and put in jail or the detention centre. We were constantly interrogated and beaten, stripped and exposed to the cold wind of an electric fan in severe winter conditions. When someone could no longer bear the stinging heart-felt pain and cried out, his mouth was stuffed with a rag. All my property was confiscated – even the only ragged winter-clothes I had were taken away.

I was taken away from the detention centre to be interrogated round the clock. Finally I was indicted on the charge of organising a "cult". I strongly contested that we are orthodox Christians truly believing in Jesus and that we are against cults and heresies. "Why am I accused of organizing a cult?" I argued, "My belief is sound. I believe in the Triune God and in Jesus who is both human and divine, being saved only through faith, and the Bible as the supreme authority. We respect the leaders and officials of our country. We love our motherland and obey the law. Wherever the gospel is preached, social order is improved. People are turned from wickedness, broken families restored, the lazy become diligent. Wherever there is an increase in the Christian population there is social harmony and unity because no true Christian would like to be against the government."

The police admitted what I said were facts. Yet because we are a systematic organisation, setting up mission branches and teams of evangelists, the government became suspicious. But they said, "According to our principles, we charge as a cult those who do not join the Three Self Patriotic Movement. Only those [house church] gatherings with fewer than twenty members and not linked with other churches are not considered as a cult, but still must be disbanded."

Then I appealed: "Do not let unbelievers determine what a cult is. Those who believe should decide. On the basis of biblical principles – a church's condition, life conduct and gospel message – they may judge whether a group is orthodox, extreme, heretical or a cult. It should not be determined by unbelievers at their whim." Nevertheless I was confined for forty days without appeal. Then sixteen of us in handcuffs were brought to public trial in Xinyang County where we were convicted of being a cult and sentenced to 2–3 years of reform through labour. Others were released after being fined several thousand dollars. Public posters outlawing the "CEF" as a cult were widely posted and reported in the news.

Because of my physical disability – my feet being paralysed – I was given medical release after 83 days and had to pay a fine. Now I am back at home, but my dear brothers are still in the forced labour prison working day and night, running and pulling broken carts. They do not have enough to wear or eat. Their wives and children must bear all kinds of burdens emotionally, physically and financially. I cannot help but cry out: "is this the lot of those who believe in Jesus and do good, to be condemned as a cult only because they do not join the political organisation of the TSPM?" How many good citizens of God's kingdom must suffer through · this splitting up of families?

This stark report is typical of the treatment being meted out to many house church Christians in many areas where the unregistered house churches are strong, particularly Henan and Anhui. Although cultic groups exist, there seems no doubt from the evidence cited above that many evangelical Christians whose "crime" is only that of refusing to join the TSPM are being persecuted in many parts of China.

A seven-fold confession of faith

Between 22–24 November 1998 leaders of four major house church groupings, including the China Evangelistic Fellowship, held a meeting in northern China to declare their basic unity in Christ in the face of persecution and to draft a confession of faith. The four groups were the China Evangelistic Fellowship based in Henan and Hebei, the Mother Church of Fangcheng, the house churches of Fuyang, Anhui (both areas of major revival) and another unnamed network.

Their confession of faith is thoroughly conservative evangelical, and covers seven key areas including the Bible, Jesus Christ, the Church, and the Last Things.[5] The following excerpts show clearly that the mainstream of the Chinese house churches are determined to "earnestly contend for the faith which was once delivered unto the saints" (Jude 3).

1. **ON THE BIBLE:** We believe that the 66 books of the Bible are inspired of God and that they were written by the prophets and apostles under the inspiration of the Holy Spirit. The Bible is the highest standard of our faith, life and service. We are opposed to all those who deny the Bible and to the view that it is out of date; we are opposed to the view that the Bible has error; and to those who believe only in selected sections of the Bible. We are opposed to interpreting Scripture by one's own will or by subjective spiritualization.
2. **ON THE TRINITY:** We believe in only one True God, the eternally self-existing triune Father, Son and Holy Spirit who are the same in substance, equal in glory and honour. We believe that God created

all things. He is the Lord of human history. He is just, holy, faithful and merciful. He is omniscient, omnipresent and omnipotent. We refute all mistaken explanations of the Trinity such as one entity with three modes of manifestation. [NB: this is probably aimed at the heterodox theology of Witness Lee former leader of the "Shouters" who upheld a modalist view of the Trinity.]

3. **ON CHRIST:** We believe that Jesus Christ is God's only begotten Son; he came to the earth by way of incarnation (the Word became flesh). In his perfect humanity he was tempted, though without sin. He allowed himself to be crucified on the cross of his own will and there shed his precious blood in order to redeem those who believe in him from sin and death. He rose from the dead, ascended into heaven and sat down at the right hand of God from whom he received the promise of the Holy Spirit, which he gives to all who believe in him. On the last day Christ shall come again the second time to judge the world. Christians receive the status of sonship, but they remain humans; they do not become God.

No one knows the specific dates of the second coming, but we firmly believe that Christ will come again. We can also know some signs of his second coming. We are opposed to the teaching that Christ has come again the second time in his incarnated form. We are opposed to all who claim themselves to be the Christ. All who claim that Christ has already come the second time should be declared heretics.

4. **ON SALVATION:** Anyone who repents, confessing his or her sins, and believes in Jesus as the Son of God, that he was crucified on the cross for our sins and that he rose again on the third day for the remission of our sins and for receiving the Holy Spirit shall be saved through being born again. For by grace are we saved through faith: we are justified by faith; we receive the Holy Spirit through faith; and we become the sons of God through faith.

We believe that God will preserve his children in Christ to the end, and that Christians should firmly believe in the truth to the end. We believe that receiving the Holy Spirit is the assurance (evidence) of being saved and the Spirit of God bears witness with our spirit that we are the children of God.

We are opposed to all who take specific phenomena or personal experience as the objective criteria for being saved. [This is aimed at both some in the otherwise orthodox "New Birth" network and extreme charismatics.]

We are opposed to the belief that one can sin because he is under grace. We are opposed to the idea of multiple salvation. We are also opposed to the belief that we can be saved by keeping the law. [This is aimed at the Seventh Day Adventists and some other fringe sects.]

5. **ON THE HOLY SPIRIT:** We believe that the Holy Spirit is the third person of the Trinity. He is the Spirit of God, the Spirit of Christ, the Spirit of truth and the Spirit of holiness. The Holy Spirit illuminates a person causing him to know sin and repent, to know the truth and to believe in Christ and so experience being born again unto salvation. He leads the believers into the truth, helps them to understand the truth and obey Christ, thereby bearing abundant fruit of life. The Holy Spirit gives all kinds of power and manifests the mighty acts of God through signs and miracles. The Holy Spirit searches all things. Through faith and thirsting, Christians can experience the outpouring and filling of the Holy Spirit. We do not believe in the cessation of signs and miracles or the termination of the gifts of the Holy Spirit after the apostolic period. We do not forbid speaking in tongues and we do not impose on people to speak in tongues; nor do we insist that speaking in tongues is the evidence of being saved.

We refute the view that the Holy Spirit is not a person of the Trinity but only a kind of influence.

6. **ON THE CHURCH:** The church is composed of all those whom God has called together in Jesus Christ. Christ is the Head of the Church and the Church is the body of Christ. The Church is the house of God built on the foundation of truth. The Church is both local and universal; the universal Church is composed of all churches of orthodox faith currently existing in all parts of the earth and all the saints throughout history.

The administration of the Church should be conducted according to principles laid down in the Scriptures. Its spiritual ministry shall not be directed or controlled by secular powers.

The mission of the Church is: proclamation of the gospel, teaching and pastoring the believers, training and sending them, and defending the truth by refuting heresies and bringing them back to the correct path. All believers are priests and they all have the authority and responsibility to preach the gospel to the ends of the earth.

We are opposed to the unity of Church and state or the intermingling of the Church and political power. [This is aimed against the TSPM.]

We are opposed to the Church taking part in any activities that seek to destroy the unity of the people or the unification of the Chinese state.

7. **ON THE LAST THINGS:** We believe in the Second Coming of Christ and the bodily resurrection of those who are saved. No one knows the date of the Second Coming. When Christ comes again he will come down in the clouds of heaven in great glory. The bodies of those Christians who have been born again and saved shall be changed and they shall be lifted up to meet the Lord in the air, and they shall receive a glorified body.

The saints and Christ shall reign for a thousand years. After a thousand years Satan shall be temporarily released to deceive all the peoples until he is cast into the lake of fire. Then Christ shall sit on his throne and judge all the nations. All those whose names are not written in the Book of Life shall be cast into the lake of fire. Those whose names which are written in the Book of Life shall enter into the New Jerusalem and be with God forever. We believe that as believers wait for the Second Coming they should be diligent in doing the work of the Lord, preaching the Word of Life, shining for the Lord on earth, and bearing abundant fruit in word, deed, faith, love and holiness.

As to whether Christ will come before or after the Tribulation we acknowledge there are different views and we cannot make any view absolute. The responsibility of Christians is to be alert and be prepared to welcome the Second Coming of Christ.

CONCLUSION: We praise and thank our Almighty Father for leading us to draft this Confession of Faith. We pray it will strengthen the faith of brothers and sisters, resist heresies and cults and together forward the great revival of the Church in China. May the Lord bless the unity of the house churches in China. May the Lord bless China, the Chinese peoples, and the Chinese Church. May praise and glory be unto our triune God. Amen. (Signed 26 November 1998)

This confession represents the mainstream of the house church movement in China. In its view of the Bible, the Trinity and the work of Christ, it stands firmly in the tradition of historic evangelicalism. However, it has a uniquely Chinese flavour, too. Various doctrinal positions which might be regarded as opposed to each other in the West are here joined in a synthesis. For example, the statement affirming the perseverance of the saints reflects historic Reformation teaching; on the other hand, denying the cessation of miracles or gifts of the Holy Spirit is similar to charismatic teaching in the West. But, again, the careful neutrality concerning speaking in tongues is very far from the extreme teachings current in some charismatic or Pentecostal circles. The statement concerning eschatology is pre-millennial and this reflects the majority view of Chinese Christians. Here again, a spirit of moderation is evident, with a refusal to dogmatise about the tribulation.

The classic Reformation doctrine of separation of church and State is maintained. Quietly but firmly the headship of Christ over his Church is proclaimed, and the right of the TSPM or the authorities to interfere in the spiritual matters of the Church rejected. However, the house churches also affirm their loyalty as Chinese citizens and reject the Church being used as a political tool to subvert the Chinese government.

Why many house churches do not register

The issue of registration has come to the fore in recent years, particularly since 1996. In certain provinces registration has been vigorously enforced. For instance, Jiangsu Province has seen special efforts to register all house churches. It is by no means coincidental that a survey of letters from Chinese Christians for the years 1996–97 showed the highest incidence of complaints of persecution to emanate from this province. While some previously unregistered churches may see some advantage in legalisation and accepting government control under the TSPM umbrella, others have remained unconvinced.

The same four house church networks who issued the Confession of Faith also published a statement on their attitude towards the government, its religious policy and the Three Self Patriotic Movement. After reaffirming their loyalty to the government and constitution, they laid out their reasons for not registering as follows:

1. Because the State ordinances on religion and demands for registration are contrary to the principles of Scripture, such as the "Three Designates (San Ding) Policy":
   a) *Designated location:* religious activities are only allowed to be conducted in registered places, otherwise they are considered illegal. But the Scriptures tell us we can meet anywhere and that so long as we meet in the Name of the Lord he will be with us.
   b) *Designated personnel:* only those issued with preaching licenses by the Religious Affairs Bureau are allowed to preach. But according to Scripture so long as preachers are called by the Lord, recognised and sent by the church, they may preach.
   c) *Designated sphere:* preachers are limited to preach only within the district for which they are assigned [by the TSPM]; they may not preach across villages or provinces. But the Bible teaches us to preach the gospel to all peoples and to the ends of the earth.

2. Because the State policy does not allow us to preach the gospel to those under the age of 18 [see Chapter 10 for further details], or to lead them to Christ and be baptised. But Jesus said, "Let the little children come unto me and forbid them not." Therefore those under eighteen should also have the opportunity to hear, and believe in, the gospel.

3. Because State policy does not permit believers to pray for the sick, to heal them, or to exorcise demons from them.

4. Because State policy does not allow us to receive fellow believers from afar, but the Bible teaches us that elders should receive brothers and sisters from afar.

5. Because State policy does not allow us to have communication with churches overseas, but the Bible teaches us that the Church is universal.

Why most house churches do not join the TSPM

The independent house churches are concerned to base all their arguments upon Scripture and for this reason they build a powerful case. In a similar vein they lay out their reasons for not joining the TSPM.

Chinese house churches do not join the TSPM for the following reasons:

1. The head of the two groups is different:
   a. TSPM churches accept the State as their governing authority: their organisation and administration are governed by the government's religious policy.
   b. House churches take Christ as their Head, and they organise and govern their churches according to the teaching of the Bible.

2. The way church workers are ordained is different:
   a. Religious workers in the TSPM churches must first be approved by the Religious Affairs Bureau.
   b. House churches choose their workers by the following qualifications: spiritual anointing, being equipped in the truth, possessing spiritual gifts, approval by the church, and having a spiritually qualified character.

3. The foundation of the two is different:
   a. The TSPM churches are products of the Three-Self Reform Movement which was initiated by the government; they

were started by Wu Yaozong who propounded a liberal social gospel type of theology; some of the TSPM initiators were not even Christians.
   b. House churches take the Bible as the foundation of their faith; they developed from the traditions of the fundamentalists and evangelicals.

4. *The paths of the two are different:*
   a. The TSPM churches practise the union of politics with the church; they follow the religious policy of the State, and they engage in [approved] political activities.
   b. House churches believe in the separation of church and State. They obey the State when such obedience is in accordance with Scripture. When the two are in conflict they will "obey God rather than man". For such obedience they are willing to pay the necessary price, which is known as "walking the pathway of the Cross."[6]

Deep theology arising from deep experience

Like the confession of faith, this apologia for the house churches shows considerable theological profundity and deep Scriptural foundations. Some evangelicals have joined the TSPM for various reasons, and there is no doubt, as we saw in Chapter 3, that the gospel may be proclaimed with varying degrees of liberty within its system, although always under ultimate government supervision. However, the house church position has the advantage of clarity and strength of Scriptural support. So the house church movement is clearly in the tradition of the Reformers such as Luther and Calvin, and their Huguenot, Puritan and Covenanting successors who paid a great price for the religious freedom we enjoy in the West today.

Some, particularly in denominations which no longer place emphasis on the full authority of Scripture, may disagree with the position taken by the house churches. However, following these public statements they can no longer in honesty denigrate the house church movement as simplistic or merely stubborn. The Chinese house church manifests a robust evangelicalism which is much needed in the West today. Their theology, far from being pursued in an academic ivory tower, has been hammered out in the face of persecution and heresy. It breathes a deep commitment to Christ and his Word and throughout there is a commendable emphasis on practical Christian living. There are important lessons to learn in Western evangelical circles from the way the Chinese Church rejects both legalism and antinomianism. For Chinese Christians, discipleship is costly, involving "walking the way of the cross" and this shows itself in ardent evangelism.

The response of the authorities

Since the Cultural Revolution the government has granted much greater religious autonomy, while insisting that Christians worship within parameters laid down by the Party. In practice this means worshipping only in churches or meeting-points registered with the Three Self Patriotic Movement. Over the last two decades the policy of religious control has varied widely at different times and in different places. In general, there has been an automatic tightening of control whenever Beijing has launched a major political campaign or an anti-crime campaign. House churches become easy targets caught up in wider campaigns against political dissidents, criminal elements and sects.

In the late 1970s and early 1980s house churches enjoyed great liberty and expansion. Deng Xiaoping had just returned to power and was busy "reversing verdicts" – that is, undoing Mao's extremist policies, including outright persecution of religious believers. Cadres were unwilling to risk being labelled as "leftists" or followers of the Maoist "Gang of Four" by continuing repressive policies. However, by 1982 the government formulated its new religious policy in "Document 19" which expected all Christians to accept a measure of government supervision under the TSPM. The policy on house churches was rather ambiguous:

> So far as [Protestant] Christians undertaking religious activities in home-meetings are concerned, these should not, in principle, be permitted. But they should not be rigidly prohibited. The religious masses should be persuaded, through the work of the patriotic religious workers [ie TSPM], to make other suitable arrangements.

This gave ample room for manoeuvre for both a liberal and a repressive interpretation of the law when dealing with house churches.

And so it has proved ever since. In 1982 the first details of major crackdowns in Henan and Anhui on house churches were reported. In 1983 the government launched the notorious "anti-spiritual pollution campaign" to bolster flagging support for Marxist orthodoxy. Despite assurances that the campaign was not aimed at religious believers, many house church Christians were jailed nationwide. For instance, about one hundred Christians were arrested in Lushan County, Henan, in June 1983. By mid-1984 the campaign was abruptly brought to a halt by Party moderates who feared a return to Maoism. Between 1985–87 the house churches again enjoyed a period of relative calm. Party moderates Zhao Ziyang and Hu Yaobang were in power and reportedly favoured a much more relaxed religious policy. However, in 1987 Party left-wingers launched a new "anti-bourgeois liberalisation campaign" aimed at unhealthy influences from the West such as democracy. Independent Christians were again targeted. However, calls for radical reform continued to be made. In 1988 and early 1989 liberal elements in the Party and the TSPM even pushed for the abolition of the TSPM and the entire apparatus of religious control.

The ruthless repression of the Democracy Movement in Beijing in June 1989 brought to an end all hopes of an imminent liberalisation of Party policy on religion. The 1990s have seen a marked increase in persecution of house church believers. Since 1996 the implementation of a stricter policy on registration of all religious meetings has added to pressures on unregistered Christians. Provincial documents stating Party policy regarding religion have become more detailed, trying to close any loopholes. However, this repressive policy has been implemented alongside the continuing opening-up of Chinese society in the economic field, which has resulted in greater freedom of movement, more contacts overseas and an influx of foreign tourists, businessmen and religious believers. Although the overall intent has been to tighten control, there are many counter-currents which are difficult if not impossible for the authorities to manage. Thus the house churches continue to flourish and expand although in urban areas they can function only as small cell groups.

Difficulties continue

There seems little doubt that the authorities have chosen to ignore the olive branch proffered by the house churches in August 1998. In the same month they temporarily detained Alan Yuan, an 85-year-old house church leader in Beijing, after he had baptised more than three hundred new converts in a factory swimming pool. This event was unconnected with the issuing of the house church statement in Henan.

However, on 26 October and 5 November 1998 police in Henan arrested over 140 house church Christians. Forty Christians were arrested when police made a night raid on a meeting near Wugang City where house church leaders from sixteen provinces were gathered. Chen Meiying, from northeast China was reportedly lashed with wet rope and beaten about the head with a police baton; she was unconscious for three days before being released, and then suffered complete memory loss. Another leader escaped, but was shot in the leg by police and is now on the wanted list.[7]

Then on 5 November about one hundred believers were

arrested in the Nanyang region of Henan, where independent house churches are particularly strong. It is believed most were released after paying fines. In December, 25 believers were also detained in Tanghe County in southern Henan. Again most were released after paying fines. On 1 December police raided a large house church in Huadu, Guangdong Province in south China. They confiscated Bibles and arrested the leader, Mr Li Dexian, aged 47, who was held for fifteen days for "illegal preaching" and had his head shaven.[8]

Repression has continued. On 26 January 1999, house-church leaders were arrested with their pastor, Mr Chu Chang'en in Fangcheng County, a centre of house church revival in Henan Province. According to one visitor "Entire villages are totally Christian in this area; that's why the government is so mad."[9]

Into the new century the sad catalogue of arrests, beatings and even torture continues. On 2 April 2004 three female members of the South China Church, Cao Hongmei, Liu Xianzhi and Meng Xicun from Hubei and Henan Provinces, testified before the United Nations Commission on Human Rights in Geneva. Ms Cao testified that the police "questioned me for about a month. They would use different ways of torturing me. For instance, they hung my two hands up on the door frame and my feet couldn't touch the floor. They used a sharpened bamboo stick to beat my hands and shoulder. I couldn't bear this tremendous pain any more so I began to scream... One used a pair of handcuffs to hammer my fingers. They began to bleed and my fingernails to break... They also used a lighter to burn my ears, my face and my lips."

On 11 June 2004 about 100 leaders of the China Gospel Fellowship were arrested in Wuhan while on retreat, although all had been released a month later. In July 2004 over 100 house-church co-workers were arrested in Changji, Xinjiang, while also holding a spiritual retreat. On 1 December 2004 police arrested Zhang Rongliang, one of the leaders of the Fangcheng fellowship, in Zhengzhou. In May 2005 police simultaneously raided 60 house churches in Changchun, Jilin Province, and another 60 house churches in nearby Jiutai. Over 100 leaders were detained, including many students and professors.

New Religious Regulations which came into force on 1 March 2005 call for strict registration of all house churches. A few younger leaders in Beijing were considering doing so, to get official permission for their house churches to undertake social-service activities. But most of the older generation I have spoken to are adamant that they will not register, as they do not wish to accept interference from the government through the TSPM.

Despite continuing arrests, particularly in rural areas, in 2005 I detected a greater boldness on the part of many urban house-church Christians and a greater freedom of manoeuvre. It remains to be seen how strictly the new regulations will be enforced. As the Olympics in 2008 loom nearer it seems unlikely the government will risk antagonising international opinion by any massive crackdown. However, sporadic repression is likely to continue, particularly in rural areas off the beaten track.

6

The "Jesus nest" – revival in Henan

Behind iron bars, hard labour ceases for a moment –
My spirit rests in peace.
Meditating daily on our Lord's love
Stepping up to higher spiritual ground.
Preparing daily to suffer physically for the Lord
Voices of humiliation enter my ear.
But persecution comes with the Lord's permission
Following the Lord with trust and obedience.
The angry eyes of people today will be
Exchanged for the smiling face of Jesus.
The temporary ruin of my body today
Exchanged for the glorious crown in Heaven.

Written by a believer in Henan while in labour camp

Henan is China's ancient rural heartland. Here at Anyang two thousand years before Christ, the Shang dynasty emperors had themselves buried in sumptuous tombs with jade and bronze artefacts that even today tomb robbers smuggle out to collectors worldwide. They also conducted human sacrifice to ensure an adequate supply of slaves accompanied them into the future life.

The Yellow River – "China's sorrow"

Over the millennia, Henan has suffered more than its fair share of human sacrifice. Wars, barbarian invasions, peasant rebellions and corrupt tax collectors have swept through the province bringing death and misery in their wake. The Yellow River – "China's Sorrow" – cuts through the northern part of the province often bringing massive floods. It deposits vast amounts of yellow, alluvial silt along its banks and has gradually built up its own course to be higher than the surrounding plain. The turbulent, muddy waters are held in place only by massive dykes. Over the last century the dykes have burst many times – or even been deliberately breached, as during the Japanese invasion. Floods have been interspersed with famines when millions starved. The last major famine occurred between 1958–61 when many Henan peasants were reduced to eating tree bark and grass. But this time the catastrophe was largely man-made, due to Chairman's Mao's disastrous utopian economic policies. In some areas two-thirds of the population perished and the total death toll in Henan was about eight million.

The peasantry of Henan – which now has a population of over 93 million – are industrious, humorous and fatalistic. Folk-religion and superstition is endemic along with a residual belief in *Lao Tian Ye* – "old father god". In this crucible of poverty, natural disasters, political oppression and despair, the Christian gospel has made its greatest triumphs over the last three decades. As Jesus said, "The poor have the gospel preached to them."

The early days

On the eve of the Communist victory in 1949 there were probably fewer than 100,000 Protestant Christians in Henan Province. By 1952 all foreign missionaries had been forced to leave. The Lutherans and the CIM were the largest societies and had succeeded in planting the gospel in many villages. However, in the land reform campaigns of the early 1950s, most of these village congregations were closed, leaving just a few churches in the towns. By 1958 when the TSPM closed most remaining churches under the pretext of "church unity" a mere handful were left in the main cities such as Zhengzhou and Kaifeng. In the days of famine and distress (1959–61)

Christians met secretly in their homes and prayed for the sick. There were conversions as people saw the power of God manifested in answer to prayer. When the full onslaught of the Cultural Revolution swept over the province in 1966 there were those who were martyrs for their faith. This suffering had a deep effect. One old lady who held on to what she believed through thick and thin led another to faith who later became a full-time evangelist.

The church at this time was virtually invisible and could have appeared totally extinguished. Henan was one area which was declared an "atheistic zone" by the authorities. But the Holy Spirit was deeply at work, and, as is so often the case, he worked in humble and surprising ways. An elderly house church leader from Henan who was himself in labour camp for many years, gives a rare glimpse of how the gospel not only survived, but even flourished, in the dark days of the Cultural Revolution.

In the late 1960s the arm of the Lord was revealed in the villages of Henan. There were countless villages where meetings sprang up almost simultaneously. This was virtually unthinkable, as believers were under constant surveillance and even exchanging a few words of Christian comfort between friends, if overheard, could lead to political persecution. The dictatorship of the proletariat was extremely effective in repressing Christians. Yet God was able to work even within that system.

When the wives of Communist Party cadres fell ill, they sought out every medical help, even visiting doctors in Beijing, but often to no avail. So many of these women came home to Henan to die. In the villages there were many elderly Christian women who had not been able to go to church for nearly twenty years. Although all their Bibles had been confiscated they were still strong in faith and knew how to pray. They went into the homes of these commune cadres and production brigade secretaries bringing the love of Christ and preaching Jesus, the Great Healer. Many of those desperate women received Christ as their Saviour. After they recovered they asked for further instruction from those elderly Christian women who were simple peasants. So many meetings actually started in the homes of local Communist cadres.

In the autumn of 1975 I happened to be passing through a rural county in northern Henan. After repairing a cart for a farmer I sat down to eat and was amazed to hear people nearby singing: "The Holy Spirit has come... " I immediately went to this house church meeting. I found more than one hundred people crammed into a small cottage and spilling into the farm courtyard. This was their normal evening meeting. After singing some hymns, an elderly brother gave an exhortation and then everyone prayed simultaneously out loud. The preacher told me that they had been meeting in a cadre's house since 1970. The cadre's wife had been very ill and sought help to no avail. She had turned to Christ and been healed very quickly. Her husband was the brigade secretary in the commune and he turned a blind eye so they had no persecution. He told me that there were also many Christians in the counties to both the west and the east. They held meetings every night, but rotated them round different villages. Every village, even every other family, had believers.

That evening I could not sleep. Like Thomas, I hardly dared to believe what I had seen and heard. Then I remembered what an elderly Christian sister had told me long before in 1964: "Do not worry that the church is now desolate and taken over by wolves and false prophets. Very soon the Chinese Church will experience a great revival." Ten years later in 1974 I had come across this sister again who told me: "I have some good news for you! In the mountains 150 kilometers away the peasants have a Christian meeting every night." At that time I did not dare believe her, as the persecution by the Communists was still so virulent.

The next day after breakfast my new friend took me to the home where the meeting was. I did some repair work and at the evening meeting was invited to preach. It was a strange feeling – my own father had been a preacher and was condemned as a "rightist" before his death. I myself had been condemned for the worse crime of being a "counter-revolutionary", but now I was following in my father's footsteps. My friend reassured me that I was in little danger as most of the meetings were held in cadres' homes! During the following year I also met with the accountant of a production brigade. His eight-year-old son had been seriously ill with leukemia. He had spent much money on medicine but finally the doctor told him there was no hope. A Christian neighbour, overhearing the wailing of the parents, came in and shared the gospel with them. They both turned to Christ. The child recovered rapidly and when they took him to see the doctor again, his white blood-cell count was normal. From then on they opened their home for meetings.

This account clearly shows that in Henan the gospel spread during the Cultural Revolution through the prayers and faith of very simple peasants. Healing in the Name of Jesus was a major factor. The same source also mentioned that around 1970 the Chinese government greatly reduced the price of radios throughout the country. Many country people from then on were able to afford to tune in to gospel radio programmes from overseas which have led many to turn to Christ in the remotest corners of the country. Other house church leaders in Henan have remarked on the suddenness with which revival came and summed up the phenomenon succinctly as

1. Mass conversions in the villages
2. The conversion of many Communist Party cadres
3. Miracles and healing.

By the time (1979–80) the first few State churches were opened in the main cities of Henan such as the provincial capital in Zhengzhou, house churches were already flourishing throughout the province. Henan became a powerhouse of revival and evangelism which the authorities and the Three Self Patriotic Movement have tried to limit and control largely in vain.

Revival in Fangcheng

Fangcheng County in southern Henan is an agricultural district with nearly one million inhabitants. Sixty years ago Henry Guinness, David Adeney and other missionaries of the China

Inland Mission travelled by bicycle with Chinese colleagues throughout the villages, and small churches were planted. Today there are so many Christians that hostile cadres have labelled the area a "Jesus Nest". As early as 1982, following some months of great revival, local Christians estimated there may be as many as 300,000 believers in Fangcheng – one third of the population. In just three communes there were then already 160,000, but they had only 43 Bibles and 27 New Testaments between them. They had to mimeograph Christian material, which was strictly illegal. In more recent years Bibles have been printed within China and sent in from overseas, but in many rural areas the supply is still far from sufficient.

That evangelism, and the revival which followed, were not without opposition and much persecution. In May 1982 Fangcheng Christians wrote a long letter to Christians overseas. It describes in graphic and moving detail what happened.

ALL WHO LIVE GODLY LIVES IN CHRIST JESUS SHALL SUFFER PERSECUTION

Dear brothers and sisters,

On behalf of the brothers and sisters in Henan I send greetings to members of the Body overseas! Today the church in Henan is being greatly blessed by the Lord and the number of those saved increases daily. The gospel of God is flourishing. All this is done not without your prayers and contributions.

Wherever there is revival, there are also trials. The revival in Henan has flourished in such a situation. If Jesus had not been crucified, nobody today could be saved – if there were no testing by fire, then true faith would not be revealed. Suffering is the means for promoting spiritual life and the ingredient for revival of the Church.

Dearly beloved, most recently the cause of the gospel in Fangcheng County, Henan, has been greatly promoted. A dozen young Christians have been imprisoned, beaten and bound, and this is the cause. They have regarded suffering for Christ as more precious than the treasure of Egypt. They started preaching the gospel in the poorest, most desolate regions. One day they went to Yangce Commune in Miyang County. No-one seemed to listen so they prayed and were greatly inspired by God. They split into groups and went preaching to many different places. As soon as they started to preach, the power of God came down. They preached with tears streaming down, so that passers-by and street-vendors, both Christians and non-Christians, stopped to listen. Even the fortune-tellers were moved by the Holy Spirit to burst out crying. Many people forgot their food, forgot their work or even to return home. Even by evening people had not dispersed. They preached until they were exhausted but still the crowd would not let them leave. When the shops and factories closed, their employees also came to listen.

However, then Satan made his move. The authorities suddenly dragged them away one by one, binding them with ropes and beating them with electric stun-truncheons. They also kicked them in the face with their leather shoes, beating them unconscious. But when they came to, they continued to pray, sing and preach to the bystanders. One girl who was only fourteen was beaten senseless. But when she came to and saw that many people were sympathetic, she started to preach again. Her words were few and spoken in a low voice but the street-acrobats and actors could not refrain from crying out, repenting and believing in Jesus. As they were being bound and beaten, many people noticed a strange expression on their faces. Amazed, they saw they were smiling. Their spirit and appearance was so lively and gracious that the crowd asked why they did not feel ashamed? They were so young, so where did this power come from? Their example caused many people to believe in Jesus.

When the Christians in that area saw them bound and forced to kneel on the ground for more than three days without food or water, beaten with sticks until their faces were covered with blood, and their hands made black by the ropes, but still singing, praying and praising the Lord – then they, too, wished to share their persecution. So the flame of the gospel has spread throughout Yangce. There had never been revival here before, but through this persecution the seeds of life have been truly planted. May everyone who hears of this give thanks and praise for the revival of the Church here.

Dearly beloved, in men's eyes this was an unfortunate happening, but for Christians it was like a rich banquet. This lesson cannot be learned from books, and this sweetness is rarely tasted by men. This rich spiritual life cannot be had in a comfortable environment. Where there is no cross, there is no victory. If the spices are not refined to become oil, the fragrance of the perfume cannot flow forth. If grapes are not crushed in the vat, they cannot become wine. Dearly beloved, these saints who went down into the fiery furnace, far from being harmed have been glorified. Their spirits have been filled with power to preach the gospel with far greater authority and to enjoy a far more abundant spiritual life. Satan was unable finally to force them to give up their faith, so they were released.

The Christian workers in Fangcheng, Sheqi and Miyang counties have all been emboldened to preach the gospel. Those who were not imprisoned felt ashamed and saw the marks of the Lord Jesus upon their bodies. They also desired to suffer that the Lord's Name be glorified. Dearly beloved, the Lord wishes to add to the number being saved working through us. Let us seize the opportunity to work for him as there are many souls still unsaved. There are many lambs wandering on the mountains without anyone to seek and find them. May the Lord Jesus place a burden to preach the gospel on every Christian's heart. May he give a spirit of prayer to every Christian so they will become a prayer-warrior. May our brethren overseas strive to meet the need for Christian literature which is so lacking within China, as God has given you the perfect environment to do this. May God grant you to be faithful unto death until he comes. The Lord is coming soon. Lord Jesus, I desire you to come! May the Lord give us hearts to pray for each other until that day. Emmanuel!

From the weak brethren in Fangcheng, Henan.
6 May 1982

This moving letter gives an insight into the spiritual depth of the work being done by God among the house churches of Henan. Many Christians there have a deep love for Christ, a deep understanding of his Word, a deep concern for evangelism and a living hope that he will come again. They are willing to suffer joyfully for the gospel's sake. The contrast with the affluent, comfortable Christianity of many churches in the West could not be sharper.

Revival in Lushan

Lushan County in southern Henan is another country area, with a population of 771,000 (1994). The Norwegian Lutheran Mission did good work planting evangelical churches in the area before 1949. In 1982 a missionary from this society visited China, met with an elder from Lushan and reported: "We had no idea that the revival in China was so deep." The elder reported that there were 90,000 Christians in Lushan, of whom 27,000 had been baptised. The others were then still awaiting baptism.[1]

In June 1987 a Christian wrote from Lushan that the Religious Affairs Bureau had conducted a religious census and was alarmed to find nearly 100,000 believers in Lushan. At first it was willing only to register the 27,000 who were baptised, but eventually agreed to register 50,000. This shows the arbitrary nature of official statistics in China! In October 1995 another Christian wrote from Lushan claiming that the number of Christians was between 90,000–150,000 or 10–19 per cent of the population.

In 1984 a house church elder who described himself as an elder in the Lutheran church gave a description of the work of God and the persecution in this area. Around 1980 the church experienced great revival. In his village of 3,000 people, 600 were Christians. For a while they met openly. They even used a public address system and carried tape recorders around when they went preaching to large open-air meetings in the villages. But by 1983 great persecution came again and they had to return to small house church meetings. In the autumn of 1983 he himself was arrested by the police and labelled a "counter-revolutionary". Any Christian who had refused to join the Three Self Patriotic Movement was arbitrarily labelled a "Shouter" and was liable to arrest.

I was working on the wheat farm when I was arrested. They came to my house and searched everywhere but they could not find any evidence. But they still called me a "counter-revolutionary" and sent me to a "study house" for twenty-four days. It was actually a prison. We were separated from each other and everyone endured severe beatings, some with lashes, some with sticks. To join this "study class" we had to pay 15RMB and donate 40 lb of rice of which we were given only a watery bowl of rice for each meal. Sixty Christians were imprisoned there and the night we were thrown together we spent two hours kneeling in prayer. They told us not to join the Shouters, not to hold meetings, not to engage in evangelistic activities and not to read Christian books from overseas. They even asked us not to believe any more. I told them bluntly I could not deny Christ whether they released me or not. But they released me after all. They repeated their "Four Don'ts" and "One Demand". Their one demand was that we join the Three Self Patriotic Movement. We expressed our firm resolve not to.[2]

The Persecution of 1983–84

The almost untrammelled growth of the house churches in Henan, and across China, was abruptly halted in 1983. The Party line set in Beijing moved to the left with the launching of a nationwide "Anti-Spiritual Pollution Campaign". The government again insisted on ideological purity, and although disclaimers were made that the main religions, including Christianity, were not being targeted, in reality many cadres at the grassroots tightened control of the church. Simultaneously, a nationwide crackdown was initiated against the "Shouters" or Local Church, an extreme offshoot of the Little Flock founded in the 1930s by Watchman Nee. They were particularly active in rural areas of Henan and local authorities often seized the opportunity to persecute evangelical house churches. Many genuine Christians were caught up in the campaign and a wave of repression flowed over Henan.

On 5 June 1983 100 Christians were reportedly arrested in Lushan, followed by a second and a third wave of arrests on 22

July and 16 August. Also in June 1983 twenty-four house church leaders were arrested in Nanyang district in southern Henan. Only two were associated with the "Shouters". Several dozen Christians were reportedly arrested during this same period in Zhenping County. Many were arrested in Fangcheng and other places and forced to attend political studies classes during this same period. The persecution continued well into 1984 and was further exacerbated by the government's launch of an anti-crime campaign, which also targeted fringe sects. The local Public Security Bureaux were given quotas for arrests. To fill the quota, Christians conducting home-meetings or doing evangelistic work were rounded up on the thinnest of pretexts.

In January 1994 two letters from a house church Christian in Henan were hand-carried to Hong Kong describing the persecution in detail:

Dear Sister,

The last days are drawing near. Angry waves are rising and unlawful acts are on the increase. Many brethren were imprisoned here. But after their release they were despised and rejected by everyone including their own relatives. Only those who have turned to the Lord will stretch out warm, loving hands when one is suffering and rejected by men. They draw near, ask after one's sufferings and health. They send the things needed in an unending stream. So everyone now knows that in all the world only true Christians are close spiritual brothers and sisters!

Brother "Li" was injured when he was beaten by the head of the Religious Affairs Bureau while he was being interrogated. At present, he has been allowed home. They wanted to give him some money in compensation, but he did not want it! He is so strong and pure and does not wish to be tempted into taking money from the authorities.

There are also two sisters who are in prison. The authorities have not bothered to investigate their case. I thought of writing to the Chinese Christian "Three Self" to see if they could help. But I know the Three Self would not be concerned in this matter. They dare not ask questions. They fear the authorities will not let them do their work. And they fear losing their monthly salaries. They are only capable of helping the authorities oppress the true believers.[3]

The second letter, undated, was written a little later:

Twenty-nine Christians have been released on bail. But another brother was interrogated at night and tortured severely. He was sent back to his dormitory but then disappeared. During interrogation one brother was bound with ropes for a long time. Now neither of his arms can move. The other brother beaten with a pistol is now in hospital in Luoyang. His faith is weak. He could not bear the suffering when he was being tortured and revealed things he should not have said. When he was sent home he was talking nonsense and his mind was disturbed.

By late 1984 the persecution had eased, and many Christians had been released although some leaders were sentenced to imprisonment for varying periods. By mid-November 1984 there were still over fifty Christians (not belonging to the "Shouters") in prison in ten counties in Henan. But the work of the gospel carried on and the house churches continued to flourish. Evangelists working in Henan reported in 1984 that in one city in the south-west, baptisms were held twice monthly, with 200 converts baptised at each meeting.

The church in Henan has been tried and refined through persecution which has continued in a spasmodic and arbitrary fashion since 1983 right up to the late 1990s. In June 1985 a Henan house church leader shared how his church had reacted to persecution in a positive fashion:

From July 1982 to January 1985 our group of Christians experienced more than 40 incidents of persecution. There were more than 1,000 incidents of people being detained from between seven days and one month. They were fined RMB30-50 and then released.[4] There were about 200 incidents of people being arrested for between one month and two and a half years, most being fined RMB50-150 and then released. Twenty-four people have been sen-

Easter Sunday service 2004, Chongwenmen Church, Beijing
– crowds exiting the first sevice.

Easter Sunday service 2004, Chongwenmen Church, Beijing
– crowds queuing for the second sevice!

Wang Mingdao – China's greatest Christian leader this century – pictured with his wife at their home in Shanghai. They were both imprisoned for 23 years for refusing to compromise their faith.

Lin Xiangao (Pastor 'Samuel Lamb') – probably China's best-known living house church leader pictured at his house church in Guangzhou (Canton).

Packed Sunday service at the TSPM church in Hothot, Inner Mongolia.

A rural house church in Inner Mongolia.

The Church has a strong presence in Shanghai: the cross atop
Muentang Church rivals the cranes on new office blocks as
Shanghai rushes into the twenty-first century.

Allen Yuan (left) baptising in Beijing, August 2000
– 300 new converts queue for baptism

A house church evangelist addresses a typical rural congregation.

A 'tin tabernacle' in south China – a typical small, unregistered city house church.

Hundreds attend this cramped, unregistered city house church in south China.

Buddhism and folk religion are also experiencing a revival – a girl kneels at a temple shrine.

Blind Christians reading braille Bibles in Guangdong, south China.

A flourishing house church Sunday school in South China, 2005.

Worshippers have to sit outside the TSPM church in Guiyang which is packed with over 1,000 people.

tenced to four or five years in prison and 55 people are under detention in addition to those already sentenced.

Whenever the Lord permits these incidents, our first reaction is to take the burden with ease in the Lord. Secondly, we feel the pain and the sorrow. Thirdly, we take action to review and investigate in depth the cause of the suffering. Finally, we confess and pray, and act according to God's will to the best of our knowledge. All this takes place through prayer, review and fellowship of the whole church before the Lord. Therefore, our hearts are peaceful as we go through trials. The suffering, persecution and arrests are steps on a spiritual ladder for each of us, the costly marks of the outreach ministry of the church. Our greatest comfort is "the Lord knows". How do we know he knows? We are clear about our salvation through the Holy Spirit. We received a clear calling and we proclaim the cross of salvation according to the truth of the Bible.

The Christians of Henan know nothing of a "prosperity gospel", but they are rich in Christ. As we have already observed, they walk the way of the cross and experience the blessing of God in deep spiritual experience, and it is this which spurs them to such effective evangelistic outreach.

7

Church growth in Anhui

Anhui has always been one of China's poorest provinces. The peasants have fatalistically endured floods and famines. In 1959–61 it was particularly hard hit by famine due to Mao's utopian policies, and many people died of starvation. In recent years the standard of living has risen for many, and Hefei, the provincial capital, has an aura of prosperity with gleaming office blocks and shopping centres. However, many rural people are still poor. Large numbers of girls leave the province to seek employment as maids and child carers in Shanghai and Beijing.

Explosive growth

Anhui has experienced explosive church growth in recent years. When I visited the main church in Hefei, there was a steady downpour of rain. However that did not deter the Christians. The main sanctuary was crammed to capacity with over 1000 in the congregation. Hundreds more sat in overflow rooms, some equipped with closed-circuit TV. Outside in the courtyard dozens more stood in the pouring rain under umbrellas. One lad sat on a window ledge; a middle-aged woman perched tiptoe on a stone to peer in through a window and catch the sermon. On Christmas Day 1994 1,500 new Christians were baptised here. In 1981, soon after the church was reopened, there were 200 believers. Today there are over 10,000.

Fengyang County in northern Anhui was particularly hard-hit by the famine of 1959. For two years a reign of terror operated in the region. The inhabitants of twenty-one villages died and there were even reports of cannibalism. Local cadres punished desperate, starving peasants, burying some alive and reducing the already meagre rations. By January 1961 when this extreme policy was brought to a halt, 28,000 people in the county (12 per cent of the population) had been punished in some way and there were 2,398 orphans.[1]

Is it too speculative to see a connection between the desperate suffering of the people in this and many other rural areas in China, and the subsequent great openness of the peasants to the Christian gospel? Utopian Maoism had failed and driven the people to despair. Many were impressed by the loving witness of the faithful remnant of Christians and willing to listen to the Christian message. Today there are 50,000 Christians in Fengyang worshipping in 48 registered meeting-points. They have no ordained pastors or elders. On 15 July 1997 a new church was opened at Songji Township in Fengyang. It cost 80,000 RMB which was borne by the local believers. Nearby Huainan City in 1997 had 11,000 believers meeting in 100 churches and meeting-points.

The house-church movement is very strong in Anhui. Yingshang and Lixin in the north-west part of the province are the headquarters of two major house-church movements of the same name. They each have spread across China and claim several million members. Their networks are among the six largest in the entire country. Another network in the west of the province covers eleven counties and three cities. They have five levels of spiritual leadership with elders responsible for 50, 200, 600, 1,000 and 10,000 believers. In the summer of 1991 severe floods devastated many parts of the province. Many people lost their homes and many churches and meeting places were swept away or badly damaged. The leader of this grouping was reduced to living in a shelter made of grass. He was under surveillance and had to report twice a year to the police. Despite both the physical and political pressures, Christians reported that the number of believers in this area had doubled from 70,000 before the floods in May 1991 to 140,000 only fifteen months later!

Fuyang Prefecture

Probably the area of Anhui that has seen the greatest revival has been the Fuyang Prefecture in the north-west of the province. Local believers report that the China Inland Mission laid a firm gospel foundation in the area before 1949. On the eve of the Communist victory there were twenty-three churches and about 100 outstations serving 29,000 believers. Numbers then shrank under the pressure of various political campaigns to only 5,000 on the eve of the Cultural Revolution. However, the last two to three decades have seen a massive revival. Two Chinese researchers based at Nanjing went to Fuyang in 1991 and in 1999 and did intensive research on the church situation. Their published reports reveal that since 1979, when the churches first resumed operation after the Cultural Revolution, the number of Protestant believers in Fuyang has soared nearly tenfold.

TABLE OF CHURCH GROWTH IN FUYANG	
Year	No. of Protestants
1949	29,000
1958	8,000
1965	5,000
1979	28,444
1980	45,744
1981	88,632
1982	118,892
1988	232,433
1989	217,325
1990	212,759
1997	252,471
1998	273,187

According to these statistics, the number of Protestants in Fuyang in 1998 was over 200 times the total number of practising Buddhists and Daoists! It is interesting to note that only seven Buddhist and Daoist temples had been reopened by 1998 as compared to 459 registered Protestant meetings – as well as over 600 unregistered house-church meetings! Thus the gospel has been free of the normal competition. However, the church faces restrictions from the local government. Even the researcher was critical in his report:

> The "Three Designates Policy" [which limits "Three Self" workers to particular buildings and parishes] in some points clearly goes against Christian tradition. Religious Affairs officials blatantly go up into the pulpits to issue their instructions, thinking that as the churches have been built with their permission they have free rein so to do. Of course, all the believers clap after they have concluded.

This is a rather revealing insight into the realities of church life and government control from an unexpected source! The researcher further admitted that over 60,000 of the Christians in Fuyang belonged to more than 600 independent house churches. This was an admission that some 30 per cent of all the believers were outside Three-Self control. Other information from Fuyang received in 1990 suggested that as many as 75 per cent of the Christians had left the Three-Self controlled churches because of dissatisfaction with the degree of political interference. The unexplained fall in the number of Christians for 1989 and 1990 (see Table) could also be accounted for by people leaving the TSPM churches.

Evidence that the gospel has spread in Fuyang in the teeth of official opposition came to light in late 1993. Two "Re-education Through Labour" documents were published in Hong Kong which showed that six house church preachers had been sentenced to between two and three years in prison. Their "crimes" were listed as "organising sessions to listen to Hong Kong gospel radio broadcasts, and receiving overseas versions of the Bible. From 31 December 1992 to 5 January 1993 they organised a preachers' training class which about sixty people participated in."

It is not surprising that the church continues to grow by

leaps and bounds. Persecution refines the Church, ensuring that only those totally dedicated to the Lord will risk everything to preach and train clandestinely in the house churches.

Mengcheng County is part of the Fuyang Prefecture and reports from Three-Self sources confirm that significant growth is taking place. By 1995 the county had thirty-two major registered meeting-points with congregations of five or six hundred people each. In addition, there are 200 "daughter" meeting-points with between one and two thousand people at each. In recent years 2,000 new converts have been baptised annually. The total number of Christians in Mengcheng according to the TSPM was more than 30,000 by 1995.

Huoqiu County

Another area of revival is Huoqiu County, just south of Fuyang. The gospel was first brought to Huoqiu as recently as 1937 by the China Inland Mission. By the time the missionaries had to leave in 1951 there was one church and two small outstations with a total of about 200 Christians. Today, Huoqiu may have as many as 30,000 believers, according to a TSPM pastor. In 2003, the TSPM magazine *Tianfemg,* reported that there were 159 registered churches and meeting-points in the county – a huge increase since the days of the China Inland Mission. However, even this does not take account of the great growth of unregistered house churches. In 1987 Christians wrote out to say that there were fifteen large churches with 1,000 people at each and many smaller house churches. They spoke of "great revival" with four services at the main church every Sunday with 1,000 at each service. There were "hundreds of house churches, and in every village". A Chinese academic researcher visited Changji District in Huoqiu in 1992 and documented the astounding growth of the church (doubtless based on government and TSPM sources):

TABLE OF CHURCH GROWTH IN CHANGJI DISTRICT, HUOQIU			
No. of registered Christians			
1978	18	1982	258
1979	36	1983	480
1980	105	1985	763
1981	143	1986	2,811

Growth of the church throughout Anhui has been through tireless evangelism and fearless witness, as well as loving service. Christians have been in the forefront of settling neighbourhood disputes and teaching the elderly to read.

Revival and heresies; too few to minister

Yet it would be wrong to paint too glowing a picture of church growth in Anhui. If the province has been a furnace of revival, it has also been the cradle of heresies and cults. The "Shouters" and the "Established King" cults have been particularly active. In more orthodox circles, the churches have been riven by disputes concerning spiritual gifts, head-coverings and the place of works and justification by faith. Some house church preachers have taken extreme positions. The reader can find more details about such sects and cults in Chapter 9. The poverty and low education level of many of the country believers, and the lack of trained leaders, has exacerbated the situation.

In 1994 there were fewer than forty registered pastors and only twenty-four elders working in the more than 2,000 churches and meeting-points operating under the TSPM in the entire province. The house churches are training young men for ministry and I was much impressed with their zeal and biblical knowledge when meeting a group who ministered to several thousand believers. Sometimes they did not even have enough money to buy food or buy rail tickets. The country people are often unable to give those who live by faith even the barest essentials. However, there are others who peddle extreme doctrines and verge on heresy. They swindle the peasants out of their meagre money and resources and bring down the wrath of the authorities on their own heads – and on the heads of numerous true believers who become the indiscriminate target for suppression.

Continued growth through persecution

In late 1995 Anhui provincial authorities launched a major drive against cults. However, in an ominous move, local leaders decided to recommend "re-education through labour for principal members [of non-governmental religious groups] whose misdeeds do not warrant criminal punishment".[2] In effect, this meant that members of any sect, cult or unofficial house church could be targeted and leaders who "repeatedly failed to repent" sent to labour camp for non-criminal offences – such as itinerant evangelism, distribution of unapproved religious literature, etc. Since then, many letters have been received from house church Christians in Anhui complaining of renewed persecution.

On 2 November 1995 a Christian wrote:

Our house church has been closed by the government. This time the churches in the entire province are being "rectified" and many churches have been prohibited. Only one church is allowed per rural district. In our rural district ten house churches have been closed down.

A Mr Niu wrote out on 23 February 1996:

Our meetings here are suffering extremely great pressure from the government. Some churches have been forced to stop meeting. But the brothers and sisters are still hungry for God so have just changed their mode of worship. The authorities say they wish to protect legal believers and strike against illegal religious organisations. This is all very well, but at the grass-roots level it becomes simply an excuse to extract money from people.

Many similar examples could be given.

Anhui Christians have suffered much. Yet the gospel continues to spread. Persecution and heresy make serious assaults on the church, but the people of God have stood firm. In 1934 there were only 38,000 Christians in the entire province. It is doubtful if there were more than 50,000 by 1949. Yet recently a TSPM pastor estimated that there are probably between two and three million believers in Anhui today – that is three times the number in the whole of China in 1949!

8

Revival among the tribes

I was standing at the back of the Holy Trinity Church in Kunming, southwest China. This old, rickety building was formerly the main China Inland Mission church in the city. Two tribal Christians who had come down from the mountains came up to me and we had a brief conversation.

"I've just been talking to the pastor here. He says that north of Kunming there are 80,000 tribal Christians meeting in three hundred fellowships? Is that true?"

"Yes, of course. Everyone is a Christian where we live!"

In many parts of Yunnan Province this is no exaggeration. There has been a great outpouring of the Holy Spirit among the Lisu, Miao, Yi, Jingpo and other minority peoples. In virtually every case, present revival can be traced back to sacrificial missionary work earlier this century. The seed of the Word of God was planted at great cost; then the missionaries often saw spiritual breakthrough and mass turning to Christ of entire communities. But this church growth has been dwarfed by what God has been doing in Yunnan over the past two decades.

The Lisu: prayer and poverty

In 1913, just before World War I, James Fraser of the China Inland Mission began Christian outreach among the Lisu people in the mountains of Yunnan along the Burma border. The Lisu had the reputation of being one of the most backward tribes in Asia. They were bound by animism and demon-worship and were perpetually drunk. Fraser, often working in isolation, fell prey to illness and depression. He saw little fruit from his preaching and the few converts soon relapsed into their old ways. Out of his despair of the situation and even

106

more of himself, Fraser was led into a deeper walk with Christ and total reliance on God through prayer. He realised the hard way that no breakthrough would come without fervent intercessory prayer. To that end he set up prayer groups in the UK and sent detailed, factual reports, honestly sharing his failures.

Spiritual breakthrough came. At a tribal feast where drunken Lisu danced and prostrated themselves to the evil spirits, Fraser's missionary companion, Allyn, broke down and wept. A powerful sense of the Spirit of God came over them all. The village headman threw away his whiskey and destroyed all the objects of demon worship in his house. In Allyn's own words:

> Then Big Tiger led the way to the spirit tree. Incense and bowls for food stood on the shelf attached to it. He broke the bowls and tore out the shelf, burning everything that could be burned. All the whiskey was poured out to the pigs. Before nightfall the whole village had professed to believe. Within a few days, the people of the next hamlet had followed suit.

Fraser wrote soon afterwards that over 400 Lisu families had come to Christ and were under instruction – a total of over 2,000 people.

Fraser developed a simple alphabetic script for the Lisu which helped lift the people out of superstition and illiteracy. The Bible, a catechism, a hymn book and other works were printed in the new script. The first Lisu books rolled off the presses in 1925. As has often been the case, the translation of the Bible into their own language gave the Lisu a new sense of identity. Today, over seventy years later, a well-known Christian Lisu scholar estimated that between sixty and seventy thousand Lisu in the Salween valley still read this script. In 1986 a government literacy drive proudly announced that two Lisu villages in Lijiang reached targets of 100 per cent and 94.7 per cent literacy – using the old "Fraser script".

Gospel work among the Lisu was later consolidated and developed by others, including most notably Isobel Kuhn who wrote many books about the Lisu church. On the eve of the Communist victory in 1949 there were about 15,000 Lisu Christians. Then came tragedy. Churches were closed and pastors imprisoned. Many Lisu believers fled across the mountains into Burma. For two decades from the mid-1950s the situation appeared very dark. Then, in the early 1970s, one elderly Lisu evangelist was released from labour camp and began to preach the gospel along the precipitous banks of the upper Salween River. Revival broke out and many Lisu returned to the Lord.

Since 1980 the gospel has spread among the Lisu to the extent that a few years ago the government was considering declaring them officially a Christian minority. In December 1997 the official China Christian Council magazine *Tianfeng* published the following report about Nujiang prefecture where many Lisu live:

> In 1980 Nujiang had 21,441 Protestant Christians. By 1989 they had increased to 66,702. Fugong County is the most typical: there is no other religion apart from Christianity in the entire county. In 1987 it had 87,090 people of whom 54,829 were Christians or sixty three per cent of the population. In some villages ninety eight per cent of the population are Christian. There are 292 registered churches in this county.

This official report shows that within nine years the number of Christians tripled in the Nujiang Prefecture. It is interesting to compare it to a Communist Party investigative report made in 1950 of Christian activity in Fugong County. In July 1950 the total population of Fugong was only 18,000 people of whom 3,437 were Christians (about one fifth) meeting in thirty-seven churches. Comparison with the 1997 report shows that since 1950 the number of churches in Fugong has increased eight-fold and despite massive population growth, the percentage of Christians has risen from one-fifth to nearly two-thirds of the population – in spite of the severe repression which lasted from the 1950s into the 1970s.

However, even these official statistics may be on the conservative side. In 1987 the North Burma Christian Mission which has had long experience of mission work among tribal people in the "Golden Triangle" area of south-west China, Burma and north Thailand, reported that there were 131,000 Lisu Christians in China meeting in 1,250 churches. A leading TSPM pastor I interviewed in Kunming in 1993 gave a figure of 200,000 Lisu Christians – or 35 per cent of the total Lisu population of 575,000.[1]

By 1996 the China Christian Council had printed 75,272 Bibles in Lisu script – a considerable number in view of the fact that there are 227,000 illiterate or semi-literate Lisu.[2] Today the Lisu are still very impoverished even by Chinese standards. The standard of living is still very low due to the mountainous terrain, poor soil and lack of communications. Annual income for many is unbelievably low – perhaps under £20 per annum in cash terms. Thousands are living at subsistence levels outside the money economy altogether. Yet in the face of this poverty, in rough stone churches perched on precipitous ravines lit by oil lamps, the Lisu cling tenaciously to their faith. The saga of how the gospel came to them and spread like wildfire over the last eighty years is one of the great success stories of 20th-century missionary endeavour and subsequent successful indigenisation.

The Miao: martyrdom and growth

On 10 July 1998 Queen Elizabeth II attended a service in Westminster Abbey to commemorate ten Christian martyrs of the twentieth century. Among the ten statues of martyrs unveiled on that solemn occasion was that of Pastor Wang Zhiming, chosen to represent all those who gave their lives for Christ in China. Pastor Wang was a Miao Christian who in 1944 was made President of the Miao Christians in northern Yunnan; a strong church had been established here by World War II. In 1951 he was ordained pastor in Kunming and was greatly loved by people of many tribal groups.

Soon afterwards, pressures on the church grew steadily. Sapushan, the CIM base-village where he worked, was renamed "Anti-Imperialism Village" during the Cultural Revolution and the church was desecrated and turned into a warehouse. An apostate, named Elder Long, helped instigate relentless persecution. Churches were closed and an atheistic "cultural centre" set up to indoctrinate the Miao believers. Although Pastor Wang had been received by Chairman Mao in Beijing in 1955, in 1969 he was labelled a counter-revolutionary. In 1973 he was executed at a mass rally before more than 10,000 people, most of them Christians forced to attend. Thirty-four other Miao Christian leaders were unjustly imprisoned in labour camps.

Yet the persecution often had the opposite effect of what was intended. Immediately after the execution, a group of Miao Christian women rushed to the official stand and denounced Elder Long who was sitting there with the Public Security officers. The whole stadium was thrown into turmoil. Twenty years later this same elder was bitterly disappointed that he had failed in his goal of wiping Christianity out in Sapushan, and expressed his indignation to a Chinese researcher that Christianity was reviving everywhere.[3]

Miao Christians associated with the CIM in Guizhou Province also suffered great persecution. According to a report by a sympathetic Mainland Chinese researcher:

The Miao teacher Yang Zhicheng and 162 other evangelists and Christians were labelled a "counter-revolutionary clique" and wrongly sentenced to labour-camp. In 1964 local cadres investigated one production brigade which had more than 100 Christians and decided the church had taken over power from the grass-roots Party organs. Suppression of religion redoubled. All the properly ordained preachers suffered restriction, which gave independent evangelists their opportunity. In 1965 in Weining there were at least 647 independent [house church] preachers – more than twenty times the number of those formally appointed in the original church.

This report is evidence that, in this area of Guizhou, persecution actually led to a multiplication of evangelism by laymen and the birth of religious activities, which formed the beginnings of the house church movement. The same researcher gives a moving account of how persecution intensified in this area during the Cultural Revolution (1966–76).

At the onset of the Cultural Revolution all religious believers were labelled "ghosts, snakes and monsters" and "running-dogs of imperialism". Some were forced to renounce their faith at special indoctrination sessions. In the Wumeng area alone, these sessions were held eighteen times. Churches were confiscated and Bibles burnt. On 28 July 1974 a secret Christian meeting of Miao people at Xinglong Commune in Weining was surrounded by armed militia and a bloody incident occurred. The "exterminate religion" campaign reached its zenith. But the Miao resisted, saying:

"The more you forbid Christianity, the more we will cling to the church. If you confiscate our churches, we will worship in caves. If you announce the extermination of the church, we will develop even more secret meetings. If you attack ordained pastors, we will use even more independent house church preachers instead. If you take action against us on Sundays, we will multiply our meetings to every day of the week and into the night."

Despite every effort at extermination, Christianity made tremendous progress in secret. Independent evangelists re-awakened the fires of religious fervour.

In 1979 a Chinese researcher visited Weining and wrote a letter to the local Party leaders about what had happened there:

A Miao, Mr Zhang Youxue, from Stone Gateway Commune and his relative Mr Yang Derong, a China Inland Mission evangelist from Hezhang went to Stone Gateway together to evangelize.[4] The commune held a struggle-accusation meeting against both of them. Afterwards Zhang was forced to commit suicide. His two sons, Zhang Mingcai and Zhang Mingan jumped into a river and also committed suicide. This incident caused masses of the Miao people to return to the church.[5]

Truly the blood of the martyrs is the seed of the Church. From death comes spiritual resurrection and revival.

In the village of Xiaoshiqiao (Little Stone Bridge) simple Miao Christians were faced with a stark choice in 1969 during the Cultural Revolution: choose between Jesus or Chairman Mao. They chose Jesus. As a result local Communist cadres told them:

> The land belongs to Mao, you cannot till it. The cattle belong to Mao, you cannot pasture them. Every blade of wood and grass belongs to Mao.

The Miao leaders were dragged off to the commune head-quarters and were incarcerated and tortured. In 1973 the villagers were forced to give up their tiny private plots – their only source of food. Relatives in neighbouring villages had to smuggle in food to them. In their long years of trial the Miao Christians drew great strength from biblical teaching on the second coming of Christ and, as in the early Church, saw suffering and the way of the cross as an integral part of the Christian life.

Even the arrest of the extreme left wing "Gang of Four" in Beijing in late 1976 and the official ending of the Cultural Revolution did not bring relief to these beleaguered tribal believers. In March 1978 local authorities launched another campaign against the "counter-revolutionaries hiding under the cloak of religion". Two hundred militia armed with rifles and machine guns surrounded the village and demanded that they give up their faith in Christ. There was no answer. So the militiamen charged up the hill and took all the men in the village prisoner. They were trussed up like pigs and carried down to the town jail. The village head was sentenced to seven years in jail but released after only one year. Eventually the cadres apologised to the people and put all the blame (conveniently) on the Gang of Four leftist leaders. The Christians replied: "We do not blame you at all. These events fulfil what is prophesied in the Bible. Christians must suffer. The gate to heaven is narrow."

Why did these simple tribal believers stand and suffer for Christ when others more sophisticated compromised or even renounced their faith? One answer is surely that they were grounded in the Word of God from the start. It is both stirring and humbling to trace the work of God among the Miao back to the beginnings a century ago.

Three missionaries: Fleming, Adams and Pollard

The China Inland Mission began preaching the gospel among the Miao in Guizhou Province in 1896. From the start, the work was born in suffering and martyrdom. In 1898 W.S. Fleming of the CIM and Pan Sheoshan, the first Black Miao convert, were both murdered. Many Black Miao came to Christ in the years that followed. An even greater harvest was reaped among the Flowery Miao. In 1899 J.R. Adams of the CIM opened a chapel and a small boys' school in Anshun, Guizhou. Adams aggressively proclaimed Christ and confronted idolatry head-on. New converts were expected to burn their "spirit paraphernalia" – charms, drums, sorcerers' wands, etc. All of it was thrown on a bonfire. "Spirit-trees" were cut down and the huts where Miao young people engaged in sexual orgies and smoked opium pipes were ruthlessly torn down. In 1902 the first twenty converts were baptised. But by 1907 Adams and his colleagues had baptised 1,200 Miao!

The new converts were thoroughly grounded in the Christian faith. No one was accepted for baptism until they had been a Christian for at least eighteen months and undergone a rigorous programme of instruction covering the entire spectrum of Christian doctrine and practice. At baptism they were given a Christian, personal name. This was highly significant as until that time many Miao had no personal names, being designated by numbers or by their relationship within the family: "Little sister" or "Big two". For the first time, the gospel gave them a personal identity. For centuries the Miao had been oppressed and driven from their homes by Han Chinese settlers and officials and local Yi warlords. They practised slash and burn agriculture, scraping a precarious existence from the stony soil of the mountains. Whole communities, sunk in poverty and despair, would periodically be swept by pagan "messianic" movements promising a great king as a deliverer. It was into such a desperate situation that the gospel of Jesus Christ came as a message of hope and liberation.

By the time Adams died in 1917 he had baptised nearly 7,000 Miao converts. The revival, which often took the form of a mass people-movement with entire clans and villages turning to Christ, swept westward to the Guizhou-Yunnan border region, and then deep into the heart of Yunnan Province itself. One day a group of dishevelled Miao arrived on Adams's doorstep, hungry to hear the gospel. They had travelled on foot for three days all the way from Zhaotong in north-east Yunnan. Adams recommended that they return and seek instruction from the United Methodist missionary, Samuel Pollard, who had recently started work in the area. Two hundred Miao descended on Pollard's mission compound, and a second revival began!

Samuel Pollard began visiting Miao homes in 1904. He soon set up a new centre at Shimenkan (Stone Gateway) on the Yunnan–Guizhou border. By 1907 1,412 Miao from seventy-one villages had been baptised. On one occasion after hearing the love of God preached, one Miao asked Pollard: "You do not really mean that God loves us Miao, do you?" After centuries of poverty and oppression they could not conceive that anyone could love them, much less the Lord of all creation. The gospel came to the Miao as a great liberating force from their traditional animistic world controlled by cruel and capricious evil spirits.

Pollard taught the new Christians to pray against demonic oppression and possession. He also applied the gospel sensitively in the wider, social context. Christian festivals filled with races, games, lantern-shows – and, of course, preaching! – were substituted for pagan sexual orgies. Concerned about their poverty and the unscrupulous exploitation of greedy landlords, he organised a savings club and helped the Miao to buy their own plots of land. For this practical Christian compassion he was nearly beaten to death by the servants of two of the landlords, and was laid aside for a year. When he returned, it was as a hero. The man responsible for the beatings was finally apprehended and sentenced to death. Pollard, in the spirit of Christ, successfully pleaded for his life: "When I'm better, I want that man to come and have a meal with me. Jesus Christ died for that man and I want to see him saved." This spirit of servant-hood and forgiveness was to provide an example and a strong bedrock of faith in action for Miao believers such as Wang Zhiming who died a martyr's death fifty years later.

Miao revival spreads

The revival among the Miao spread west into northern Yunnan. Two Miao lepers in Wuding County, north of Kunming, had heard the gospel from their compatriots. Pollard, already overworked in Stone Gateway, graciously invited the China Inland Mission to pioneer a new work. In 1906 Arthur Nicholls set up a new and thriving Gospel Centre in Sapushan. The work spread from the Miao to the Yi and Lisu communities nearby. By the early 1950s 12,000 Christian Miao, Yi and Lisu lived in this area. The CIM had built over 200 churches and outstations, and ran clinics, primary schools and a Bible college.

Since the early 1980s the Miao churches in Yunnan and Guizhou have again emerged strongly. In both provinces, despite the persecution which lasted from the early 1950s to the late 1970s, there has been massive church growth. In 1950 in the Hezhang district of Guizhou there were 9,800 Miao Christians meeting in fifty churches, according to a local government report. By 1986 they had grown to 23,000 believers meeting in ninety churches. In the Wumeng Mountains of the same province the fierce persecution which drove Zhang Youxue and his sons to suicide (see above) led to amazing church growth. The government discovered that in 1986 the Miao believers in Wumeng had grown ten-fold from about 3,000 in 1950 to 30,000. When I visited the provincial capital, Guiyang, in 1993, a leading pastor told me that there are now 300–400,000 Protestants in Guizhou compared with fewer than 20,000 in 1949. At least half (200,000) of them are Miao believers.

In northern Yunnan the Miao and Yi have returned to Christianity in great numbers. In Luquan County in 1950 there were about 1,600 Black Yi meeting in fifty-two churches and chapels. In 1994 the official Christian magazine *Tianfeng* reported that there were now 50,000–60,000 Christians among the Yi, Miao and Lisu in Luquan meeting in nearly 300 churches and meeting-points. Neighbouring Wuding County had about 5,600 Miao and Yi baptised Christians living near the Sapushan CIM HQ in 1950, together with 2,700 Lisu Christians making a total of about 8–9,000 committed Christians in the area. In 1988 on a visit to Kunming I was told by a local preacher that there are at least 30,000 Christians in Wuding meeting in over 100 churches and meeting-points. The seed of the Word of God first planted by the CIM has borne much fruit.

Similarly, the early Methodist work in Zhaotong has survived and flourished. In the summer of 1988 the Rev Huang Guiying, a female pastor of Miao nationality, visited the UK. The following year, she reported that there were 130,000 Christians in Zhaotong prefecture, mainly Miao, served by over 400 Christian workers. However, she herself was the only formally ordained pastor for this huge number of believers. In 1993 when I visited a senior pastor in Kunming, he informed me that there are actually 150,000 Christians in Zhaotong.

The total number of Christian Miao in Yunnan has been estimated at 50,000 by another Kunming pastor. However, given the very large numbers of Miao believers in Zhaotong, Luquan and Wuding – and there are Miao Christians in other areas, too – this figure seems very conservative. A Western Christian with much experience in tribal work in south-west China has estimated that there are about 150,000 Miao Christians in Yunnan.

Communist Party researchers estimated there were about 100,000 Christians in Yunnan in 1950. Today there are officially 800,000 according to a Christian Council spokesman. This means the church has grown eight-fold since the Cultural Revolution. About three-quarters of the believers belong to minority groups such as the Lisu, Miao and Yi. However, only about 60 per cent have been baptised, because of the dearth of Christian workers in the province to cope with this huge increase. The entire province had only ninety-one registered pastors at the end of 2001, although they were aided by 640 elders and over 1,300 preachers and evangelists. The number of registered churches has increased from 800 in 1982 to 2,200 in 2003, and in addition there are over 1,000 registered meeting-points. However, poor communications, illiteracy and poverty are major obstacles to proper pastoral care and biblical teaching for the rapidly growing church in Yunnan. Five enormous prefectures have no ordained pastors at all.[6]

Too few Bibles, too few pastors

The revival and church growth in Yunnan is staggering. But the downside is that many of the believers are impoverished and poorly educated, even illiterate. There are about 600 elders and over 1,000 registered preachers in the province to aid the overworked pastors. But this still means a ratio of 1:500 in terms of Christian workers to believers, and many of the preachers themselves have minimal education. Pastor Huang from Zhaotong reported that in 1989, in some areas, there was only one Bible shared between 2,000 Christians. Hopefully, the dire shortage has been eased somewhat in the last decade. However, quality Christian literature is still in short supply in Yunnan and many Christians, especially tribal minority ones, cannot afford to buy the modest selection of titles available in the large churches in Kunming.

The tribal churches in Yunnan and Guizhou have survived and multiplied at great odds and under great persecution. According to recent visitors – the few who have been able to reach the high mountain villages, as tourists and outsiders are generally discouraged from going there by suspicious local authorities – there is something of a "Shangri-La" atmosphere about these remote Christian communities. What can be more moving than to hear Miao choirs sing Handel's *Messiah* in full harmony? Yet the deep and genuine devotion of these tribal believers should not blind us to the real dangers they face. Poverty and illiteracy are still endemic, leaving them prey to extremism and false cults.

Ominous progress

Perhaps most ominous of all, is the continual process of assimilation to the "higher" Han Chinese culture in the valleys and the cities, and the inexorable process of modernisation and urbanisation. Fifty years ago the aboriginal tribal churches of Taiwan were flourishing. Today their young people leave the mountain villages seeking employment as cheap labour in the factories of Taichung and Taipei. Fresh and innocent tribal girls are forced into prostitution in the cities. The Christian tribal peoples of Yunnan and Guizhou are much more numerous, but they are not exempt from the same impersonal forces of "progress". Yet the gospel has brought them new life and hope, and in most cases given them a written language and a cultural identity which otherwise would already have been swallowed up by the surrounding, dominant Han Chinese culture. Perhaps one cause for hope that they will survive, and their churches not go under, is the fact that in areas such as Wuding and Luquan quite sizeable numbers of Han Chinese now worship together with the tribal Christians, attracted by the gospel message and testimony of these simple people.

TABLE OF CHURCH GROWTH IN YUNNAN		
YUNNAN LOCALITY	CHRISTIANS IN 1949–50	CHRISTIANS IN 1990–2000
NUJIANG PREFECTURE	14,800	100,000
Inc. FUGONG COUNTY	3,437	50–60,000
ZHAOTONG PREFECTURE	11,889	150,000
WUDING COUNTY	8,000	30,000
LUQUAN COUNTY	1,600	60,000
WEIXI COUNTY	500–600	5,000
TOTAL YUNNAN PROVINCE	c.100,000	c.800,000

9

Signs and wonders

Pastor Ye in south China told me how one day he came across several people praying for a child in his church courtyard. The little girl had fallen unconscious and been rushed by her mother to the local clinic where she was pronounced already dead by the doctor. In despair, the distraught mother carried her daughter to the church. Pastor Ye took the child from her mother and found the body already chilled. He laid hands on her and prayed, but nothing happened. Then he and all the church members knelt and prayed earnestly. He prayed that the Lord would save the child and that until then he would stay on bended knee. Shortly afterwards, the child began to cry. She was given some milk, but vomited it up. She was then taken to the hospital and this time admitted. She suffered a relapse but Ye and others stayed with her and continued to pray. She finally made a complete recovery, and in 1992 celebrated her eleventh birthday.

This remarkable story was later published in a Christian magazine in Hong Kong.[1] It did not take place in a dubious pseudo-Christian sect on the wilder fringes of the unregistered church, but in the courtyard of a registered TSPM church and after the prayers of a TSPM pastor. Pastor Ye was well aware that he was taking a considerable risk in praying for the girl's healing and that he and his church could have got into serious trouble with the authorities and even be blamed for her death. Miraculous healing and exorcism (*yibing gangui*) are distinctly frowned upon by Religious Affairs cadres. But Ye felt he had no alternative faced with a mother's need. Later, she wanted to bear witness at the church to the miracle, but he carefully refused, fearing the repercussions. Yet deep in his heart he knows that miracles are a Christian reality. "Did not Jesus heal the sick and cast out demons? How can we deny these miracles?"

Pastor Ye's attitude is shared by the overwhelming majority of Chinese believers, apart from a few pastors and theological teachers in the TSPM seminaries who cling to the now rather old-fashioned liberalism they imbibed pre-1949. Chinese Christians adhere to a robust biblical supernaturalism which believes in a sovereign God who can answer the prayers of his people in remarkable ways. Eighteenth-century rationalism with its deism and "God of the gaps" theology, which has so emaciated late 20th-century Western Christianity, has had little influence in the Chinese Church. Struggling to survive in a Marxist environment which prides itself on being "materialist", Chinese Christians have wholeheartedly accepted the supernatural worldview presented to them in the Bible.

Mixing in the demonic

A few words of caution are in order at this point. In the West, many stories of healings and miracles in China have been circulated with little attempt at verification. Some frankly incredible stories have been used to boost fund-raising. A degree of healthy scepticism is in order, particularly concerning very second-hand reports from the Chinese countryside. Chinese peasants in many areas are still steeped in much superstition on which witches, occultists and sect leaders thrive. In Daoist and Buddhist folk-religion, it is common for people to have remarkable dreams, see visions and be taken up into heaven and to converse with immortals, perhaps even the Jade Emperor himself.

From a Christian perspective it may be said that, in God's providence, the preaching of the gospel has met with ready acceptance by Chinese peasants who have no difficulty (unlike Western rationalists) in believing in the supernatural worldview of the Bible. Where there is clear biblical preaching and teaching (as there often is in both TSPM and house churches) this is a positive thing. However, where Scriptural truth has not been presented clearly, some "believers" may be left in a twilight world of folk-religion with a thin veneer of Christianity. They believe that "Jesus heals" but have no clear understanding of his atonement, or experience of conversion. They are left in a position in which they are still open to the demonic, and continue the practices of folk-religion using Christian terminology. This is a good part of the reason why so many sects such as "Lingling", "Lightning from the East", et.c have sprung up in the last two decades.[2]

A clear instance of this mixture of folk-religion with Christianity occurred recently in central China. A large crowd of country Christians were engaged in loud and ecstatic worship. The impression is sometimes given that this rather extreme form of worship is the norm throughout China, which it is not. However, more seriously, two peasant women were delivering "prophecies" in a trance-like state. A Chinese Christian friend who had been a TSPM pastor in north China was quite horrified by this. She had preached widely in the countryside and succeeded in upsetting the local authorities, so she could not be accused of toeing the "Party line". However, she told me that she had prayed for, and exorcised, peasants who had been demonically inspired and had "called down the spirits" (*tiaoshen*) in an exactly similar way. The only difference was that the people she had dealt with had been practising folk religion, while the two peasant women used a gloss of Christian terminology. Otherwise, the practice was identical and she had no hesitation in calling both demonic.

Don't accept everything; don't reject everything

So low levels of literacy and education in the countryside, combined with a mindset often steeped in native Daoist and Buddhist folk-religion, lead to syncretism and the development of cults. We should be cautious in accepting every story of miraculous healing which emanates from China. However, the opposite danger of rejecting every such report on *a priori* grounds that miracles no longer happen is also very real for many Western Christians whose thought-processes have been more moulded by a narrow scientism than they would care to admit.

In some areas of China, Pentecostal or indigenous churches laid a strong emphasis on faith-healing before the Communist takeover, and this tradition is still strong today. In Guangxi, for example, many Zhuang minority people believe in the power of shamans to heal the sick – usually for a substantial fee. Today, in some villages, Christians have prayed for the sick without charging. As a result, in Guiping the number of believers grew from a few dozen to over 200. Local shamans regard the Christians as their enemies and even vandalise their properties. Guangxi has been deeply influenced by the Christian and Missionary Alliance which holds that Jesus is the perfect Healer.

In the 1920s Rev Zhong Zhentang of Yulin was suffering from tuberculosis and went to the Queen Mary Hospital in Hong Kong for a cure. Doctors told him his case was hopeless. For three months he called on God in prayer to heal him, and completely recovered. He returned to Guangxi praising the power of God and telling everyone of his experience. It is not surprising that, to this day, there is a strong belief in the power of God to heal the sick in Guangxi. Christians gather around the pastor after the service to ask for a prayer for healing. Christian doctors and pastors in Guangxi when interviewed were understandably cautious (because of the authorities' opposition to "feudal superstition") but admitted they believed in the power of prayer, while not using healing as an excuse to reject medical treatment or to inveigle people into church.[3]

Work of the Spirit noted by authorities

In China even the authorities have openly admitted that many people have become Christians after claiming to have been healed in answer to prayer. The phenomenon is so widespread, that even allowing for exaggeration and syncretism, there is plenty of evidence that an unusual work of the Holy Spirit has been taking place. In the Yangzhou district of Jiangsu Province, for example, many people have been drawn to church because of the healing power of Jesus. They are not always sick themselves: the experiences of healing by family members or friends have been a powerful testimony.

In Taixing, a large city in the Taizhou district, the revival of Christian activities owes much to the healing of a Miss Zhao Su'e, a clothing sales-girl. She began to work in 1989 but one morning fainted, spat much blood, and was rushed to hospital. Her white blood cell and platelet levels were found to be far below normal. After resting at home for two months she continued to spit blood so was admitted to the Liberation Army hospital in Suzhou in October 1989. Her parents were Buddhist, so they paid a visit to the Hanshan Temple. Her mother prostrated herself before the idols 500 times – but to no avail. The doctors told Miss Zhao her chance of survival was only 1 per cent, and she had only six months left to live. She was twenty-one years old.

The cancer spread rapidly and the family were grief-stricken. Then a Christian who was visiting his sick wife in the next ward told her that only Jesus could help. She listened to the gospel intently and one day said excitedly: "If there is such a God in the world, I would follow him to the end." She learnt how to pray and entrusted her life totally to God. Where medicine failed, God's help intervened. Gradually the cancer cells decreased and her white blood cells and platelets increased. The doctors could not figure it out. Although it was an army hospital and all doctors held military rank higher than that of a company commander, they turned a blind eye when she prayed and sang with her new-found Christian friends. They finally admitted that something was at work outside their experience. Miss Zhao was finally allowed to go home in May 1990. When she came back for a check-up, her marrow was found to be healthier than that of a normal person.

While she was convalescing her mother came to Christ. Su'e continued to pray for her father and younger sisters. She gave testimony in the Suzhou church and asked the Christians to pray with her. Then on New Year's Eve 1989 her father told his entire family that he, too, had decided to follow the Lord. At first, Su'e could find no Christians in Taixing. But gradually she made contact with ten others. They applied for permission to reopen the old mission built by American missionaries but long occupied by other units. Fortunately, one of her relatives was Party secretary of the county and the church was quickly reclaimed. The church was reopened in Taixing in September 1992 and attracted 1,000 people to the rededication service. By 1994 there were between five and six thousand Christians in Taixing County. Almost every village now has Christian meetings. Su'e continues to be very active in local church-work.[4]

In nearby Huangqiao the lady in charge of the local meeting-point, Chen Heying, can also testify to God's healing power. She had throat cancer for three years and no doctor dared operate on her. She first came in touch with Christians in June 1991 and was baptised in August 1992. Now she sings every day for the Lord and bears witness to her friends and relations. When she first believed, Huangqiao had only a handful of Christians; now there are about 500.

The testimony of Chen Guifang in Quxia, Jiangsu, is even more remarkable. Ten years ago there were no Christians at all. At that time she had been bedridden for eight years with liver cancer, unable to eat anything, and existing on glucose through a tube. In early 1986 her nephew shared with his aunt the good news of Christ. Unable to speak, she just nodded her head in acceptance. She found herself very relaxed and soon afterwards was able to drink and sleep well. She began to pray disjointedly: "Jesus, I want you, save me!" The next evening she felt remarkably comfortable, broke into a sweat and – for the first time in eight years – asked for something to eat.

Yet she still had a swollen liver, a tumour under her armpit and a hard boil in her buttocks. She was taken for recuperation to Zhangjiagang although her family did not expect her to survive. However, after one month's stay in the home of her sister whose husband was a deacon of the church, she made a full recovery. She rushed back to Quxia and gave testimony. More than ten people believed in Christ as a result. She shared her testimony by singing three songs:

1) "I want Jesus every day. I want him when it is bright sunshine and when it is covered with black clouds. I want him every hour."
2) "Enter my heart, Lord Jesus. Come now, never go away. Lord, come and live in my heart."
3) "Mighty and all-powerful, the blood of the Lamb is victorious. Mighty and all-powerful the blood of the Lamb helps us to be holy."

Her repertoire of gospel songs may have been limited, but no one can accuse her of preaching heresy, or deny the reality of her simple faith. Three of her relatives were converted and joined her in preaching the gospel. In 1985 they set up their own unregistered meeting-point. By 1994 there were more than 300 Christians in Quxia compared with none ten years before. In 1989 the government took action and surrounded the building. Each of them was interrogated and their names taken. They were warned not to meet again. However, most came back the following Sunday and for the next few years they were not interfered with.

Such instances of healing leading to conversion are commonly reported by Christians. Here is an example taken from a letter written recently by a Christian in Anhui Province:

One day in May, my father was knocked down by a car right in front of our house. The doctor diagnosed a broken chest-bone and another fractured. My father was taken to a small hospital and only given the same medication every day to reduce the pain. We were worried that the bones would not be healed in this way. At this difficult time we prayed together that the Lord would help my father. The Lord did work a miracle. About a week later the bones began to heal and two weeks later my father could even walk for short distances. Some people had said for sure that he would at least be bedridden. Others said he would never be healed. They were so surprised that he could walk. As a result we have become a Christian family now except for my elder brothers. Many people in our village have turned to Christ, including young people.

Demon possession and folk practices

Demon possession is still quite common in the Chinese countryside because of the resurgence of Buddhism, Daoism and folk beliefs, all of which have a strong occult tinge. One of the standard works on demon possession was written by John Nevius, an American Presbyterian missionary in the 19th century, as a result of his long experience of working in the Chinese countryside. Today, much of the strength of idolatry and demonism has been broken in China, particularly in the north, where the Communists did a more thorough job of destroying shrines and educating the peasants. However, it would be a grave mistake to state, as some have done, that Mao totally eradicated traditional religion, unwittingly preparing the way for the gospel.

Today folk practices are rife in many areas, and not just in the countryside. Some years ago I was introduced by Pastor Lin Xiangao (Pastor Lamb) in Guangzhou to a young city lady who had recently been delivered from an evil spirit. Dabbling in fortune-telling and Buddhist occult practices she had heard voices following her down the street wherever she went. After much prayer she was completely delivered to become the quiet, neatly-dressed young Christian I chatted with briefly. Pastor Lamb does not make a fuss about such things, yet he is quite happy to pray for healing and to exorcise those who have been afflicted by evil spirits.

Most experienced Christians in China take the same practical attitude. I remember meeting two nurses who were house church leaders in Suzhou. They were quite clear in their definitions of mental illness or schizophrenia, and of demonpossession. They were quite able to distinguish the two and describe the different symptoms. The deluge of interest in the occult in the West means that cases are on the rise and that Western Christians, too, need to be aware of how to deal with those afflicted in this way.

Government officials and researchers have admitted in recent years that the Church has grown greatly, particularly in the rural areas, because of the influx of new converts who have claimed healing in the Name of Jesus. Their attitudes vary from perplexity to downright hostility.

The case of Liu Qinglin, a house church evangelist in Inner Mongolia, is typical. Liu was converted at the age of thirty-one when he came across a copy of the Bible. Although he was uneducated, like many peasant Christians in China, conversion spurred him on to read God's Word and raised the level of his literacy. In 1984 he began to preach the doctrine of Christ crucified in the remote area of Moguqi in the far north-eastern part of Inner Mongolia where temperatures drop to minus 40 degrees Celsius in winter. In those early days more than fifty people turned to Christ through his preaching.

Remarkable stories of healing

In 1985 a young man suffering from pulmonary tuberculosis spent more than 3,000 RMB at Moguqi's two main hospitals, but in vain. He was taken to Liu's house, where Liu cared for him and gave him massage, which helped him to breathe better. He became a Christian and returned home and after a week was completely better. This young man had a relative called Wen Qinglu who was himself a doctor of Chinese medicine. His mother had been suffering from pulmonary emphysema for two years and he himself had fallen ill. Through the young man's witness the entire household of seven people turned to

Christ, and two weeks later Mr Wen recovered and was able to walk.[5]

Thereafter Liu Qinglin's fame spread rapidly through the region and many people were converted, mostly through receiving healing. By 1989 the number of baptised believers was nearly 3,000. Liu attracted the hostile attention of both the TSPM and the local authorities and was arrested three times. On 3 January 1989 the Inner Mongolian TSPM passed resolutions which included the clause: "the making of converts must be done in strict accord with church regulations and is not permitted to be done by unordained persons." According to unconfirmed reports, Liu may have died while in prison.

A remarkable testimony was published in 1990 in China. The author, She Guoqing, was an engineer, then aged 68. He wrote as follows:

I am 68. In 1952 I changed my profession from the army to work on a farm. My wife is Yang Shenying. She believes in Jesus Christ and has brought our three children to faith. Because of my hardness of heart I would not accept Jesus as my Lord for a long time. I had an atheistic education. The thinking was that when a person died he just turned to ashes. I smoked, drank, played cards and my health suffered. I did not believe in heaven or hell nor acknowledge I had sins.

One day sudden illness struck. This time I was not able to rise from my bed. I deteriorated to a very critical state and was close to death. Suddenly, I heard much noise and relatives crying. I felt myself floating in the dark like an observer before the bed. I saw my thin body, my yellow face. Then I was led by an unseen force into a long, dark tunnel seemingly without end. I walked with great effort towards the end where there seemed to be a glimpse of light. At this moment I heard in the distance behind me someone calling: "Papa! Papa!" I recognised the voice of my eldest daughter.

About this time a person in white was pulling hard from the back. I woke up, opened my eyes and saw my daughter kneeling by my side, crying and pleading with Jesus to save me. I also saw that I was dressed in a dead person's clothes. I asked my daughter what had happened. She told me: "You were dead for two days. Uncle and grandfather quickly put the funeral clothes on you. They wanted to put you quickly into the coffin, have the funeral and then the burial in case your body would rot in the high temperatures in Yunnan. I was very much against this as I felt you had not believed in Jesus and would not go to heaven. I could not bear to see you go to hell. So I desperately begged Jesus to bring you back to life, so you could accept Jesus... and then you could die. This is the reason I did not allow our relatives to put you in the coffin for burial. I did not leave your bedside, even for a minute. For two days and nights I cried out to Jesus unceasingly for his grace. I would not get up from the floor until he answered my prayer. Now Jesus has performed this miracle and brought you back to life."

After hearing my daughter's account, I was finally touched by her faith and God's grace which had touched my heart and melted it. I kept saying "Thank you, Lord". I now want to use my second life granted by God to be his witness, to preach the gospel, to bear much fruit and to glorify his Name.

The people in my village saw the wonders God had done in my life and began to believe that God is real and alive. Many accepted his salvation and accepted Jesus as their Lord and Saviour. This news spread all over the village. My new life is a gift from God and so I don't worry about it anymore. I no longer lust after reputation, position or enjoyment. I only want to devote my life to preaching the gospel.

Mr She's experience, although placed firmly in the Chinese cultural context, tallies remarkably with "near death experiences" recorded in the West. It would be dangerous to build doctrine or Christian experience on such occurrences. However, there seems little doubt that Mr She himself was soundly converted as a result of his experience, has led many others to Christ and has devoted his life to preach the gospel. Such stories are not uncommon among Christians in China. What is remarkable about Mr She's account is that it was published openly in 1990 in the pages of the TSPM-controlled *Yanjing Theological Seminary Bulletin* in Beijing. The TSPM normally strongly discourages any emphasis on healing or on signs and wonders. The present writer is very uncomfortable with the orchestrated healing meetings which have become common in the West. What is usually different about the Chinese accounts is that they record remarkable answers to prayer by individuals for themselves or their families when faced with real-life crises rather than in a hyped artificial atmosphere of "healing meetings".

Some DVDs circulated in the West give the false impression that the entire house-church movement is wildly charismatic. In fact, the mainstream in the cities is quite conservative evangelical, even fundamentalist. It is true that in some rural areas unhealthy influences have been brought in from Hong Kong, South Korea and elsewhere. Most Chinese worship meetings, whether in house churches or TSPM churches, are characterised by reverence and holy awe.

Wang Mingdao, whose writings are still very influential in house-church circles, roundly denounced what he considered to be the excesses of the early charismatic movement in Shandong province in the 1930s. He did not take a strict cessationist view, and gave an "emphatic yes" when asked whether God could still heal in answer to prayer. But he was sceptical of those who were always falling over and having dreams and visions: "What sinners need most to hear is the gospel of saving grace. What believers need most to hear are God's rebuke, teachings, promises and exhortations and not dreams, visions and tongues, which are no substitutes."[5]

More recently, Allen Yuan in Beijing, who himself came from a traditional Pentecostal background, spoke out against charismatic excesses. He stated: "I don't speak in tongues. I don't think a person has to speak in tongues to be saved. We should pursue being filled with the Holy Spirit but not in the way the charismatics do. We should be biblically balanced."[6] Along with Samuel Lamb and many other leaders, these men cannot be pigeonholed into our Western boxes.

I remember one of my first meetings with an elderly house-church leader in Beijing. She was a medical doctor who had retired early despite pleas from the authorities that she continue, so much did they value her services. However, she retired to devote herself full-time to Christian ministry. I remember knocking on a red door and being ushered in by this smiling lady. I explained briefly who I was. "Come in! Come in! We are just praying for a young couple whose baby is ill."

It transpired that the couple had taken their baby to hospital because of what looked like a dark birthmark, quite common in Chinese babies, and quite harmless. But this case was different and the hospital staff were not able to diagnose the disease. Dr "Wang" herself was unsure. "I have just been counselling them and sharing the gospel with them for the last hour. Now it is time to pray together for them and seek God's hand of healing on the child." She, her daughter, the young couple and myself bowed our heads in prayer. It was all so simple and natural. I was profoundly moved by her holistic ministry in which the gospel of Christ and the need for repentance and faith were obviously central, and yet healing, whether by medical means or in answer to prayer, also had a place.

Perhaps in the West, where positions on healing have become sharply polarised, we need to learn from our Chinese brothers and sisters.

10

Ravening wolves

In late 2005, I was visiting one of the large TSPM churches in Chongqing when I was approached by a young man who claimed to be a house-church leader. However, as our conversation progressed, he avoided answering quite simple questions and I became increasingly suspicious. He made great play of our being in "the End Times" and of a new, secret, revelation. But about what that revelation was, he remained tantalisingly silent. In retrospect, it seems almost certain that he was a "scout" for the cult "Lightning from the East".

On many issues, TSPM and house-church leaders remain at loggerheads. But, as to which is the most dangerous cult in China today, they are in complete agreement. Over the last five years on my various travels all over the country, when I have enquired about which is the cult most active in a particular area, the answer has almost invariably been "Lightning from the East" (LFE). But what is this mysterious cult?

According to the latest Chinese research, the founder of LFE is Zhao Weishan, who fled to America (where he sought asylum) in June 2001. Zhao was originally with the Shouters but eventually founded a new cult, which believes that the age of grace is now over; it has been replaced by imminent judgement. The only way of escape is to believe in the new female Messiah – a Chinese woman surnamed Deng, believed to live near Zhengzhou in Henan Province. A young Christian researcher who has written a book on cults in China believes she is not only Zhao's puppet, but also mentally ill, even demon-possessed.[1]

LFE works clandestinely because it has been outlawed by the government. Its workers mainly target existing churches, especially house churches. These "moles" infiltrate churches for months, and are experts in imitating Christian language and behaviour. They look out for the most spiritual leaders and play on their desire to go further with the Lord by dangling the promise of "new revelation" in front of them. They also use money, blackmail, false miracles, kidnapping and physical beating to force Christians to become their workers. These are classic cultic brainwashing techniques and can be very effective. Their methods are very similar to traditional Chinese secret societies and those of the sinister, shadowy world of "black society" – the Chinese criminal mafia.

LFE pulled off its most outstanding coup in mid-April 2002, when it succeeded in kidnapping virtually the entire top leadership of the mainstream evangelical house-church network, the China Gospel Fellowship. Thirty-four leaders were lured to various locations with the promise of intensive Bible training offered, supposedly, by a respectable Singapore-based evangelical training centre. In fact, it was an elaborate, highly co-ordinated "scam". The house-church leaders were released only after one of their number escaped, and members appealed in desperation to the government and police for help.

Over the last five years LFE has spread its tentacles to virtually every province of China. It has devastated poorly-taught rural house churches, taking over up to 50 per cent of the existing churches in some places. It is even active overseas, having set up several bases in North America, and has been known to engage in giving out tracts outside large Chinese churches in California.

But LFE is not the only cult active within China. The Chinese government, as of 2004, recognised fifteen illegal cults. Three of these were Buddhist – the remaining twelve were all pseudo-Christian.

In early 1992 rumours spread throughout the large Korean (Chaoxian minority people) community living in north-east China that the end of the world was imminent. Cultists from South Korea had visited the area and spread their false teaching. In the village of Yinmahe an unbalanced cultist announced that the date was fixed for 9 June 1992. On that day true believers would ascend into heaven and see the Lord. In a grim re-enactment of the Jim Jones' "People's Temple" mass-suicide in Guyana, he persuaded many people that killing themselves was the pathway to bliss. At the last moment the police were tipped off and burst in to prevent a tragedy. Twenty-three people including seven children were saved from mass suicide.[2]

Many other gullible "believers" have not been so fortunate. In March 1990 a strange preacher walked into a village in Fangcheng County, Henan, a centre of Christian revival already described. He announced that Jesus would appear soon on the banks of a nearby river. A large crowd of peasants gathered and waited all night for the second coming. One man could not contain his eagerness and walked out into the strong current. Nineteen others followed him. All were swept away and drowned in the frigid waters.

The Chinese Church is undergoing massive growth and revival, but the forces of darkness have launched a strong counter-attack. The last two decades when the Church has seen rapid expansion, have also seen the growth of numerous heresies and cults. We should not be surprised by this: in New Testament times, and whenever there has been revival, false teaching and extreme practices have led many astray. Paul contended with extreme manifestations at Corinth and John denounced the gnostics. In more recent times, Jonathan Edwards, George Whitefield and the Wesley brothers were greatly used by God, but alongside spectacular conversions and church growth they also had to contend with extremism and false doctrine. The Chinese Church is no different and it would be very wrong to paint an idealised picture ignoring the darker side and the intense spiritual warfare taking place.

Cults: real and misperceived

Jehovah's Witnesses have been active in Shanghai, and Seventh Day Adventism is strong in many areas. Mormons are sending in English teachers and using their wealth to gain influence. However, in general, the traditional Western cults have made few inroads into China. Much more dangerous have been new, indigenous cults which have sprung up over the last twenty years.

The first cult to make a nationwide impact in China were the "Shouters" in the early 1980s. An offshoot of the biblically-based "Little Flock" founded by Watchman Nee in the 1930s, the "Shouters" looked for inspiration to Witness Lee, Watchman Nee's chief lieutenant. While Nee endured long imprisonment in labour camps eventually suffering martyrdom in 1972, Lee sought to take over the movement from the safety first of Taiwan and then southern California. His views on the Trinity were reportedly unorthodox, and his control of the "Local Church", as it became known, was increasingly author-itarian. In China the wide dissemination of his books in the early 1980s led many "Little Flock" believers – and, sadly, often the younger, keen members – to wander into the paths of extremism. In some cases, ill-taught followers ended up pray-ing in the name of Lee and regarding him as little less than a new Messiah. Others, however, appear to be genuine evangeli-cal believers caught up in an extremist group.

The movement in China was characterised by strong hostil-ity to both the Three Self movement and the government. Lee had developed close political ties with the Nationalist authorities in Taiwan and made no secret of his virulent anti-Communism. In China his followers sought to take over assemblies, indulged in aggressive evangelism and denounced the government. In July 1983 the authorities responded by launching a nationwide crackdown. Thousands were arrested and many key leaders imprisoned for long periods of time. However, this, and the death of Lee himself on 9 June 1997, has not destroyed the movement which still remains strong in many areas.

Many other cults have mushroomed in recent years. Usually they have been created by some "charismatic" figure, often a poorly educated peasant with a gift for preaching. This person claims to be the Messiah and attracts a following. Most of these cults flourish in the strange world on the very fringes of the Christian Church where fragments of Christian belief meet with traditional folk superstition. In spite of fifty years of Communism, traditional Buddhism and Daoism have experienced a new lease of life, together with palmistry, witchcraft, seances, fortune-telling and every conceivable type of occult activity. The local Chinese press often fulminates against this "feudal superstition" yet it remains a fact that at almost every pedestrian overpass in the cities you will find people practising fortune-telling undisturbed whereas anyone daring to sell Christian literature would soon be arrested by the police.

The rapid growth of the Christian Church, which in many areas has outpaced its ability (whether registered or unregistered) to provide solid biblical teaching, has led inevitably to extremism, and to a large fringe element who are vulnerable to ever more bizarre heresies. This does not mean that the heart of the revival movement is unsound. Sometimes Christians overseas – especially those who have had contact only with the "official" church and its political spokesmen – have been too ready to accuse the house churches of being hotbeds of heresy and almost deserving the repression meted out by the authorities. My own experience, having met with godly house church leaders in many provinces, is very different. The heart of the house church movement (or movements, as many different streams are involved) is led by dedicated men and women whose knowledge and practice of the Scriptures puts most Westerners to shame.

However, it would be foolish to deny the existence of a "fringe element" and the growing menace of cults. In 1996 the China Christian Council published a useful booklet entitled *Uphold the Truth – Resist Heresy* which contains valuable information on the main cults. House church leaders such as Pastor Lamb in Guangzhou have also mimeographed booklets opposing heresy. While travelling in southern China in late 1998 a young house church leader gave me a privately-printed booklet which also critiques several of these cults from a biblical perspective. Since then, several books have been published within China giving much valuable information.[3]

Even listing the main cults and heresies shows the extent of the problem:

CULT/HERESY	FOUNDER	ORIGINAL AREA
Shouters (Huhanpai)	Witness Lee (Li Changshou)	National
Established King	Wu Yangming (executed)	Anhui
The Lord God Cult (Zhushen Jiao)	Liu Jiaguo (executed)	Hunan
Ling Ling Cult	Hua Xuehe	Jiangsu
Mentuhui (Disciples)	Ji Sanbao	Shaanxi
Eastern Lightning	Zhao Weishan (in USA)	Heilongjiang, Henan
Three Grades of Servants (Sanbanpuren)	Xu Shuangfu (arrested April 2004)	?
New Testament Church	Zuo Kun	Taiwan
Cold Water Cult	Huang Huanting	Guangdong

Many of these cults are now nationwide, having spread to most major cities and even to far-flung areas such as Xinjiang. The Disciples, for example, originated in the poverty-stricken district of Ankang in Shaanxi Province (north-west China). Their founder, Ji Sanbao, who may originally have had connections with the "Shouters", formed a tightly hierarchical organisation. Fervently apocalyptic, they urge farmers to stop their work, and students their studies. By 1995 the cult had spread from Shaanxi to Hebei, Sichuan, Shandong, Yunnan and even Xinjiang. In Sichuan it spread rapidly to more than seventy counties and twenty major cities. The Sichuan Public Security Bureau estimated that in 1995 it had over 100,000 followers in Sichuan, meeting in 4,000 gatherings. Several serious incidents ensued, including one in which local people spread a rumour that the Disciples had poisoned the water supply. Enraged, they attacked sect members and twenty people were killed and thirty-one injured.

In Shaanxi the sect converted nearly 100 Party members as well as more than eighty local People's Congress delegates. The government, thoroughly alarmed, took swift counter-action and in 1995 declared it illegal and raided meetings in Sichuan, Shaanxi and Hubei. In April 1995 they investigated more than 3,000 members in 600 towns and villages. Over 2,000 meetings were closed. In Shaanxi the army and militia were called out and over 500 members deemed "destructive elements" were arrested as well as eighty "hardcore" leaders. In early 1996 a Christian in Nanchuan City in Sichuan wrote out that registration of all Christian meetings had been strictly enforced with the aim of eliminating the Disciples. Genuine Christians in the area had been wrongly targeted.

In 1995 a senior leader of the Three-Self Patriotic Movement expressed serious concern to the government that many Christians had been wrongly labelled as belonging to the "reactionary Disciples" organisation. Apparently, two investigation teams had been sent out, but returned with conflicting reports: one stated the Disciples were a dangerous cult, the other that they were genuine Christians, harming no one! He was worried that although the Disciples were believed by the government to have 300,000 members, there was no hardcore evidence that they existed as a specific grouping at all! Many government reports were based on hearsay. More alarming, some officials were openly advocating that people be labelled as "Disciples", as otherwise they could not be arrested because Christianity is a legal religion in China.

This highlights one of the many undesirable side effects of these new cults. True Christians, especially those meeting in unregistered house churches, are often caught up in the campaigns to crack down on the cults. This was particularly true in 1983–84 when there was a major drive against the Shouters and many evangelical Christians were wrongly arrested and even imprisoned. Local government cadres have little detailed knowledge to distinguish *bona fide* believers from cultists. They also rely for information on leaders in the Three Self Patriotic

Movement, part of whose role is to inform the government of "abnormal" religious activities. Those who are politically subservient and hostile to evangelical religion may take the opportunity to accuse genuine Christians who meet outside the "Three Self" umbrella.

Definitions are crucial

The TSPM leader pointed out that the problem of definition of a cult is crucial. In China, once labelled a cult, a religious group is outlawed, its members face fines and "political re-education" and its leaders imprisonment and even execution. In the case of the Disciples, he stated that there is no clear definition and that the boundaries between "Disciples" and true Christians is difficult to draw: "Because of this there is the possibility that the broad mass of believers will be labelled as 'Disciples'. Striking against them will be most unfortunate and will worsen relations between officials and the masses."

Ironically, three years later in August 1998 beleaguered house church leaders in central China raised exactly the same question with the authorities in an open letter pleading for dialogue and an end to persecution. They called on the central government to "spell out the definition of what is a 'cult'. This should be according to recognised international standards and not just according to whether people attend or do not attend "Three Self" churches."

Unfortunately, as we approach the Millennium, it appears that the Chinese government has largely ignored this wise advice, both from the senior levels of the TSPM and from the house churches. The indiscriminate crackdown on cults and house church Christians continues. In some cases the persecution proceeds from abysmal ignorance bordering on the laughable, if it were not for the fact that innocent Christians are being punished. One of the most blatant examples surfaced in Red River County (Honghe Xian) in a remote corner of Yunnan inhabited by the Hani people, many of whom have turned to Christ.

On 30 June 1998 the local newspaper published a long article attacking Christians meeting in five towns in the area. About 425 Christians were gathering in eighteen meeting-points. The local authorities declared them an "illegal religious organisation". They were accused of being a "heretical cult" for separating themselves from the traditional idolatrous customs of the Hani people. Leaders were arrested in the middle of the night. However, what reveals the sheer ignorance of the authorities is the fact that the newspaper openly published that twenty "illegal missionary books" were confiscated including "The Old and New Testament", "Hymns of Praise" and "A Biblical Look at the Three Self" – all books legally printed within China by the China Christian Council! Local cadres clearly had no idea, or chose to ignore the fact, that Christianity is a legal religion in China and that Christians have freedom to read Bibles printed within the country.

The authorities are clearly extremely nervous of all new religious movements. China's history is punctuated by peasant rebellions and the rise and fall of dynasties. Very often those rebellions originated in secret societies and cults with a strong sectarian basis. In the mid-19th century China was ravaged by the pseudo-Christian Taipings whose ideology mixed Old Testament iconoclasm with motifs from traditional folk religion. This incendiary mixture resulted in a nationwide rebellion in which twenty million people lost their lives. The Communist Party came to power as a secular movement which rallied the peasants under the messianic leadership of Mao Zedong. It is ironic that this same government which until recently applauded the Taipings and highlighted every peasant rebellion has, since the death of Mao, become increasingly conservative and made efforts to suppress any manifestation of religious, let alone political, unrest in the countryside.

The "Established King" cult

The rise and fall of the leader of the "Established King" cult is a grim illustration of how the authorities deal with any religious cult deemed subversive of the State. Wu Yangming, a peasant from Anhui with only primary education, professed faith in Christ in 1979 at the age of twenty. However, by 1983 he had been drawn off-track into the activities of the Shouters. In the 1983 crackdown on the Shouters, and again in 1986, he was arrested by the police and in 1987 imprisoned for one year. On release he discovered his place had been usurped by others so he set up his own organisation and proclaimed himself to be the "Established King". In 1989 he was rearrested and sentenced to three years "re-education through labour" but managed to escape the following year. Over the next five years he eluded the authorities and established a growing network of supporters who engaged in widespread evangelism of the new teaching.

The "new gospel" centred around Wu himself, who twisted Scripture in outrageous fashion to "prove" he was the Messiah. He proclaimed: "Jesus is already dead. Now only the 'Established King' is the One True God and the Lord of Heaven!" In fact, every reference in the Bible to Jesus was soon replaced by the "Established King" to whom special hymns of adoration were composed. Every cult member had to learn them – if not, they were forced to kneel on the ground until they could sing them by heart.

The cult spread rapidly from its base in Anhui to more than twenty of China's thirty provinces. However, the authorities did not become fully aware of its activities until 1993. In October 1994 cult members in Shanghai distributed tracts denouncing the Communist Party as "the Great Dragon drunk with the blood of the saints" and announcing the world would be consumed by fire within two years: "All who do not believe in the 'Established King' will die! Only those who believe in him will obtain eternal life!" Unsurprisingly the government moved to suppress what they now considered to be a blatantly "counter-revolutionary" organisation.

They were aided in this by Wu's reported sexual escapades. About 80 per cent of his converts were women and girls. Strict segregation of the sexes was practised outwardly. However, secretly Wu reportedly engaged in sexual intercourse with more than 100 women and was always accompanied by an entourage of a dozen girls. Eventually one of them reported him to the police who tracked him down after a ten-day manhunt. Wu was arrested and on 29 December 1995 was executed by a local court in Anhui, accused of being the founder of a counter-revolutionary organisation.

Wu's sect has uncanny similarities to the Taipings of the mid-19th century. Both claimed to follow the Bible but in reality owed more to traditional Chinese folk-religion and secret-societies. Both set up strict feudalistic hierarchies demanding absolute obedience. And both leaders originally enforced puritanical sexual standards but indulged themselves in sexual licentiousness. Finally, both strongly opposed the government and were ruthlessly suppressed.

How widespread is the problem of cults?

Many have spread to virtually every province. The problem seems to be growing as the Church, both registered and unregistered, struggles to combat false teaching with a lack of trained pastors and preachers and a lack of teaching materials. Some observers have expressed fears that the Chinese Church will be taken over by heresy. Others have begun to attack the house churches, virtually equating them with cults. Both these views are, in my view, extreme and unwarranted.

Available statistics from TSPM and government sources, although incomplete, do go some way in helping to formulate a realistic picture of the size of the problem. The following table gives some idea of the scale of the problem:

TSPM/GOVERNMENT ESTIMATES OF CULT FOLLOWERS	
Shouters	200–250,000
Mentuhui (Disciples)	300,000
Established King	nearly 1,000,000
Lord God Cult 10,000	
Lightning from the East	over 1,000,000
Three Grades of Servant	500,000 (House-church estimate)
Cold Water Cult	1,000

An internal document listing numbers of Protestant churches and house churches in Henan suggested that well below 10 per cent of all meetings in that province (which all agree has been a hot-bed of heresy as well as revival) belong to cults and sects. In Jiangsu, the Lingling cult reportedly had no more than 15,000 members at the height of its influence in 1994 – yet Jiangsu officially has more than one million Protestant Christians. That is equivalent to only 1.5 per cent of the total Christian population.

Taking the admittedly limited evidence available, it seems reasonable to assume that nationally no more than 5 per cent of the overall "Christian" population may be involved in pseudo-Christian sects. That figure may, however, be considerably higher in certain areas when a cult makes initial headway before being targeted by the authorities and its members scattered and "re-educated".

The threat facing the Chinese Church from sects and cults while serious, is not yet chronic. We may go some way with Marxist sociologists in agreeing that as long as poverty and illiteracy remain endemic in China's countryside, then it will be a rich spawning ground for bizarre sects and cults. It is also sadly true that on the fringes of the Christian Church there are a growing number of heterodox groups. The ultimate answer to the sects is for Christians in China, as elsewhere, to be rooted in Scripture. For that to become a reality many more Bible colleges need to be opened than are at present permitted, and restrictions need to be lifted on the mass printing and distribution of Christian literature within the country and on its importation from abroad.

11

Suffer the little children

There are over 500 million children under the age of 18 in China. Also, according to the religious regulations laid down by the Chinese Communist Party, no child under eighteen may be baptised or become a member of a church. You will always see a scattering of children attending church with their parents or grandparents in the large city TSPM churches. They are the privileged few. Children from non-Christian homes are unlikely to attend. They may do so occasionally, but if they come too regularly it is likely that the news will leak back to their schools and pressures be brought to bear. The Party is anxious to channel promising children into its youth organisations and then into the Party itself. In practice some 500 million children and young people in China are "off-limits" to the Gospel – a shocking situation.

It is fashionable now in the West to write off Chinese Marxism as a fraud and a sham in which no one believes anymore. It is certainly true that people do join the Party to "make friends and influence people" and to get a foot higher up the ladder of promotion without believing a word of the jargon of "Marxism-Leninism-Mao Zedong Thought". Very few people apart from some diehard "leftist" Maoists believe in Maoism with the fanatical, quasi-religious faith of so many young people during the 1950s and 1960s. However, one should not write off Marxism in China yet.

Schoolchildren taught God does not exist

This is especially the case where the young are concerned. Even a cursory browse in any State bookshop will reveal that all the school textbooks from primary level upwards are still written from a narrow Marxist, materialist perspective. The entire educational system in China is based on the presupposition that atheism is true and that science has disproved religion. Evolutionary theory of a crude, 19th-century kind that has long been abandoned in the West is still instilled into the children. As a result, young people grow up taking it for granted that God does not exist.

I remember clearly an incident in Chengdu a few years ago. My hotel was next to a large primary school. Early in the morning the children were standing in serried rank in the playground. For a good fifteen minutes they chanted the words: "I love the Communist Party! I love the Communist Party!" over and over again. It was a chilling reminder that Marxist ideology is still propagated throughout the educational system, and that hundreds of millions of children are on the receiving end.

Sunday Schools and children's work of any kind are glaring by their absence in most TSPM churches in China. Pastors sometimes deflect foreign visitors' enquiries with such excuses as "the premises are too small". Amid the modest range of Christian literature produced by the China Christian Council, there is not one book or booklet for children. There are no children's Bibles and no Sunday School materials available legally in China for children or teachers. At a TSPM meeting in Shanghai in the early 1980s there was a discussion about teaching the gospel to children. Many Christians at the meeting insisted that according to the words of Jesus himself to "let the little children come unto me", there must be preaching of the gospel to children. No decision was taken, but later on the Party passed down the order that there was to be no instruction of children in the faith.[1]

Some signs of change, but difficulties continue

However, since 2000 there are encouraging signs that this state of affairs is slowly changing. Many TSPM and house churches do operate Sunday schools, youth work and young people's camps, and in some areas – particularly large cities and coastal provinces – the "under-18-year-old" rule is not applied with any vigour by local officials. Such work is done quietly and in such a way as not to draw official attention. In one church I visited in Fujian Province I was overjoyed to hear dozens of children singing Bible choruses in a downstairs room during the main Sunday morning service. Children's work here seemed well organised. In contrast, the "Sunday school" in a huge city church in north China's Liaoning Province which had a membership of over 5,000 people was tiny and "ad hoc". A young woman squatted on a plastic stool on the floor of a small room reading from the Bible to no more than four children. The pastor was proud of the fact that they even dared to have a children's meeting but obviously nervous of official intervention.

Such meetings take place in some churches but are not called "Sunday schools". They are advertised among church members as "crèches" to which Christian parents can deposit their children so that they do not disturb Sunday worship. There they can be taught a few songs and given a Bible story. In this way, the church has some excuse if any over-zealous official should come prying. However, such crèches are by no means the norm. Many, probably most, churches do not dare go so far. In some country areas where control is still very tight, it is reported that the presence of hard-line Maoist officials leads to children being turned away from even entering the doors of a church.

In late 1997 authorities in Wenzhou, Zhejiang Province, took action against a flourishing Sunday school operated by a large church in the area. In a letter dated 21 November 1997 a local Christian gave a rare glimpse into some of the problems faced by our brothers and sisters in China as they seek to share the gospel with children:

> Recently the government sought to suppress and wind up our Sunday school. But thanks to God's great power and the tenacity of our workers we can now continue quietly as long as we do not call it a "Sunday school", but change the name. They have also tight-

ened control on what materials we can photocopy. Our teachers lack materials so it is very difficult for them to teach the children well. They also lack training.

Another letter from Hebei Province in north China dated 25 February 1997 shows the persecution those running Sunday schools may still face:

> Several of our church-workers enthusiastically started Sunday school work. But later the local school teachers and even some parents were strongly opposed to it. Then the police made several investigations and persecuted us. Each teacher was fined 200 RMB. So we were forced to wind up the Sunday school, although one in a neighbouring village has gradually been consolidated.

And in August 1997 a house church believer in Anhui shared this:

> In just the space of a year we have set up another house church in addition to the original one and are about to start a third. Thanks to God's guiding and help we have also set up a Sunday school. Up to seventy children attend. This is a very important work but we lack teaching materials. As it is a new work we are not gifted in leading it. Moreover, in China to do Sunday school work is a dangerous enterprise. The law lays down that it is forbidden to lead children under the age of eighteen to faith in Jesus. If they discover us, then the lightest punishment is detention and a fine. The heaviest punishment is three years in labour-camp. This Spring Festival [February 1997] we had a sister who was arrested and was forced to confess that she had led three little friends to faith in Jesus. She was detained for four days and fined 1,200 RMB. Ours is a very impoverished region, so most people do not earn that much in a year. Please pray for us. And please send some materials on how to teach Sunday school.

It is humbling to read such accounts and to realise that despite intimidation and persecution, many Chinese Christians are seeking to obey Christ in outreach to children.

A mixed picture

However, it is to be feared that in some areas of China the very concept of children's work has faded into oblivion. In Shanghai and some major cities there are still a few old ladies with practical, but outdated, experience of Sunday school work from the 1940s or even the early 1950s. But in vast areas of China such people are few or non-existent. I remember quizzing a house church leader in Yunnan on the subject. "The children?" He looked bemused. "They are too young. They disturb the meetings for the adults." That seemed to be the extent of his concern.

Of course, some house churches do have vigorous children's ministry. Pastor Lamb (Lin Xiangao) in Guangzhou has had a flourishing children's and young people's work. What a joy it was to attend a special Easter youth celebration a few years ago. With people sitting on the rickety wooden stairs and squashed into every nook and cranny one could hardly breathe! First the Sunday school put on a Bible play in costume. Then the older children sang, accompanied by violins and a whole range of instruments. In the West, thousands of meetings like this take place and are unremarkable. But to see this in China was an overwhelming experience. I almost wept.

Pastor Lamb's efforts to reach children with the gospel have not gone unnoticed or unopposed. On 10 February 1998 three officials of the Religious Affairs Bureau called at his house church. Here, in his own words, is what happened:

> They said, "Sunday school is illegal". I said, "China agreed to the law of the United Nations that children can follow their parents to believe in Jesus. If we register, our faith will be restricted. I'll not register even if you arrest me again."

Many people pray for Pastor Lamb and so far the new, restrictive religious laws have not been implemented against him. But it is a sobering thought to realise that it is his flourishing children's and youth outreach which has aroused the ire of the authorities.

Children are the future of the Chinese Church and there is no doubt that the lack of Sunday school work and children's ministry constitutes a serious weakness in what is otherwise a flourishing scene. When emphasis has been given to children's work, children themselves have often taken the initiative, quite spontaneously, to share the gospel at school with spectacular results. One Christian worker from south China shared in late 1998 that out of his church of more than 2,000 members, more than 200 were children who regularly attended meetings. "These children are extraordinarily hungry to know God. They have quite a deep knowledge of the Scriptures."

In September 1996 a Christian from Shaanxi in north China wrote:

> The church here has been persecuted by the "Three Self" and forced to stop meeting. The Christians have been fined. But our leaders are preparing to start up meetings again. Many of the children here love to listen to Bible stories, and they love me to teach them hymns. Recently the children learnt about the persecution and the fines and they prayed about the situation. A few days ago I went back and the situation had improved considerably. The children continue to pray with me. We have up to twenty come. Every time I see them they demand Bible story books, but every time I return I have to disappoint them.

Growth, and some exciting new projects

Despite all the pressures and difficulties, the vision to engage in children's ministry is spreading. In one area in eastern China almost every church has a Sunday school which is seen as a vital component for building up the church's life. Besides having to operate in a situation where such work is still forbidden, the churches here also lack suitable Sunday school materials. The teachers have to modify materials from Hong Kong or other countries. These churches also focus on the children's parents. They organise meetings with parents regularly to help them understand the importance of teaching God's Word to children. They also hold summer camps for children. In 1995 "only" 200 children participated; but in 1998 over 1,000 children took part.[2]

In late 1998 while visiting south-west China I was reliably informed that the TSPM churches in Guangxi province had held a meeting to discuss children's work. There are other signs that, despite official pressures, more attention is being given to this vital ministry. In March 1997 a house church leader in Henan wrote:

> In our county town there is not one child who has been born again in our church. Nearly every family of believers has children and there must be 20-30 children altogether. But none of them goes to meetings as there is no suitable house for them to meet. Please pray that God will supply Sunday school teachers and a suitable place to meet!

In August 1998 a Miss Wang wrote from Shandong Province, describing how God has called her to become involved in Sunday school teaching:

> I have a vision for Sunday school work and have already been involved in this for nearly a year. But I have never been properly trained nor had teaching experience. When all twenty of the children I am teaching decided to follow Christ I simply wept. I have witnessed God himself at work. These children were able to confess their sin and believe in the atonement of Christ. The Sunday school work in our area is relatively recent: just over a year old in one church and only a month old in another. But from just a handful of children we now have nearly one hundred. Now we have four classes. One problem is the wide age-range. Another is the lack of teachers. We have only five and they are all in full-time employment with little free time. We are making this a matter of urgent prayer. Just last summer more than thirty of the children were converted. We need systematic training.

All across China there are similar situations. As China continues to open up, churches overseas, particularly in the overseas Chinese world in south-east Asia and North America, need to give top priority to training culturally-sensitive children's workers and Sunday school teachers and trainers. Already, a few have been visiting China to train Sunday school teachers. However, many more are needed. It goes without saying that much more Christian children's literature is needed. Various groups have published children's Bibles, Christian comic books and song-tapes. I recently even came across an excellent comic book of a Chinese girl's conversion from occultism to Christianity. But there still seems to be a lack of co-ordination by the various agencies. Welcome as all these efforts are by Chinese Christians, they are really but a drop in the ocean in the great task of evangelising China's 400 million children.[3]

12

Party members find Christ

Mrs Su is a retired lawyer, a former Communist Party member – and a Christian. She lives with her husband and aged mother in an old house in one of the ancient *hutongs* (lanes) in Beijing, which are fast disappearing before the bulldozer. Many years ago Mrs Su became a Christian, but as a Party member she had to keep her faith secret. Party members, by definition, must not have any religious belief. Their guiding ideology is still "Marxism-Leninism-Mao Zedong Thought". However, God spoke to her and she was convicted that she should no longer be like Nicodemus and keep her faith in a strictly private compartment, but profess Christ openly. She went to the Party Secretary in her university where she was teaching law and politely stated that she wished to rescind her Party membership as she had become a Christian.

The Party Secretary took back her Party card and cancelled her membership. Then he looked at her and told her bluntly that she no longer was allowed to teach at the university. She had been fired. In the months that followed she tried many openings for teaching posts throughout Beijing, but every door was closed – no one wanted to employ a person who had dared to defy the Party and was therefore politically suspect. Her decision to follow Christ openly had been costly, but one she does not regret. She lives modestly at home, supported by her husband. Every day people from all over the city, and from further afield, visit her for spiritual counsel and prayer. God has opened up a ministry of encouragement that has more than made up for the job she lost.

Communist Party today

There are 63 million Communist Party members in China. That is more than the population of the UK. Yet they are a minority – only 5 per cent of the population. The Party maintains absolute political control, but recognises that the majority of the population are not Communists. By a sophisticated "United Front" strategy the Party ensures that those with other belief-systems, including Christians, outwardly obey Party policies whatever their private beliefs may be. It was only during the madness of the "leftist" years (roughly 1958–78) that Mao and the extremists in the Party sought to indoctrinate the entire population and turn every Chinèse into a "New Socialist Man".

Today the Party is an elite club whose members enjoy many privileges – not least the power and the *guanxi* (connections) which enable many members to make money in business and finance. It goes without saying that this has resulted in the most blatant corruption which has riddled the Party from top to bottom. As the Party is self-policing, periodic anti-corruption drives usually execute or imprison a few scapegoats in lowly positions, leaving high Party officials unscathed.

Party members, along with the three-million-strong People's Liberation Army, are indoctrinated in atheism and forbidden to take part in religious worship, let alone become practising religious believers. The only exception to this rule is in certain minority areas such as Tibet and Xinjiang where the local population are overwhelmingly Buddhist and Muslim, so to avoid total isolation cadres are permitted to attend religious meetings and even, to some extent, to hold religious beliefs.

For years the Party has sought to infiltrate and destroy the Christian Church from within, and during the 1950s it was highly successful. Certain key pastors and church workers were actually working for the Party within the church. In the 1930s and 1940s the YMCA and the YWCA in China became recruiting grounds by Party underground workers of keen, left-leaning

Christians. Today, a good proportion of the elderly TSPM workers who hold political power in the registered churches come from this background and are regarded justifiably with suspicion by Christians.

In his book *Christianity in Communist China* (1969) George Patterson gave unique evidence from a defector from the Guangzhou Religious Affairs Bureau. In the early 1950s "Xiao Feng" was instrumental in setting up the Religious Affairs Bureau in Guangzhou. At that time officials had no knowledge of religion, and their one guide for the work of controlling and infiltrating the churches was a series of lectures by Stalin entitled "Foundations of Leninism". It is often forgotten now in the West that China was then closely allied with the Soviet Union and that the whole panoply of religious control set up in China owes much to Stalinism. "Xiao Feng" claimed that the originator of the Three-Self Patriotic Movement, Wu Yaozong, was a secret Party member directly responsible to the Propaganda Department of the Party.

Attempts to control the Church

The Vice-Director of this Party organ gave secret directives for a "divide and rule" strategy to control the Protestant churches, playing on their existing denominational divisions. Xiao Feng also revealed the existence of "hidden strength" Party operatives who were infiltrated individually into the churches to subvert it from within. These were secret, "underground" Party members who were openly religious leaders or prominent figures in public life who ostensibly had no connection with the Party. Although Xiao Feng was in charge of religious affairs in Guangzhou for years, he was totally unaware of this more covert means of control. Both the Beijing Union Theological Seminary and the Nanjing Theological Seminary had been brought under Party control by the mid-1950s by this method and the Three-Self Movement used to control the churches on a national scale. It is not surprising that older Christians in

China still remain deeply suspicious of the Three-Self because they suffered greatly from the 1950s onward.

However all this activity, both covert and open, to control the Church has dismally failed. In 1979 the Head of the United Front Work Department in Zhejiang Province reportedly admitted that every effort to destroy the Church had failed, and that history had plainly shown this to be the case. Far from Christianity disappearing without trace, it had survived and multiplied under persecution, reappearing with renewed force after the Cultural Revolution. In a stroke of bitter irony to hardline cadres, the very areas such as Wenzhou and Henan which had been designated "atheistic zones" have today become the centres of church growth and revival.

Conversion of Party members

No exact statistics can be produced for the number of CCP members who have become Christians. By the nature of the case, many prefer to remain secret believers. However, there is enough evidence from reliable sources including documents from the Communist Party itself, to suggest that the number is quite considerable. In September 2004 the Hong Kong Chinese-language magazine *Zheng Ming* which has excellent Mainland sources, claimed that as many as 3–4 million Communist Party members had become Protestants or Catholics, or attended church services. This would mean that one in every fifteen Party members who is supposed to strictly adhere to atheistic Marxism has switched allegiance to the Christian faith. That this is possible is certainly borne out by other evidence. In 1986 house-church Christians in a large city in Anhui reported that at the end of June in that year forty-six new believers had been baptised – including four Party members.

In late 1988 researchers in Hong Kong received a copy of an internal news-sheet prepared by the New China News Agency for senior Party workers. It included a long article on *Christianity Fever* confirming the massive Church growth taking place on a national scale. But what is of particular interest was the following paragraph:

> According to the Communist Party Organization Department in Wenzhou City an investigation was made in Pingyang County during a Party rural "rectification campaign". There were found to be 108 Party members in this one county who had believed in Christianity. About one half had believed because they themselves or family members had met with sickness or other disasters and no-one in the Party organisation had bothered to care for them.

Here was important evidence that large numbers of Communist Party members have turned to Christ, attracted by the love of his people in contrast to the lack of concern shown by their fellow Party members.

The problem of Party members becoming Christians is so acute that it has attracted the attention of Party leaders and academicians at the highest levels. In 1990 a survey revealed that in six major cities (Beijing, Tianjin, Shanghai, Guangzhou, Chongqing and Chengdu) the number of people joining the Communist Party had plummeted, while those becoming Christians had soared. In Tianjin, for example, those joining the Party had dropped by 80 per cent between 1987 and 1989 whereas the number of people joining the Christian Church had more than doubled between 1984 and 1986.[1]

In 1995 the magazine *Modern Religious Studies* which is written by Marxist researchers bemoaned the phenomenon. In an article headed "Investigations and Thoughts Concerning Party Members Turning to Religion", the author stated:

> We are confronted with an inescapable problem: in certain villages of the Linyi district of Shandong Province, some Party members have turned to religion. According to a survey by the end of last year [1994] many Party members had believed in Christianity in this region. ... This has had a bad influence on the masses.

He went on to paint a lamentable picture of Party members

refusing to pay their dues and even forgetting when they had become members. Why had so many of them become Christians? The writer squarely places the "blame" on itinerant house church evangelists who proclaimed healing in the name of Christ.

> More than 60 per cent of rural people who turn to religion do so because of sickness, and the percentage among Party members is even higher.

Many grass-roots reports from Christians themselves include reference to Party members turning to Christ. In one area north of Shanghai, many Party cadres became Christians between 1989–91. In fact, the village Communist Party Secretary was converted and became one of the key local house church leaders! In Beijing a Christian dentist has shared the gospel with high Party officials (even while she was extracting their teeth!), and several have believed. In Heilongjiang, right in China's far north on the border with Russia, the Party chief of a large town came to Christ in the late 1980s through the witness of his own brother who had previously been an inveterate gambler. Since coming to faith he has resigned all his Communist Party positions and is now a house church leader.

Communist Party "alarmed"

The central government has been so alarmed by the spread of Christianity among Party members that on at least two occasions over the last decade it has taken action to limit its effects. According to the Hong Kong magazine *Zheng Ming*, on 21 January 1995 it issued a new set of eight regulations to bring recalcitrants into line. The government had discovered that in major cities and in the advanced coastal region between 7–9 per cent of all Party members had joined some form of religious organisation. If family members were included, then the figure was as high as 18 per cent. Moreover, this rate of defection to religious organisations was accelerating at a rate 12 per cent higher than the Party's normal recruitment rate. The central authorities took drastic action: all Party members and cadres who had joined religious organisations were to be instantly expelled from the Party and dismissed from their official posts. Those who had attended religious worship but not yet formally joined a religious organisation were to be allowed to remain in the Party if they "repented" their error. Otherwise they, too, would be expelled. These regulations were circulated to Party organs throughout the country.

On 12 August 2004 the CCP Central Committee authorised the Central Organisation Department and the Central Propaganda Department to issue a new decree cracking down on Party members who dared to hold religious beliefs. No Party members or leading cadres are allowed to join any religious organisation either openly or secretly. Those who do so are to be expelled from the Party. In just three years, in half a dozen provinces including Hebei, Henan, Jiangsu, Zhejiang, etc., over 230 high-ranking Communist Party cadres were expelled or forced to take premature retirement because they had joined religious organisations. And this is just the tip of the iceberg.

In 1995, detailed evidence had emerged from the Party itself of the extent of Christian "infiltration" of its own ranks. "Ming Bao", probably Hong Kong's most respected Chinese-language newspaper, published a long report on 31 August 1995 under the headline "More Party members believing in Christianity alarms the Communist Party". The article stated:

> Recently a large number of Communist Party members joined the ranks of Christianity in the Bijie district of Guizhou Province. According to a survey by the Religious Affairs and Public Security Bureaux in that region, in 1991 there were only 150 Party members who had joined the church. But by 1995 the number exceeded 2,000. For example, in Nayong County alone there were 23 Party members registered as church members of whom eighteen were cadres in national organisations. More than one hundred Party members regularly attended church activities there. Eight of the

core leaders of the banned underground church organisation known as "Life Church" were Party members who had left the Party to become Christians. The survey revealed that Party members who became Christians were not just ordinary young people but old cadres who had been in the Party for decades. The Vice Principal of the Party School in Nayong who had been Area Party Secretary for over twenty years, joined the Christian church on his retirement in 1984. The Party Vice-Secretary in Zhijin County who had served in the 1950s and in the 1970s was Commune leader is now a leading light in the church.

The conversion of leading Party members has led to the growth of Christianity by the thousand and in the tens of thousands. The prestige of Party and local government organs has dropped. In some remoter villages people obey the pastor rather than the village Party head.

Horrified, the government despatched an investigation team to report in depth on the situation. They came up with the following reasons for so many Party members becoming Christians:

1. FAMILY BACKGROUND. In Dafang County a young girl grew up in a Christian home. She later joined the Party but continued enthusiastically to attend church. When an official from the Religious Affairs Bureau asked her to choose between Christianity and the Party, as Party members are not allowed to join the church, she replied: "If that is the policy, I suppose I must resign from the Party."

2. OPPORTUNISM. Cadre Li from a local veterinary clinic who joined the church in 1991 stated: "I joined the Party Youth League in the same year. But I never applied officially whereas it was my own free will to join the church."

3. PARTY CORRUPTION. Some local Party organs were corrupt causing members to lose hope. An old man in Dafang County who had been a Party member since 1952 fell ill, but no one from the Party came to visit him. Church members came to see him, bringing some gifts, and he was so touched he became a Christian. An old Party member in Nayong County who had

joined in the 1950s was quizzed by the local Party Secretary as to why he had joined the church. He replied: "I have seen through you. You wave the banner of Communism but do not practise true Communism. The Party does not allow superstition – so why, when someone in your family died, did you follow all the old superstitious customs?"

To this amazing Party internal report, we might add one more very significant reason:

North-western Guizhou is an area where the gospel was firmly planted pre-1949. Thousands of Miao tribespeople turned to Christ. Many stood for their faith and even died for it during the decades of persecution (see Chapter 7 for details of the Miao church in Guizhou). It is precisely this area where today many Communist Party members have turned to Christ. God has honoured the faithful sowing of the seed. Today he is reaping a harvest even from among those who were reared in atheism and sworn enemies of religious faith of any kind.

13

Intellectuals find Christ

We are all weeping,
Because the sun deserted us,
The earth is full of dry leaves
The sky suffocates with cloudy rain.

We are all weeping –
Fresh air stained with mud,
A young child is no longer innocent,
The weather-beaten old man shuts his eyes tightly.

We are all weeping –
The white snowflake has lost its truth;
These days the moon is sleepless.
Who will grant us
A song of integrity?

                             (Anon. Written in China after 4 June 1989)

It was late 1965. China was a closed country on the eve of the Cultural Revolution. In London University there were still a handful of students from the Mainland studying English. At that time I had just started studying Chinese at the School of Oriental and African Studies and had become a Christian. I was eager to share my new-found faith with people from China. A special meeting was arranged by the British Council for a few of us and I found myself in eager conversation with two young men of my own age. We got on famously as long as the subject was studies or sport. However, when I tried tentatively to broach the subject of God and Christianity, their attitude suddenly changed. Their curt rebuttals are still engraved chillingly in my memory.

"We are atheists. There is no God. We believe in Chairman Mao."

The other joined in angrily: "I am from Shanghai. I have visited the atheistic museum and seen with my own eyes the bones of the orphan children killed by the missionaries and used in their medical experiments."

This was said with great earnestness. There was no point in pursuing my feeble attempts at witnessing further and the meeting broke up. Such was my first inauspicious meeting with Mainland Chinese students over thirty years ago.

A year later the Cultural Revolution broke out and the London Chinese students all volunteered to return to China to take part. I have not a shadow of doubt that they volunteered willingly: what was the point in remaining in "imperialist" Britain when the fulcrum of history had moved to socialist China where a "new, Socialist Man" was in the making?

Through their eyes

Looking back, it is difficult to convey the atmosphere of those days. I remember trying to buy a Chinese Bible in one of the Chinese bookshops near the British Museum in Great Russell Street. The Chinese assistant, who was a Maoist, looked at me with incredulity and actually laughed in my face. He and the students could not comprehend how any thinking person could seriously consider Christianity as an option. It belonged firmly to the era of pigtails, opium and imperialist exploitation of China and its final flickering embers would soon be extinguished by the Red Guards.

For Chinese students and intellectuals, and especially the generation brought up and indoctrinated in the 1950s and 1960s, Christianity was a hated and despised foreign ideology – "the opiate of the people", as Marx had succinctly put it. The young Maoists saw themselves as the final wave of an atheistic tide which had been gathering for a half-century. After World War I, Chinese intellectuals became increasingly estranged from Christianity. Bertrand Russell visited China and thinking Chinese turned increasingly to humanism and socialism. The spectacle of Western "Christian" nations destroying each other in the bloody trenches of Flanders did little to aid missionaries preaching the gospel of love in China. The Bolshevik Revolution in Russia in 1918 pushed some Chinese to consider Communism as the remedy for China's many ills.

The decisive defining moment for most Chinese intellectuals was the "May Fourth Movement" of 1919 which denounced the Western powers for transferring former German colonies in China to the Japanese and sought a renaissance of Chinese culture on modern, humanist lines. Most Chinese intellectuals were still not Communists, but some leading figures of the movement went on to found the Chinese Communist Party in 1921 in Shanghai. Many were becoming increasingly hostile to Christianity, which they viewed, not without cause, as being linked with Western political and cultural imperialism. Between 1922–27 an "Anti-Christian Movement" was unleashed across the country with Communist Party support culminating in the withdrawal of most missionaries to the coast in 1928. The withdrawal proved temporary but was a foretaste of the final exodus in 1950–51.

When the Communists took power in 1949 they could therefore draw on this previous anti-Christian tradition which found sympathisers among the intellectual class far beyond the bounds of those who were members of the Communist Party. In 1966 the young Red Guards could see themselves as the culmination of this tradition as they desecrated and closed churches, dealing – as they thought – the final death blow to a foreign, outmoded, anti-scientific religious superstition.

More than thirty years later, every Sunday morning, large numbers of students from Beijing and Qinghua Universities – the Oxbridge of China – sit crammed on benches in the Haidian Church just a stone's throw away from Beijing University. With Bibles on their knees they sit quietly drinking in the hour-long sermons. In the main church in Nanjing I visited a Wednesday-evening young people's meeting which was packed with 200 students and graduates in their late teens and twenties. They listened with interest and respect to an elderly woman in her seventies expounding an obscure Old Testament passage for more than an hour. In the UK such a scene would be incredible. Clearly something has happened to cause this great reversal among intellectuals.

The Cultural Revolution

One cannot over-emphasise the magnitude and importance of what has taken place in China over the past twenty-five years. The young Maoists who in 1966 saw themselves as on the cutting-edge of history, a decade later realised that they had walked into a cul-de-sac from which there was no exit. The dreams and hopes of Chinese intellectuals had been gathering force since the early decades of the 20th century and found their focus in the archetypal Great Leader – Chairman Mao. But instead of leading them upwards to the socialist utopia, he dragged them down into an abyss of poverty, class-struggle and death. In 1966 and 1967 the Red Guards worshipped "The Chairman" – by the early 1970s many were secretly cursing his name after he had called in the Army to suppress disturbances and ship them to far-flung and inhospitable corners of the country. This was called "sending people down to the country-side to learn from the peasants". The result in actuality was the blighting of millions of lives.

Intellectuals suffered heavily under Mao. They were stigmatised as the "ninth stinking category" – placed below landlords and capitalists on the Maoist list of "ghosts and demons" to be attacked. The "Anti-Rightist" movement of 1957–58 had led to the imprisonment of many intellectuals who had dared to speak out even mildly against the new regime. The Cultural Revolution was the final crescendo in a series of political campaigns which crushed the intellectuals as a class under the juggernaut of the Maoist "dictatorship of the proletariat". It was only in 1978 when many intellectuals were rehabilitated by Hu Yaobang and Deng Xiaoping that they were allowed to return to their universities and lectureships from labour camps and factories all over the country. By that time many had lost the most productive years of their lives digging ditches instead of doing research in physics. The loss to the nation was incalculable as was the personal anguish and bitterness. Some never returned: they had died wretchedly in some village hovel far from home. Others had committed suicide in despair.

The death-throes of Maoism

The past two decades have seen the death-throes of an entire worldview in China. Maoism was a pseudo-religion with its own scriptures (the Little Red Book of quotations from Mao), its daily political study-sessions, its worship ("morning and evening reporting to the Chairman") and even its miracles – documented cases of people undergoing surgery without anasthaesia being "cured" by the application of suitable "Quotations" by unqualified bare-foot doctors. All this has vanished with scarcely a visible trace. Most pictures and statues of the "Great Helmsman" have been removed from view, and copies of the *Little Red Book* and Mao badges fill the bric-a-brac stalls. The "Marxism-Leninism-Mao Zedong Thought" of China's present leadership is a thin varnish for the unbridled capitalism which surely has the Chairman turning in his marble sarcophagus in Tiananmen Square.

The intellectuals and students, as a class, were simultaneously the most cowed and the most enthusiastic supporters of Maoism. The collapse of Maoism as a worldview has left them in a spiritual and ideological vacuum which is hardly filled by the pale ideological reconstructions of the Deng and post-Deng eras. For some, disillusionment set in during the Cultural Revolution. Red Guards came to faith through secretly reading the very Bibles they had confiscated. Others were set thinking by the Christian content of banned novels by such authors as

Dostoevsky. The first hints to the outside world that something profound was happening in many hearts became apparent in the early and mid-1970s. Some of the Red Guards who swam to freedom in Hong Kong made a point of immediately asking for the nearest Christian church.

When the first churches were reopened in 1979–80 observers were surprised by the number of young people and students who attended them. After the suffocating decades under Mao, intellectuals and students were free to explore spiritual paths previously forbidden. Spiritual hunger has been fed by the translation and publication of works of Western literature which directly or indirectly point the reader towards Christianity. Works by Bunyan, Milton, Augustine and even C. S. Lewis have been published in China. Christian books as a category are few and far between in State bookshops and can usually only be obtained on Sundays at "Three Self" churches, but the serious searcher can find any number of literary works which give broadly Christian answers to questions concerning the nature of man and the meaning of life. In many Chinese universities it is now accepted that the Bible has had a profound influence on Western literature and art and students are free to study it.

Christianity in the student world

In China's universities and colleges, one significant influence often overlooked has been the witness of elderly Christian academics who returned to their posts after they were rehabilitated in 1978. On the eve of the Communist victory in 1949 there was a significant awakening across China among university students. The Chinese Inter-Varsity Fellowship (IVF) was at that time the largest Christian student organisation in the world. Missionaries such as David Adeney and Leslie Lyall of the China Inland Mission, who were deeply involved in student outreach, witnessed amazing scenes in Beijing. Normally reserved Chinese students sang and testified in the streets as they returned from conferences where there was a deep sense of the presence of God and outpourings of the Spirit leading to many conversions. Many students were converted under the soul-searching preaching of Wang Mingdao, later to suffer long imprisonment for his refusal to compromise his belief in the supremacy of Christ over even the Communist Party.

The new converts, too, soon had their mettle tested: the IVF groups were banned from campus and broken up. Christians who sought to engage in open apologetics against atheistic Marxism came under severe criticism and many were eventually shipped to labour camps. One teacher in south China was imprisoned for many years for having opposed the Marxist theory of evolution. Much later after his release he told me that many died in the camp, but God wonderfully sustained him and enabled him to lead six others to Christ.

Those who survived such testing experiences returned to their posts in universities and colleges all over China. Now elderly, they had kept the faith after a lifetime of suffering and privation. Deep in practical experience of God's faithfulness they have had a tremendous impact on the younger generations of seekers. One such man was Professor Feng of the Chinese Academy of Sciences. For many years until his recent death he openly witnessed to young people in the church near Beijing University ("Beida") and held an informal after-meeting for students. Professor Feng was one of China's top physicists and widely respected. He wrote a detailed book on the relationship of Christianity and science and insisted that when it was published in Hong Kong it should bear his name. He was fearless in his witness to Christ and led many students to faith. One of them studying at "Beida" describes how his life was changed by the Professor:

> My starting point was that Marxism was useless. It justified the massacre in Tiananmen Square with its teaching that the end justifies the means. I wanted to make sense of that evil and to find an answer that could take away my anxiety and depression... All my

careful study of Taoism, Buddhism, Confucianism and Chinese classical religion had brought me hopelessly to the bottom of the tank where I couldn't move. So I headed off to a nearby Three-Self church. To my surprise it was packed with more than 1,000 people crammed into the building. An even greater surprise was to see quite a number of my student friends. I had assumed I was the only one with doubts, but obviously not. What arrested me was the Scripture reading from John 8:23-24 "If you do not believe that I am the One I claim to be, you will indeed die in your sins."

I knew I had to get a Bible and ordered one from the church bookshop although they said it would take weeks to arrive. I went back to Beida with my mind ablaze with the staggering possibility that Jesus Christ, who was a man, was also God. Then my quest was over! An older student who spotted me at church invited me to attend a meeting the following Sunday after the service, where a professor would talk about the Christian faith. "Say very little about it – he holds these meetings quite unofficially and the Three-Self authorities might not be too pleased to hear about it."

The Professor was a nuclear physicist, very well known and reputedly one of the brightest minds in China. Everyone knew he had cut short a lucrative career in the US to return home in 1955 in order to help the rebuilding of China. The Party thanked him by making him dig ditches for twenty years. Now about seventy, he was restored to his academic post. We students crowded into a small room. There were about twenty of us and he held us spellbound with his brilliant apologetics for two hours. He spoke about the absolute truth that never changes. In order to be taken seriously it had to derive from a source who is still alive, unlike Confucius, Marx or Mao. The only giver of truth still alive is Jesus Christ. He spoke of the connection between truth and love, with the only example of unconditional love extended to us in Christ, even though we do not deserve it. He spoke of the power of love that can change people.

What really convinced me was the professor himself. There was passion and conviction in his words. It suddenly occurred to me: "he believes every word he says." This was incomprehensible to me, being used to lecturers who hated what they had to teach. Coming from one of the most intelligent men in China it was impossible not to take him seriously. I suppose that talk sealed my conversion.

Now I had a faith that could tell me what God was like. As I learned to pray I gradually felt the hatred leave my heart. I found love there instead. I felt the fear leave me too. I am no longer concerned about going to jail. I even attend a house church which is forbidden in China. We meet secretly, sing quietly and discuss the Word of God in low tones. I am probably facing jail or at least a lifetime of discrimination. But I pray my testimony will be like Paul's when he faced trial: "For me to live is Christ, but to die is gain." (Phil:1:21)

Many students could give similar testimonies. And there are many senior faculty like Professor Feng who are leading them to faith by teaching and example, although not all dare to be so open. Before the Revolution there was a high number of Christians working in the medical profession because of the large number of Christian-run hospitals and missionary clinics. Even today, this influence still lingers with many older doctors and nurses maintaining a significant witness for Christ in the now State-run hospitals. One foreign visitor to a Chinese hospital discovered that many of the older staff were keen Christians – but none of them dared openly attend the local State-church for fear of losing their positions or being otherwise discriminated against. In some cases, doctors and nurses are fairly open about their faith, praying with their patients. In others, this would be strictly forbidden and quite dangerous.

The tide becomes a flood – "June Fourth"

Throughout the 1980s more and more intellectuals were converted. In February 1989 a Chinese newspaper published a long article about the phenomenon of "Christianity Fever" and highlighted the large number of conversions among intellectuals:

> When the tide of "Christianity fever" first began it seemed most of the believers were elderly and illiterate, but in the last few years there has been a big change: according to the authorities in Shanghai 20,000 people have become Christians there over the last three years and one quarter of them are intellectuals and young

people. Among them are university professors, doctors, writers, engineers and students.[1]

But it was after the failure of the democracy movement in 1989 that the tide became a flood. On 4 June 1989 the aspirations of a whole generation of idealistic (and perhaps naïve) students were crushed in Tiananmen Square. Demonstrations in more than sixty other Chinese cities were also suppressed and the leaders arrested. However, ideologically and spiritually it was Maoism and the "dictatorship of the proletariat" which were dealt a death-blow. "June Fourth" was a watershed: from then on no self-respecting intellectual in China could seriously defend the political system. The stifling of political dissent has only led to a deeper, spiritual questioning.

In the decade since the tragic events in June 1989 much evidence has accumulated of a profound work of God among Chinese intellectuals. In one university a year later one official confessed that not a day had passed without a student asking him about faith in Jesus Christ. Christian students reported that they had never had so many opportunities to share the gospel. In 1990 a seminar at Beijing University on the history of Christian music attracted 200 students at its first session – and over 400 at its second. There was a big demand for the music tape which accompanied the sessions. One song – "You are My Hiding Place" – was aired (in Chinese) over the campus broadcasting system for several weeks. All over China small Bible study groups mushroomed on campuses. Some groups have been meeting in student dormitories, others in the homes of the Chinese Christian faculty. In some campuses whole dormitories of students became Christians.

In south China, soon after the events in Beijing, over 200 students came literally knocking on the door of the local TSPM church seeking answers to their anguished questions. One Chinese scholar studying in the UK summed up the heart-searching of many thousands of intellectuals, both young and old:

Since the June Fourth massacre of student democracy activists in Beijing I have been unable to believe in Communism and I have no faith in the Party. But what is there to put in their place?

What, indeed? The Holy Spirit has been working in hearts and minds drawing many intellectuals to faith in Christ. Often, the process is tortuous as serious-minded people who have been deeply traumatised by suffering and political persecution seek genuine answers to their questions. One wife of a scholar shared her spiritual pilgrimage as follows:

> I felt the warmth and love of Jesus drawing me to him from the very start. I saw it in the eyes and on the faces of Christians, and especially in the life of the Christian girl who worked with me in the Chinese restaurant. But for a long time I did not dare commit myself, because always in the background was our former Chairman, Mao Zedong. To us as a family, and to me as a child, Mao meant everything. But then the day came when he was respected like that no longer. The idol was broken and my world fell apart. I could not bear it if Jesus were to prove an idol, too. It would break my heart.

To such people the gospel comes as a healing balm. Trite presentations of formulae to be believed and much quoting of texts by Westerners eager to "do evangelism" are most likely to be rebuffed by thinking people who have already suffered the mind-numbing recitation of the "Thoughts of Chairman Mao". It is the love of Christ expressed in practical caring and friendship, alongside the sensitive explanation of Christian truth, which has led many to faith.

After the millennium

Events in recent years prove that the revival of interest in Christianity among China's intellectuals shows no sign of slacking. Major bookshops across the country now stock an interesting (although by Western standards still very limited) range of titles dealing with Christianity. Works by Augustine and Luther have been translated, and titles dealing with patristic Christianity, the Reformation and the history of Christianity in China are now freely on sale, although the print runs are generally quite small. Some fifty privately-run Christian bookshops have sprung up in major cities, catering mainly for educated urban believers.

In late 2005 I shared my fears with a house-church full-time worker among university graduates that the wave of materialism sweeping the country might be making the task of leading intellectuals to Christ more difficult. His reply both surprised and encouraged me: "Many intellectuals have a profoundly pessimistic outlook on life. They are under no illusions about the negative trends in society and the pressures they are under to get good jobs after graduation. As a result, many are still extremely open to the gospel message. In the east China region centred on Shanghai there are some 60 universities – I reckon about two-thirds now have student Christian fellowships."

Chinese around the world *or* "the Diaspora"

After 1989 most activists in the Democracy Movement fled overseas. They found large communities of students and graduates from China already studying in many countries. Some are on State scholarships but increasingly, people are privately funded. There are about 100,000 Mainland scholars with their dependents in the United States and a similar number in Japan. Germany, France, Australia, Canada and other countries also have thousands. In Britain there may be as many as 10,000 Mainland Chinese scholars. In the freer atmosphere overseas, some start attending church out of curiosity and many more come to faith through meeting local Christians who befriend them, invite them home and share the gospel.

Some of the former Democracy Movement activists have become Christians and are providing intellectual leadership for the growing number of Mainland Chinese Christians living and studying overseas. Yuan Zhiming was a prominent dissi-

dent who had helped draft an open letter from seventy prominent intellectuals to the Chinese government in May 1989. He
was also the author of several books and over 100 articles, two
of which brought him national awards. But after "June Fourth"
an arrest warrant was issued and he spent two months in hiding in China before escaping.

In 1990 he started studies at Princeton University. A
Communist Party member who had also spent time serving in
the People's Liberation Army, it was only gradually that Yuan
came to see flaws in the Communist view of human nature. So
he became a humanist. In lonely exile in the United States he
was invited to a Chinese Bible study. "That's how we studied
Mao's works during the Cultural Revolution," Yuan remembers
ruefully. "But he deceived us, so I was very suspicious of that
type of Bible study group." It was the warmth, love and sincer-
ity of the group which broke down his suspicions. "I had just
barely escaped China with my life and had seen so much deceit
and evil. Seeing people trust one another was wonderful." Two
months later he confessed his faith in Christ and in April 1991
was baptised. He recounts his story as follows:

> From a loyal Communist Party member to an enthusiastic democ-
> racy fighter, to a devoted Christian – from the ideals of
> Communism, to humanist philosophy, to Christian culture – these
> three systems of thought and two transformations encompass such
> great distances. What can I say? Only that I have come to this place
> because of God's mercy and calling. If I say that the first transfor-
> mation (from Communism to humanism) was due to my indepen-
> dent thought and rational judgement, then what did I do for the
> second transformation? I did not do anything. I just reached out
> and took the first step of opening my heart to receive the Holy
> Spirit, who had been knocking all along at the door of my heart,
> and passively, spontaneously, ran to embrace the home of my soul!

Since his conversion, Yuan has worked tirelessly lecturing
and writing, seeking to introduce the Christian faith to others

in the worldwide Chinese diaspora. But in the longer term he would like to return to China.

For the most part, the Mainland Chinese today are empty people with empty hearts. The Communists have never believed the traditional Chinese religions and now people don't even believe in Communism. With the move to a capitalist economy they believe only in money. If the Chinese, especially their leaders, do not have a transcendent spirit, faith and convictions, then regardless of the banners we raise, we will be unable to bring about any good results.

Another prominent dissident who has become a Christian is Han Dongfang who sought unsuccessfully to set up free trades unions in China, and is now living in Hong Kong. In an interview given in 1993 he described how he had come to faith in Christ:

I remember very clearly the first time I saw someone I knew die, and this left a void in my heart I could not understand. So I was afraid of death and started to wonder where we came from and where we were going to. I made some contact with Buddhism and Daoism and went to temples and burnt incense. My mother died when I was fifteen and I went even more to the temples. I was aware that there was a force outside this world which was motivating it.

After I was in prison in Beijing, I believed more in fate and after I came out went more often to the temples to worship Buddha. My first contact with Christianity was in early 1989; a fellow student faced with the choice of joining the Party or being baptised, chose to be baptised. He invited me to church but I never went while still in China. However, I started reading the Bible from Genesis and used this against him, saying, "Why did God create this and that on the second day? Why seven days? – why not eight days?" He had no answers, merely suggesting I go see a pastor.

I actually became a Christian later in America in an extraordinary way. I needed a driving license and a friend suggested I ask a pastor to interpret for me as in New Jersey one needed to take the driving-test in English. So I got to know a pastor. Even though I was still spitting up blood from my illness he said people wouldn't worry if I came to church. So I started attending a fellowship totally comprised of Mainland Chinese, called "Echo". After joining, I experienced a sensation I had never felt before except with my closest family relations. It was love – not just conventional motions, but a genuine caring. But at that time I still had not decided to be baptised: I told the pastor that to choose a religion was an important step about which I needed to think more deeply. After fifteen months two Mainland friends told me: "To believe in God is not to trust in any pastor or fellowship. We can only come to know God through the Bible." I knew this was right, so later I was publicly baptised before returning to China.

Han also has some searching advice for those who, like himself, are in danger of being crushed underfoot by a monolithic system, or responding in kind:

Since my conversion my greatest strength has been love and tolerance. When one has experienced these things oneself, one can overcome different problems. When hate meets with love everything is transformed. Of course, one's own heart is transformed and one's opponent is not necessarily capable of transformation, at least not as quickly. But gradually what I call the "invasion of love" is extremely effective against hate.

Han's involvement in workers' rights is motivated by his Christian beliefs and he sees the gospel as the only hope for China:

I tell people: China cannot be saved by democracy, nor by a multi-party system. Only Christianity can save China completely. Christian doctrine is incarnational and world-affirming, so the future of Chinese society and its development depend on Christianity. If Christianity cannot expand in China then China has no hope.

Such words from a Mainland intellectual would be unthinkable only thirty years ago and show how far the gospel has rooted itself in the consciousness of many thinking Chinese.

Chinese government response

The Chinese government has taken note of this religious revival and is thoroughly alarmed. In June 1994 the Communist Youth League and the State Education Commission conducted an opinion poll of young people either attending or working at colleges and universities. 47 per cent of the young cadres polled did not believe in socialism or communism. 88 per cent of the 670 young researchers questioned did not believe. 76 per cent of young workers and cadres at State-owned industrial and mining enterprises did not believe. (The Party has always prided itself on its traditional support among the workers.) Of 760 students at eight universities and colleges, including some who were Party or Youth League members, 77 per cent responded they "did not believe".[2] Many other surveys and articles have led Party leaders to talk openly of a "crisis of faith" – not of faith in religion, but of faith in Marxism.

Conversely, the collapse of Marxist ideology among intellectuals has seen a groundswell of interest in religion. An April 1994 report by the Party's State Education Commission revealed that more than 12 per cent of the upper-class men in eight key universities believed or had contact with a religious faith. This figure was three times higher than the remnant hardcore of believers in socialism and Marxism. State Vice-Minister Li Lanqing, responsible for education, admitted: "There is a sense of being lost. Religious belief implies that Western ideological concepts have not only corroded our youth, they've likewise had a market in our social and political life." As Buddhism, Daoism and Islam are hardly Western religions, this is a clear statement from the top levels of the Chinese government that it is the revival of Christianity which is causing the greatest concern.

The fact that the government continues to issue repressive measures against Christian activities among intellectuals is clear evidence of the growth of the faith in academia. On 21

August 2004 the State Council authorised the Ministry of Education to issue a decree banning all religious activities in institutes of higher education. Teachers and students who are Party members but join religious organisations are to be expelled from the Party without exception.

That this was no mere paper decree became evident nearly a year later. Several hundred house-church believers were arrested in a major swoop by the Public Security Bureau in the north-eastern province of Jilin. What was remarkable was that the majority of them were not rural believers, but were students from the universities in the area. Several professors were also detained.

It is no wonder that Christian activities on campus must still largely be clandestine. China has the dubious honour of being the major country from which Christian students are still officially banned from participating in the International Fellowship of Evangelical Students (IFES). I have no doubt that when restrictions are lifted, the Chinese contingent may again be the largest, as was the case 60 years ago.

Looking more widely, the 19th century saw the decay and fall of Confucianism as China's guiding ideology. The 20th century has seen the rapid rise and equally rapid decay of Marxism as its replacement. Could the 21st century see the firm implantation of the Christian gospel at all levels in Chinese society, leading to its flowering as the basis for a new moral order? We must avoid simplistic and triumphalistic analyses which see China from Western, politicised perpectives. Nevertheless, there are reasons for hope of a continuing spiritual and social transformation.

14

Evangelism explosion!

In March 2005, Mr Wu Dongsheng, a professor at Nanjing University, wrote a useful book on Chinese cults, published by the Social Sciences Academic Press. While researching cults and the Protestant churches in northern Jiangsu Province he casually revealed evidence of the staggering growth of the latter:

According to the authorities, who in 1998 did a survey of five muncipalities in the northern part of the province, by the end of 1997 there were 752,248 Protestant Christians in these five areas, and 2,581 registered churches and meeting-points. S City had more than 180,000 believers, and the number of rural believers in the four counties in this municipality had increased thirty-onefold since 1982. In 1984 one of these counties had only 872 believers, but by 1997 the number had grown to 48,000 [nearly sixtyfold growth in just thirteen years]. Since 1985 the number of Christians in X City has grown annually by more than 10,000, and there are now more than 200,000 believers. In Y City between 1995 and 1997 the number of legal churches and meeting-points has grown each year by more than 50.

In reality, the growth of Christianity has led to confusion in a minority of registered churches and to the springing up everywhere of privately set-up meeting-points [house churches]. The so-called private Christian meeting-points mean those that have not registered with the Religious Affairs organs. They have formed spontaneously and have quite a number of the religious masses attending. Statistics taken in 1997 reveal that in the five municipalities in the northern part of this one province there were more than 1,700 private meeting-points with more than 57,000 people attending. For instance, in one county of H city there is one permitted meeting-point for every one to two villages. In some areas there is a "topsy-turvy" situation in regard to registered and unregistered meetings. For example, in a certain place in L city there are only six registered meetings, with 2,850 believers, but there are 163 private meeting-points with around 4,500 believers...

... According to the same 1997 statistics there were 1,580 self-appointed [house-church] evangelists in these five municipalities – more than 80% of the total in the entire province. At the same time, there are some "Three-Self" patriotic members and [registered] evangelists who set up private meeting-points in their homes or undertake illegal religious activities in privately set-up meeting points, disturbing proper order in religious activities. A certain Mr Cai who was a permanent committee member of the TSPM in this northern area of the province held private meetings in his home and under his influence four more were set up in four nearby villages, drawing in over 100 villagers.

I have quoted this researcher at length because it is prima facie evidence of the grass-roots expansion of the church, and of the runaway growth of the independent house churches. It shows that, despite continuing restrictions and even arrests, the local authorities are unable to control the spread of the gospel. Moreover, there are keen Christians under the TSPM umbrella who are quite prepared to break the rules and engage in evangelism, setting up house churches illegally or co-operating with existing house churches.

It is good to have a Chinese academic confirming what we already know from a vast array of information from house-church sources – that the church in China has largely multi-plied over the past 30 years owing to spontaneous evangelism at the grass roots. Itinerant evangelists have travelled from village to village with the Good News. Of course, there has been excess and even heresy and the development of cults, as we have seen in Chapter 10 previously. But it is my conviction after over 20 years' first-hand contact with the house churches that the heart of the movement is thoroughly biblical, evangelical and led by the Spirit of God. It is a constant joy to meet Chinese believers – often farmers and working people – who share the same faith that I have. They accept the full authority of Scripture as the infallible Word of God, the atonement of

Jesus Christ as the only way of salvation from sin and all the evangelical certainties of the historic Christian faith. It is nothing short of miraculous that this faith has re-emerged triumphant after thirty years of the worst persecution the church has ever suffered. Let us look at some specific examples of how ordinary Chinese Christians have spread the gospel throughout the country.

At the end of January 1991 some of the Little Flock Christians of Xiaoshan County in Zhejiang Province were conscious that Christ's coming could be very near. The young believers felt a deep burden to spread the gospel far and wide. After earnest prayer, several went out to Guangxi and Hunan provinces to preach. Soon they returned with the good news that several dozen people had been converted. This electrified dozens of house churches in Xiaoshan who caught the vision to evangelise. In each church between six and several dozen Christian young men were sent out by their house churches. Most were farmers, and the mainstay of their families, but they gladly sacrificed their worktime and income to preach the gospel. They set off in pairs in mid-March 1991 for Hunan, Shandong, northern Jiangsu, Sichuan and other places all over China.

Those left at home were fully behind the young evangelists: they set up 24-hour prayer chains with twelve bands of prayer-warriors each praying for two hours every day. So it was not just a few hundred young people involved in evangelism, but the united effort of thousands of Christians throughout the Xiaoshan district. According to the report of this mass evangelism programme which was written in Xiaoshan in May 1991 the Holy Spirit was mightily at work:

> It seemed that the brothers just had to open their mouths to speak and people would express a desire to receive Christ. One pair of preachers after just a few days reported that three hundred people turned to Christ. When the two dozen evangelists from one house church returned, they reported that 1,300 people had received sal-

vation. This was the power of God, as how else could so few cause more than a thousand people to believe? Young evangelists from another church had never preached like this before, so when they arrived at their destination they knelt down and prayed fervently. Then they preached to the bystanders and on the first day forty friends believed. On the second day more than two hundred turned to Christ. It was God who added to the number that were saved so that they themselves were amazed.

The preachers returned with many testimonies of God's grace and power to change lives:

One brother witnessed on the train to a married couple who were both university graduates. They said they wished to believe in Jesus and asked for a Bible. He lent them his New Testament and by the time they got off the train they had already read through John's Gospel. Others knelt down on the ground to pray, not caring what other bystanders thought.

The gospel brought by these conservative Little Flock Christians was no milk-and-water message downplaying the cost of Christian discipleship. One evangelist was concerned that a man he had spoken to the first time about the gospel had refused adamantly, but the second time expressed a desire to believe. Fearing he was not genuine in his faith, he warned him that he might well face difficulties and persecution. The man replied: "Even if I am arrested and locked up I will still believe!"

Even though the Little Flock are not "charismatic" in the Western sense of the term, they reported signs and wonders following the preaching of God's Word. One pair of evangelists were staying on a farm in Hubei Province. Suddenly their host's wife fell senseless to the floor. Her husband told them she did not suffer from epilepsy so they suspected demon possession. They urged him to repent, which he did, and then they knelt down to pray for his wife. She recovered and became a believer, too. They then moved on to another village to preach with surprisingly poor response. They soon learnt that a notorious medium lived there who was preventing people from turning to Christ. They went to her house and preached Christ whereupon she believed and many more in that village then became Christians. It is notable that in both cases of deliverance the powerful preaching of the gospel message of salvation was sufficient to break the bondage.

By the end of May 1991 most of the evangelists had returned to Zhejiang. Although no direct count was made, they estimated that over 10,000 people had been saved as a result of this two-month evangelistic outreach. The house churches in Xiaoshan continued to send workers out to do pastoral and follow-up work. Older, more experienced brethren were also despatched to conduct baptisms and to oversee the establishment of new churches.

This "evangelism explosion" was unusual in China where open campaigns of this sort are often impossible. However, the Xiaoshan initiative only highlights in a spectacular way what has been happening more quietly and usually on a smaller scale all over the country.

The early days

Since the 1950s Chinese Christians were often involuntarily scattered across the country. Some were sent for years to labour camps in remote regions such as Xinjiang and Qinghai. Others were wrenched from their families and despatched at the Party's bidding to distant villages. Believers often found themselves to be the only Christians in an area where no missionary had ever come and where there was no gospel witness. In hostile environments they used myriad inventive ways to share their faith and lead others to Christ.

In the twilight years of the Cultural Revolution before the death of Mao in 1976, a young factory worker was asked by her family to burn incense to the Buddha. She obeyed, but like many young people brought up under atheism did not really understand what she was doing. One morning while exercising in the park a woman with a very kind appearance attracted her attention. She found herself pouring out her heart, and the woman shared the gospel with her. She gladly accepted Christ. Within three months she had led ten other factory workers to faith. Within eighteen months they had set up a house church meeting for prayer and worship and had held two baptismal services in which a further twenty new converts were baptised. In such ways, house churches sprang up in many cities.

Mrs Zhang, converted in 1948, was a pillar of a city church in Guangdong in southern China. As the church reeled under the assaults of the continuous political campaigns of the 1950s and 1960s, she steeled herself for martyrdom. Then, suddenly, she was sent "down to the countryside" on the orders of the Party. She found herself in a remote mountain town where she knew nobody. She set herself to pray and deepen her communion with God. One day she overheard a conversation between a child and his mother.

"Who told you that there is no love in the world except the proletariat class love?" "My teacher!" the little boy replied, having been brainwashed by Communist reductionism of everything to the class struggle.

"Oh, no!" said his mother. "There are many kinds of love... the love of your parents, the love of your elder sister... "

"And there is a Book which tells us that the love of God is even greater," Mrs Zhang found herself interjecting.

The woman smiled: "Oh, do you also have this Book?"

"Why, do you?"

"Yes!"

Mrs Zhang had providentially found another believer. Through her new acquaintance she was introduced to five other Christians. She discovered that for three years it had been too dangerous for them to meet together for fellowship. She encouraged them to pray and finally invited them to her house.

It was market day. The town was full of peasants from outlying villages selling their surplus produce – pigs, chickens, ducks and melons – as well as rice and peanuts which, strictly speaking, were still forbidden by the State. In the general chaos the local cadres were distracted. It was the perfect day for an unobtrusive Christian meeting. Mrs Zhang decided to set up some stoves downstairs and invite the farmers in to cook their own food. She charged 10 cents for fuel, salt and condiments. Over the next few months her makeshift cafè grew from three tables to seven. She got to know many people and to share the gospel with them on market days, while the Christians met upstairs, shielded by the general hubbub.

On 3 March 1973 a Hong Kong Christian visited this house church. He found about a dozen believers meeting, with bread and cups laid out on a wooden table for the Lord's Supper. Mrs Zhang spoke on "The Christian's prayer life". She had never received any theological education but spoke from rich experience of living on God's promises. In the middle of the sermon, a boy's voice was suddenly heard calling from the café downstairs:

"Mrs Zhang, we've run out of salt!"

It was the pre-arranged signal to be careful as a suspicious stranger had walked in. Mrs Zhang abruptly stopped talking, and a heavy silence fell for a while. However, the moment of danger passed and the believers quietly hummed a hymn together before receiving the communion. At the close of the meeting, which lasted for just under an hour, the visitor shared how Mainland Christians could listen to gospel radio broadcasts. Many wept. Mrs Zhang then gave out names of particular people open to the gospel to be prayed for, and the meeting dispersed.

A few years later this group had doubled in size to twenty-four members and had set up another house church in a neighbouring village. The Production Brigade chief in this village came to Christ through Mrs Zhang's witness. He had suffered criticism from the government as a "capitalist" because he had built up his bee-keeping business. They eventually forced him to give it away. In his bitterness and emptiness he readily turned to Christ. He in turn led four of the villagers to faith and greatly influenced three young intellectuals to seek God, who had been "sent down to the countryside" by Mao.

Visiting Shanghai for a month in the winter of 1973 a Hong Kong Christian became well acquainted with the house churches which were already growing in China's largest city. Meetings of up to thirty or forty people were held in homes and sometimes quietly in corners of parks. At this era before the death of Mao this was quite dangerous, so friends were stationed outside the door washing clothes or sweeping so as to alert the gathering to suspicious visitors. Some groups were already meeting two or three times each week. There was a great shortage of Bibles. Usually, passages of Scripture would be copied and distributed for study, rather than precious Bibles being carried to the meeting at the risk of their being seen and confiscated.

At Bible studies a chapter would usually be taken and studied verse by verse. They sang hymns but very quietly; many hymns were of their own composition and set to Chinese folk-tunes which were less easily distinguished as Christian hymns by outsiders. A few Christians had carefully preserved old records of Christmas carols which were listened to in the privacy of the home. Great emphasis was given to prayer. Sometimes the leader prayed, at other times all prayed quietly out loud together, or took turns to pray. The focus of their prayers was their own growth in grace, for Christians still imprisoned and for God to grant greater freedom for the preaching of the gospel.

Their mode of evangelism was necessarily secretive and personal, centring on close friends and relatives. Through a Christ-centred life radiating peace and joy they sought to influence others. When they showed interest they would ask them if they knew they were sinners and introduce the Christian faith, only later taking them to meetings. Once a person showed real interest, the Christians always asked the others in the fellowship for prayer support.

Thus the Church grew, both in the cities and the countryside, adapting itself in its style of worship and evangelism to local conditions in a natural and flexible manner. In fact, throughout China the house churches have developed and flourished as an indigenous movement which has shown a remarkable gift for acculturalisation. The survival and growth of the Church has been overwhelmingly a grass-roots lay movement. Ordinary people have exercised extraordinary faith, living out the truths of the Scripture.

Evangelism in the registered churches

Evangelism in the TSPM-controlled churches is circumscribed by numerous regulations. Over the past two decades a whole welter of detailed prohibitions have been promulgated by provincial and local authorities all over China. Preaching may take place only in the registered building. For instance, religious affairs regulations for Zhejiang Province published in the *Hangzhou Daily* clearly state that: "No organisation or individual is permitted to do evangelistic work outside the premises of a [registered] place of religious activities."[1]

Evangelism and ministry may be conducted only by approved persons (i.e. pastors, elders and registered helpers). Evangelism by itinerant preachers is strictly forbidden. No Christian literature may be produced or distributed except the limited quantities made available by the China Christian Council. In some churches I have visited these restrictions are prominently displayed at the entrance as a warning to Christians that they must obey the Party's injunctions. The Party has no desire to foster church growth and does its best to hinder and restrict it.

However, in spite of many bureaucratic restrictions registered churches continue to flourish and experience massive growth. In Zhejiang Province in one year (1992) 75,000 new Christians were baptised in registered churches. In Jiangsu Province the number of Christians associated with the registered churches has grown from 125,000 in 1985 to over one million by 1998 – an average annual growth rate over thirteen years of over 60,000.

In north China I visited a large TSPM city church. The young assistant pastor related how the church had been experiencing revival in recent years. The church members had bravely held a democratic election and voted off the church committee two notorious political stooges. As a result, many house church Christians in the city had returned to the TSPM church to worship, saying, as they put it, "God's temple has been cleansed." All over the city house groups sprang up and there was a wonderful spirit of unity among the believers as old animosities were buried. Entering that church for Sunday morning worship one experienced something electric in the atmosphere of fervent, yet restrained, worship. The pastor told me that in 1995 over 1,000 people had come to Christ and been baptised and added to the church, whose total congregation now numbered 6,000.

Vigorous evangelism is being carried out in some TSPM churches. On the 14 and 15 November 1997 the main church in Wenling County, Zhejiang Province, conducted evangelistic services. That week eighty believers held special prayer meetings. Christians brought their unsaved friends and relatives and each evening the church was packed with 4,000 listeners. Newcomers heard the gospel in the main church while many Christians watched on closed-circuit television in five other rooms. On one night alone over 600 people made a commitment to Christ and signed up for baptismal classes. They were added to a flourishing Christian community: Wenling County already has 72,200 believers (7.3 per cent of the population) meeting in 101 churches.[2]

Evangelism in TSPM churches is limited by a plethora of Party regulations. In some areas these are strictly implemented, in others the Christians have considerable leeway to spread the gospel message. It is encouraging that in many registered churches, despite restrictions, pastors and church members are engaging in evangelism and witness.

House church evangelism in the 1980s and 90s

Since the late 1970s there has been a veritable explosion of evangelistic activity across China by house church Christians. Christians now give out tracts on buses and trains, seeking to engage passengers in conversation. If there is any problem from the conductor or the authorities they simply get off at the next stop! In Shanghai young Christians have given out tracts standing at the exits of the new underground system. Commuters take a leaflet expecting it to be advertising TVs or patent medicines. Again, if there is any fear of arrest, the young evangelists melt into the crowd or move on to the next station.

Even where there is tight control, quite large-scale and effective evangelism can be carried out. As early as July 1982 house churches in Henan sent out seventeen evangelists to Sichuan – a very needy province with over 100 million people. Some of the preachers were arrested but others returned, reporting requests for help from a wide area. More than ten teams were then sent out. Since that time there has been great growth in Sichuan, too.

In 1986–87 an elderly preacher recorded in his diary the details of an extensive evangelistic tour of east and central China which makes for stirring reading:

> In the evening we had a large meeting with about four hundred people. There were so many that the place was full and the courtyard outside standing-room only. The Holy Spirit was powerfully at work. I spoke on the Second Coming and when I had finished, people surged forward like a tide and more than two hundred wanted me to pray for them. Thanks be to God, they all obtained peace before leaving. In just two or three days we saw more fruit than normally in a week. From morning to evening there was preaching, collective confession of sin and earnest prayer.
>
> We then stayed for six days in C County. We met a leading sister who asked us to go to two places where the peasants were hungering for God's Word. One meeting-place was very big. On the first day between 400-500 people came. The rooms and the courtyard

were jam-packed with people sitting and standing. I preached twice and prayed for healing for several hundred people. More than 260 people were baptised and my colleague baptised forty in another village, so in all more than three hundred people turned to the Lord.

The first day I preached on "Christ stilling the waves" and the hearts of the congregation were so moved they wept. After the meeting many sick people came to me for anointing with oil and prayer and more than one hundred were healed. One man who had been crippled for years was completely healed on the second day. On the last day Wang preached and when he spoke about David Livingstone's testimony in Africa, many were moved. The Christians of the entire city were inebriated with the love of the Lord. We saw the power of revival and of the Holy Spirit. If the situation would permit, and we had more freedom, we were completely convinced that all the major cities would experience revival. Originally there were only eighteen Christians here. Now there are more than 2,000.

Such spectacular evangelistic activities are largely limited to rural areas where control is less tight. Most evangelism in China is still carried out discreetly through personal outreach to relatives and friends in the local community. However, the results can still be as extraordinary in the long term, as a report from Jiangsu province reveals:

One town in the east of the province had no church at all. The first believer was a lady whose teenage son died tragically in 1989. This woman could not eat or sleep, but was drawn to Christ after listening to gospel radio programmes. She said to herself: "If I believe, I will be OK." So she went in search of a church but found none. Finally she came to a village that had previously been a labour-camp and saw a cross, painted above the door of a house. She went in and discovered two elderly Christians. They introduced her to another couple who preached the gospel to her and led her to Christ. She returned home and shared the gospel with many others. By late 1991 the church in that area had grown from just six believers to over two hundred in the space of only two years. They meet in three house churches and listen regularly to gospel radio for spiritual support.

Into the 21st century – house-church training

In the new century, rural house churches are struggling to train the large number of poorly educated believers, as well as to conserve younger leaders, many of whom are leaving for the cities in search of a better life. Training remains vital.

In late 2003, four of the largest six rural house-church networks gave detailed statistics of their basic Bible-training programmes. The China Gospel Fellowship, the Fangcheng church and the two large Anhui-based networks (Lixin and Yingshang) altogether had 130 basic Bible training schools. Of these, 104 were one-year training programmes, and only twenty-six were two or three-year programmes. The average number of people at each training centre is 20–30. This means these four large networks have about 3,900 people in training – this compares very favourably with the TSPM seminaries, who only have under 2,000 students in full-time seminary training at any one time. If the Wenzhou and other large networks, as well as the many city-based conservative house churches, are taken into consideration, one might hazard a guess that perhaps 10,000 or so house-church believers are receiving some form of full-time Bible or theological training.

However, the downside is that these rural house-church centres are very rudimentary, lacking the most basic facilities. Very few have any libraries and even fewer have computers. The temptation for well-funded overseas Christian organisations and foundations to pump in huge sums is understandable, but to be resisted. For the house churches to maintain their vital evangelistic zeal and trust in God, they must continue to be largely self-supporting.

In the cities, the situation is much better. House-church leaders are downloading quality Christian materials from the Internet and developing their own tailor-made curricula. Well-qualified theological trainers – mainly Overseas Chinese – from Hong Kong, Taiwan, Singapore and North America – are quietly slipping in to give intensive seminars. Tapes, videos and DVDs are being well used. For instance, in Beijing I was recently given an excellent DVD containing material to combat the "Eastern Lightning" cult. Still, much more needs to be done. However, the days when egotistical Western preachers sought to have their books and preaching materials which were fine for Pasadena or London translated into Chinese, with little thought of cross-cultural adaptation, are long gone. Much excellent material already exists in Hong Kong and Taiwan and needs only to be transposed into "simplified" script. Increasingly, high-quality materials are being produced within the Mainland and can be circulated widely in creative ways there or published overseas, then reimported.

To the ends of the earth

For a number of years, Chinese Christians have caught the vision for cross-cultural evangelism. In 1947–48, even before the revolution in 1949, some groups had a burden to reach the unevangelised peoples of north-west China, especially the Muslims of Xinjiang. The "Back to Jerusalem Band" glimpsed the awe-inspiring vista of God's purposes down the centuries. First, the gospel from the time of the apostle Paul moved steadily westward to Greece, Rome, Germany, Britain and then the United States. But then in the 19th century the Western missionaries took it back east to China. Chinese Christians believed that, before the second coming of Christ, it was the responsibility of the Chinese Church to take the gospel west to Jerusalem, thus making the circle complete. The "Back to Jerusalem Band" did pioneer work in Xinjiang but never got further because the border was then closed. However, their vision never died and was taken up by others in more recent times.

Today there are churches, both TSPM and unregistered house

Worshippers pour from the TSPM church in Guiyang after the Sunday service.

Massive churches in Wenzhou loom high in 2005.

"Seeking the Lord" – new Christians at a Chongqing church, 2005.

An unregistered open-air house church baptism – tens of thousands are baptised like this every year.

In north China house church Christians break the ice in a cave to hold a secret baptismal service.

Children sometimes accompany their parents to church – but 400 million under-18-year-olds are officially prohibited from joining church activities, and from being baptised.

These children are the lucky ones – they are enjoying Sunday School at a house church.

Miao girls in festal costume.

The author and his wife with house church believers, South China, 2005.

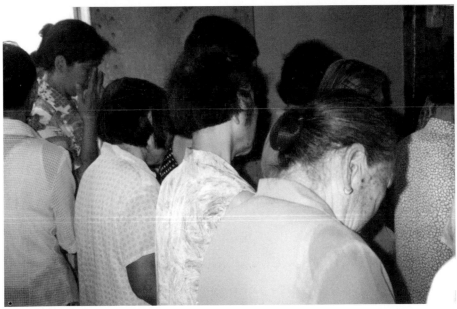

These Christians in Wenzhou, deep in prayer, reveal the secret of the Chinese revival.

churches, in most towns in Xinjiang. There are at least 130,000 believers in Xinjiang (according to TSPM estimates), in contrast to fewer than 200 in 1949. They exist among the large Han Chinese population which has moved into the region from further east. However, some Chinese Christians have a burden to reach out to the Muslim Uygurs, a few of whom have been converted despite formidable religious and cultural barriers. The Uygurs traditionally despise the Han as "idolaters and pork-eaters". The Han, for their part, often look down on the Uygur and there have been frequent clashes, some serious, between the two racial groups.

Even many Han Chinese believers in Xinjiang regard evangelism to the Uygurs as an impossible task. One elder, challenged on the subject by a house church evangelist responded by shouting, "You're crazy!" Yet barriers have been coming down. In 1988, forty years after the first Chinese missionaries set foot in Xinjiang, God poured out his Spirit on some house churches in southern Henan and gave them the vision of taking the gospel to Israel via Xinjiang. They began to learn Uygur, and in 1992 the first house church evangelists arrived in Xinjiang. They were aware that there were many Chinese Christians already in the area, so they contacted the local churches and worked with them. More recently, other evangelistic teams have arrived from Shaanxi, Anhui and Zhejiang provinces.

In 1997 house church missionaries in Xinjiang developed a new evangelistic strategy after waiting on God together. "Love every household" aims to evangelise the whole town or village in which the church is situated. Firstly, believers with the gift of evangelism are identified in each congregation. They are then formed into small groups of two or three evangelists. Secondly, the area is divided into four districts (north, south, east and west) and the number of residential and work units in each estimated. The teams of evangelists from the congregations located in a particular district are responsible for the evangelism of all the homes and factories in the area. Areas with strong churches help out those with fewer. No tracts are used in evangelism as the words and lives of the Christians are seen as the best means of communicating the gospel.

Each church seeks God for ways to make contacts with non-Christians. For instance, groups of evangelists went from house to house selling soft drinks and collecting bottles free, arousing the curiosity of people. By August 1997 this strategy was being used in seven different locations in Xinjiang. An immediate consequence was a revived zeal among the churches, greater vision and closer co-operation in practical evangelism. The aim is that all the Chinese in northern Xinjiang should hear the gospel and that 50,000 people will become Christians. Then the strategy will be taken to southern Xinjiang. When that is completed they pray that the Lord will move all the churches to evangelise the Muslims.

Similarly, other Chinese Christians have been called to Tibet, which remains the last largely unevangelised area in China. Chinese Christians have moved to Lhasa with the deliberate intention of sharing the gospel. Today there is at least one house fellowship (and possibly three) in the city. Again, they are largely attended by Han Chinese but there is a scattering of Tibetan enquirers and converts. This is a small, but significant breakthrough in a citadel of spiritual darkness which for centuries has resisted the gospel.

I know a Chinese lady aged about eighty who has travelled twice to Lhasa from Beijing as an evangelist. She did not have enough money to go by air, so took the long distance bus from Chengdu across the high mountain passes. The journey took several days. When the bus reached 15,000 feet, she passed out and blood gushed from her nose. Yet she went on to deliver her bundle of tracts. Such is the dedication and self-sacrifice of many Chinese Christians to spread the Good News.

There are altogether fifty-five minority peoples in China, although the publication in 2000 of the mammoth handbook *Operation China* showed that, in fact, this is a very artificial official Chinese government classification, and the real figure of diverse ethnic groups is closer to 500! Most have never heard the gospel or the church among them is very weak. Chinese and Western Christians need to work in partnership in the arduous task of translating the Scriptures and preparing Christian radio programmes and books and tracts. These "minorities" number well over 100 million people. The very term is misleading given their numbers. They *are* in the minority – but only compared to over 1.2 billion Han Chinese.

As the following table shows, there are many huge people-groups in China still largely unreached. Much Christian effort is concentrated on Amazonian tribes with just a few dozen or hundred people, but the Uigurs, Miao and Hui, each numbering over 9 million souls, are comparatively neglected in respect of gospel outreach.

CHINA'S MAJOR NATIONAL MINORITIES		
NAME OF GROUP	POPULATION (in millions)	AREA
ZHUANG	18.5	Guangxi
MANCHU	12.7	North China
HUI	10.7	Ningxia, North China, Yunnan
MIAO	9.5	SE China
UYGUR	9.1	Xinjiang
YI	8.3	Sichuan, Yunnan
TUJIA	7.4	Hunan
MONGOL	6.3	Inner Mongolia, Qinghai
TIBETAN	5.7	Tibet, Qinghai, Sichuan
BOUYEI	3.2	SW China
DONG	3.1	SW China
YAO	2.8	SW China
KOREAN	2.1	NE China
BAI	2.1	Yunnan
HANI	1.6	Yunnan
DAI	1.6	Yunnan
LI	1.4	Hainan
KAZAK	1.4	Xinjiang

(Figures for 2000 taken from *Operation China*, by P. Hattaway)

A missionary church

Some house churches are already seriously engaged in cross-cultural evangelism within China to over 100 million "minority" peoples. China, in fact is a vast mosaic of different "nationalities".

The vision of taking the gospel "Back to Jerusalem" is again inspiring some Chinese Christians, but this is only part of a much wider concern to engage in cross-cultural evangelism, firstly within China, and then overseas. This vision is diffuse and only in the initial stages of implementation. It is unfortunate that it has been aggressively marketed overseas by a few leaders who have often been mistakenly perceived as being key leaders of the house churches. In most cases they are no longer so, and have been largely out of touch with the house churches for five years or more, since they left China. The BTJ vision is current among some, mainly rural, house-church Christians, but I personally met a graduate at one of the TSPM seminaries who spoke soberly of undertaking strategic planning for future cross-cultural mission from China. No one person, church or organisation either within or outside China can claim to represent the BTJ vision, let alone the house-church movements. BTJ has unfortunately been exaggerated out of all proportion by some people overseas. Claims that certain leaders now overseas represent 50 or 75 million house-church Christians are adamantly rejected by the real leaders within China who repeatedly have told me that no one leader is in that position. Between 2003 and 2006 I did intensive research in many places across China, visiting many house-church leaders, including one of the original pioneers who went out in 1949 and is still living in Kashgar. Other Christian organisations, with over twenty years of experience working in the Mainland, have also been quietly monitoring the situation, and there is now general agreement about the facts of the situation.

The consensus is that a few hundred Mainland Christians are in some form of training for BTJ – not 100,000, as has been widely believed overseas. There are a handful of training schools beginning to train workers for cross-cultural evangelism within China and then overseas – not 30,000, as has been claimed. As we saw earlier, the total number of basic Bible schools (nothing to do with BTJ) of four of the largest house-church "streams" totalled just 130 in 2004.

An article published in late 2005 in the American Christian magazine *China Source*, which represents the mainstream evangelical China ministries there, explained the true situation very succinctly and fairly:

> Many supporters of BTJ do not choose their words carefully from the pulpit and present the 100,000 figure as a fait accompli. Most China ministries estimate the number of current BTJ workers and trainees in the hundreds... Are we faithful and transparent in how our ministry handles finances? Do we present the financial need accurately without misleading the donors?... If funds were raised on the 100,000 figure then there is a significant issue of integrity...

The Christian who wrote this has been involved in China ministry for over twenty years. It is sad that a vision given to humble Chinese Christians back in the 1940s with quiet encouragement from their China Inland Mission friends has somehow mutated fifty years later into a money-raising movement outside China, with often little reference to the views of the real house-church leaders inside China. The publication of books and open dissemination of much information on websites has already reportedly attracted the unfavourable attention of both the Chinese government and certain Arab governments. The polarisation between the majority of respected house-church leaders inside China denouncing BTJ spokesmen overseas and what they perceive to be the excesses of the BTJ movement, and the vociferous support for it overseas in pentecostal, charismatic and some evangelical circles has certainly not helped the development of long-term, strategic cross-cultural mission and evangelism from China, which is surely what all true Christians along with the present writer pray and long for.

In reality, the rural church networks, despite their undoubted zeal, are not best placed to undertake cross-cultural mission. Henan, the nursery of revival and explosive house-church growth for over thirty years, has one million Hui Muslims but effective house-church outreach to them is negligible, according to local sources. In early 2005 one of the handful of trained house-church evangelists to the Hui (Chinese Muslims) told me a true story to illustrate the lack of even basic knowledge of Islam among most house-church believers. In 2003 or 2004 a Wenzhou businessman who was a fervent Christian felt called to go to Xinjiang to reach out to the Muslim Uygurs. However, when he got there he had to start a business to justify his presence to the authorities and the local people. So he set up – a pork-processing plant! In this way he immediately became the most "unclean" person in the entire region and effectively destroyed any chance of befriending the local Muslims.

While acknowledging the zeal and effectiveness of the rural believers in their own cultural milieu, it seems more realistic to accept the fact that educated Christians in the cities and those with business contacts overseas are much better placed to pioneer the first steps in cross-cultural mission – first within China, and then, as they gain experience, to the wider world. The role of the "diaspora" of Mainland Chinese students and graduates converted overseas, familiar with English and other languages, and who then return to China, will be a key one in cross-cultural evangelism. Students and graduates have often played a strategic role in worldwide mission from the US and the UK and there is no reason why China should be different. This, of course, does not mean that every future Mainland missionary will have to have a degree, but those who are well educated and articulate are certainly better placed to gain cross-cultural training than poorly educated farmers.

What is truly exciting is not the hype widely created overseas, but the fact that the shoots of cross-cultural mission are beginning to emerge in China. Chinese house-church leaders rightly see the 100 million minority peoples in China (Muslims, Tibetans, Mongols, Miao, etc.) as a God-given training ground. It makes no sense to send out a large force of hurriedly trained Christian peasants from central China to the Middle East when they have major problems of adjustment to moving into an urban environment in their own country. However, there is much evidence that God has been quietly calling Chinese people to go out to Xinjiang, Tibet, SW China, etc. and begin pioneer evangelism. Some families have even "migrated" to remote regions to share the gospel with Tibetans and Muslims in NW China. But those most effective are usually those who make the least publicity. Often, they are unaware of "the BTJ Vision", and go out in simple obedience to the call God has given them. I came across one such evangelist recently in Yunnan. He has a long-standing training ministry to the Miao churches in SW China. Hmong churches across the border in Vietnam heard of how God was blessing his ministry and invited him to go there. As a natural development of his existing ministry, God was calling him without any fuss to take this new step of faith. I am sure that if I had not come across him, nobody overseas would know anything about his ministry. He was certainly not pleading for funds, but looking to God for supply in line with the original pioneers and the authentic mainstream of Chinese house churches today. In 2005, leaders of a large house-church grouping in Wenzhou said they were considering the possibility of training some of their members with a view to future mission overseas; they were adamant that they did not want funds from overseas. Financial support from abroad so often compromises the integrity of those it is aimed at helping. One is forced to ask: if so many of the godly house-church leaders both young and old are refusing to ask for money from overseas, then why are others busily looking for funding, and why are some overseas seeking to raise millions of dollars, which they must know will only corrupt the house churches and cause division?

The Western churches have had plenty of teething problems in developing missions since the days of William Carey. We are still trying to live down some of those mistakes today: paternalism, colonialism and a confusion sometimes of the gospel with a European or American "civilising mission". Then, until recently, who would have expected the South Korean churches to become a major force in world missions? The Koreans, too, have struggled to engage in cross-cultural mission. Yet God has wonderfully overruled the mistakes of his fallible workers, and the cause of the gospel has advanced worldwide. The Chinese, too, will make their mistakes. But who can doubt if they are given space that in time a genuine Mainland Chinese missions movement will emerge – perhaps linked in creative ways with the flourishing Overseas Chinese churches in SE Asia, North America and elsewhere – to become a major force in world mission. The Chinese house churches, with their strong eschatological sense that the church is in the Last Days and must vigorously preach Christ to the lost before the second coming, have recovered an authentic New Testament theme which Western missions are in danger of losing.

This Gospel of the Kingdom shall be preached in the whole world as a testimony to all nations, and then the end will come.

15

Lessons from the church in China

Recently I was having a discussion with some North American mission leaders. They claimed that China already has the largest community of evangelical believers anywhere in the world. I demurred: on the statistical evidence available, the United States still appears to have the largest number. However, China, with perhaps over 50 million, is definitely second, and is rapidly catching up. If present rates of growth continue, then in the next decade or two China will overtake the States to become the country with the largest number of Bible-believing Christians. For a country where as recently as 1978 no churches were allowed and Christianity was effectively outlawed, this is overwhelming evidence of a deep work of God and revival on a massive scale.

No other church in the world has experienced between thirty–fifty fold growth on such a scale in the short space of thirty years. The question has to be asked: why China? There is no simple answer, yet faced with this extraordinary phenomenon, let me cautiously make some observations.

Sociological explanation leaves gaps

There seems little doubt that the Cultural Revolution was the defining moment which destroyed the utopian illusions of a whole generation, and in its devastation of Chinese society and culture prepared the ground for the gospel far more effectively than most Christian evangelism. A deep wound was gouged in the collective Chinese psyche, which has yet to be fully healed. Families were torn apart. Vast numbers of people were falsely denounced and imprisoned. The "Great Helmsman" was ultimately shown to be responsible for the death of millions. The collapse of the Mao cult left many groping in desperation, their worldview shattered.

Moreover, the events of the last four decades have shaken the deeply-ingrained humanism of the Chinese people. For centuries children learnt the basic Confucian teaching "human nature is basically good". However, Mao deliberately sought (and to a large extent succeeded) to destroy this ancient ethical basis of Chinese society. Confucius, with his gentlemanly stress on self-control and moderation, was reviled. Absolute loyalty to the Party and the "Great Leader" was inculcated. Denunciation of one's neighbour, and even of close family members, became a patriotic duty. Through the cynical twists and turns of tortuous Party policy with its unending political campaigns, Chinese faith in the essential goodness of human nature was severely shaken.

For the intellectual classes, another defining moment was the tragedy of 4 June 1989 when Party leaders turned on their own children, the students, and the ugliness of raw power which was intent on survival by ruthless suppression became apparent to all. The Christian doctrine of original sin and its outworkings now makes sense as never before to thinking Chinese people. While in the West there is often an embarrassment in the churches to preach the depravity of human nature, and even a trend to preach "self-esteem" and a humanistic view of the essential goodness of human nature, in China the actual events of the past half-century have driven millions to face honestly their own guilt and sinfulness before a holy God. The message of Christ as the only Saviour from sin sounds with new power and meaning to the ears of those disillusioned by atheistic materialism.

Chinese Christians often state that the revival in China has little to do with them, but everything to do with a sovereign God. The political events of the Communist era in China have been totally outside the control of the Church, which in 1949 was a tiny minority. Yet with the benefit of hindsight, Mao's negative policies have done much as a preparation for the gospel. More positively, the unification of the country, the building of modern roads, railways and telecommunications and the imposition of Mandarin as a universal means of instruction, have indirectly helped it spread.

In this respect, the situation in China is not unlike that of the Roman Empire in the time of the Apostles. Yet the factor of God's sovereignty is often ignored. As we have seen, it would be quite possible – indeed, historically, it was almost certain – that the Church should have been completely obliterated by the Cultural Revolution. Yet the opposite has been proved to be the case – the Church has grown astronomically just as Maoism has gone into steep decline. God is sovereign Lord of history. At the very epoch when Western Christianity appears to be going into terminal decline (with some significant exceptions) he has been pleased to raise up a strong and vigorous Church in a country where thirty years ago all the experts stated Christianity had been finally eradicated. "The wind blows wherever it pleases." (John 3:8)

Here we may mention the reasons usually given by Chinese researchers and academics for the growth of the Church. A surprising amount of research has been done in China itself. The views of Sha Guangyi, a cadre in the Minorities and Religious Affairs Office of Jiangsu Province are fairly typical of such Marxist researchers. Quoting Lenin's dictum that "the deepest roots of religious prejudice are poverty and ignorance" he seeks to prove that the recent rapid growth of Christianity is due to superstition, poverty and ignorance. The majority of new converts in northern Jiangsu (93 per cent) are female peasants, and 60–70 per cent of them have been converted because of claimed healing of their illnesses. The peasants are steeped in "every type of superstition, fatalism and old customs which provide a fertile seedbed for the growth of Christianity".[1]

His arguments are superficially attractive. The gospel never comes to those in a sociological or cultural vacuum; God is pleased to use various means to draw people to himself. These sociological arguments do have some weight: many poverty stricken and sick people have turned to Christ. Far from seeing this as an embarrassment, it is cause for rejoicing. However, sociological arguments alone cannot explain the revival taking place in China today. Sha's reasoning is flawed.

In the first place, the argument that traditional Chinese religion provides a seedbed for Christianity does not hold water. In most areas of China, traditional religions have also made a come-back on a large scale. Christian converts in rural areas burn their idols and cut themselves off from superstitious customs at the risk of upsetting their neighbours and village communities and inviting persecution. With superstition rampant in the villages already, there seems no logical reason why large numbers of peasants should go against the tide of local opinion and custom to become Christians if all they have in mind is changing one superstition for another.

The argument that "Christianity Fever" has taken hold only in poor, backward areas of the country can only be taken so far. The Church has, indeed, seen great growth in impoverished regions of Henan, Anhui, Guizhou and Yunnan. However, it can also claim major gains in cities such as Wenzhou and Shanghai which are the most economically and technically advanced and prosperous in the entire country. Moreover, large numbers of students and educated young people all over the country have converted to Christ over the last decade. These facts tend to be conveniently ignored by many Marxist analysts.

Western researchers have offered more plausible reasons for the revival. For instance, Hunter and Chan in their detailed *Protestantism in Contemporary China* offer the following ten major factors for growth[2]:

1. The parallels between Christianity and traditional Chinese folk religion (this is a similar argument to Sha's discussed above).
2. Its highly flexible and successful organisational form, especially in house churches.

3. Christianity has benefited from the perception that it is a "Western religion" since China's "open door" policy largely abolished Maoist hostility to Western influences.
4. Protestantism has a powerful religious and moral message, which is attractive in a rapidly changing society.
5. Many Protestants are members of families or communities that have been Christian for some time, and the Church is strongest in those provinces where missionary effort was most successful before 1949.
6. Protestants are active in evangelism, and the house churches have a lively oral culture focusing on healings and miracles which many find attractive.
7. Christianity is a rationalistic and non-wasteful religion, able to survive in an industrial society better than traditional folk religions.
8. Christian forms of worship and music are very attractive which provide communal emotional release.
9. Christianity is diverse, ranging from highly charismatic to staid and liturgical worship. In a country as huge as China, this means Christianity has something for everyone.
10. It offers self-respect and enhanced personal identity to those whose self-worth is threatened by society, most notably women, national minorities and alienated youth.

How to respond to these arguments

Taken together they do appear to offer a plausible sociological explanation for the revival. Some arguments, however, are much stronger than others.

For instance, we have already seen that the flexibility of Protestantism, especially in its house church form, has been a major factor in its survival and growth (2); that Christianity has a strong and attractive message in today's Chinese society (4); that there is a direct continuity between the gospel planted by evangelical missionaries a century or more ago and today's revival, as we saw at the beginning of this book where the revival in Wenzhou was traced back to its humble beginnings (5); that vibrant evangelism has been a major factor (6), and that many sectors of society have found the gospel to answer their deepest needs (8–10). Few would dispute that these are important factors. But we have to ask the question: do they satisfactorily explain in full the phenomenon we are witnessing in China today?

We have already seen that Christianity demands a complete break with idolatry and folk religion. Family pressures, and in some cases even pressures from local cadres sympathetic to Buddhism, are strong disincentives to convert – yet many do. If Christianity is only a variant form of syncretistic folk religion, as the argument seems to imply, why do so many rural people not stick with the various Buddhist and Daoist sects they are familiar with? While making due allowance that syncretism does exist on the fringes of Christianity, the majority of Christians make a radical break with idolatry and superstitious customs. (See (7): both cannot be right!)

Point 2 stresses the flexible organisation of the house churches but other religions such as Buddhism and Daoism also have flexible structures. Indeed, many devotees attend temples only at major festivals a few times a year, which is much less rigorous than most house churches where attendance every Sunday is compulsory and additional meetings may be held nearly every day of the week! Many secret societies and new cults which have sprung up in recent years also meet in cell-groups. Yet in a lot of areas it is evangelical Christianity which has outstripped the traditional religions.

Point 3 puts forward the idea that the "Western" image of Christianity has great attraction. This is certainly true today, when some young city people may even be drawn to Christianity as a fashionable "fad" rather than experience genuine conversion. However, the revival began during the last years of the Cultural Revolution well before Deng Xiaoping returned to power in 1979. It began largely in rural areas which were totally beyond Western influences, and was in full-swing there by the early and mid-1980s when that influence was still only beginning to take hold in the major, largely coastal, cities. In fact it can be argued that the indigenous nature of rural Christianity accounts for its popularity and success.

Point 5 underlines one of the central messages of this book: that where the Word of God was strongly planted by missionaries, today there is often a revived Church. However, the great growth in Henan and Anhui is far inland from the coastal areas where the Church was strong. Today there are flourishing churches in many areas of China where there was none even a decade ago. The revival has extended far beyond the traditional areas where the Church was strongest: today, provinces such as Xinjiang, Qinghai and Heilongjiang where the Church was tiny before 1949 now have rapidly growing Christian communities.

Point 7 is true, so far as it goes. In backward tribal areas where much money is wasted on pagan festivals (pigs are slaughtered and sacrificed, much alcohol consumed, etc.) Christianity has an attraction as an alternative, cleaner and cheaper lifestyle! However, Marxism also attacked pagan superstition and has had a free-hand for half-a-century to attack wasteful customs. Now it appears to have failed; yet Christianity, which was on the point of extinction, or non-existent in many areas, has made a spectacular recovery. Even in modern urban areas it has often enjoyed rapid growth, whereas from a Marxist viewpoint it should have died out completely when the last few churches were closed in 1966. Certainly, Marxism claims to be the more "rational" and "materialist", yet Marxism in China is suffering a "crisis of faith" (*xinyang weiji*) – not Christianity!

Points 8, 9 & 10 are reasonable, but are inadequate as explanations. Some Chinese have been attracted into churches by the music, which is very different from the strident anthems favoured by the Party. Many, doubtless, find cathartic release in Christian meetings. Again, the Church is a haven for women, downtrodden tribal people and alienated youth – but the revival is also attracting high-calibre intellectuals and even Party members, as we have seen.

It has been pointed out that most of the arguments raised by Hunter and Chan apply equally, or even more, to overseas Chinese communities such as those in Taiwan and south-east Asia, where the Church is free to engage in aggressive evangelism and where every form of Christianity, with lively music and even charismatic healing is freely tolerated.[3] The freedom to evangelise is far greater than in China. Yet the stunning growth seen there is absent.

So while some of the sociological explanations given by both Western and Chinese academics for the growth of the Church in China may well be true, they do not adequately explain the phenomenon. We do not reject sociological explanations *per se*, as God is pleased to work through human means – that is surely the message of the incarnation. Theological and sociological explanations can coexist as different "models" of the same phenomena. However, we strongly resist reductionist sociological explanations that make no room for God or for biblically-based, theological critique.

An analogy here may be helpful: an academic might spend years researching the life of Mozart, and describing in minute detail his musical manuscripts: the paper, the ink used to write the score, the patterns of the notes, etc. etc. His scientific findings in that sphere would be perfectly true. Yet if the man himself is tone-deaf and unable to appreciate aesthetically a Mozart symphony, then despite the truth of his scientific analyses, he has completely missed the point. Similarly, any "explanation" that leaves God and the power of the gospel out of its equations is also inadequate.

The role of suffering

It is worth noting that suffering is absent from the lists of reasons for church growth, from both the Chinese and Western academics. (From the former because of political constraints, from the latter probably because it is outside their experience.) Yet the suffering and testimony of Christians under persecution has been a major factor. Those who survived long years in labour camps were released by 1980 to return to ministry in churches and house churches all over the country. Their principled stand not to compromise the gospel has deeply influenced younger Christians. Suffering has refined the Church. Men such as Wang Mingdao learnt the simple but difficult lesson not to fear persecution. For them, the truths of the gospel were more precious than life itself.

Today, the continued suffering of a minority of house church leaders carries on that refining process. Some have even told me that they do not look forward to the day when China is "open" to the gospel. They prefer the present situation of limited freedom and periodic crackdowns as more conducive, in God's providence, to produce true disciples from the ranks of the millions of new converts. They are often aware of the shallowness of spiritual life in the churches in the West, and have seen the havoc wrought in Eastern Europe by the total collapse of Communism and the subsequent freedom, with its inroads of materialism, pornography and the mafia.

The role of suffering in the Chinese revival is proof of its supernatural origin. What attraction is there for house church Christians to walk for hours in rain or snow to unheated meeting places? Or to risk discovery with resulting beatings, fines and imprisonment? What benefit does a young seminarian gain after spending several years in a cramped dormitory in an under-funded TSPM seminary, with the prospect of years as a junior church worker living on a pittance? Only the fact of the gospel and the loveliness of Christ as the "pearl of great price" can explain such sacrificial dedication.

Some lessons to draw

The visitor to China cannot but be struck by the vibrancy of Christian life across the country. I believe that our Chinese brothers and sisters can teach us much, and help redress some of the imbalances that have become apparent in church life in the West.

- **The authority of Scripture:** The Chinese Church is solidly founded on the Word of God. The Church is overwhelmingly evangelical, and this fact has been admitted even by some of the TSPM leaders who espouse liberal theology. Chinese believers hold the Bible to be inspired and inerrant. The only few exceptions are to be found in some of the TSPM seminaries and among some TSPM pastors who cling to a rather old form of theological liberalism popular in the 1930s and 1940s.

    The contrast between the growing evangelical Chinese Church and the diminishing main-line denominations in Europe and the United States is sharp. The various "theologies" which have been produced over the last half-century in the West have done nothing to halt overall spiritual decline. The abandonment of Scripture as God's own revelation has decimated the churches. In China, however, we are confronted with an exciting phenomenon – a grass-roots Church that is orthodox, evangelical and eager to hear and obey God's Word.

    Hunger for the Word of God is everywhere. Christians walk miles to attend meetings. Once arrived, they are happy to listen to preaching that usually lasts at least an hour, and often much longer. Many, especially older believers, have memorised long sections of Scripture. The universal use of one version – the "Union" version – has helped maintain doctrinal and spiritual unity. This centrality of the Bible has been lost in the West, not only in liberal denominations but also by some evangelical or charismatic churches where preaching is at a discount, and the focus has been switched from the rock of God's divine revelation in Christ to the shifting sands of religious emotions and subjectivism. (Francis Schaeffer called it "super-spirituality".) The one clear lesson from the Chinese revival which the Church in the West desperately needs to hear is that there will never be revival in the West without a wholehearted return to the Bible as the sole standard of faith and practice.

- *Obedience:* The Chinese are a practical and hard-working people. This is reflected in the way Christians live. Those trained in academic theology are rare, but many are receiving biblical training with a strong emphasis on discipleship. The Lord said: "If you love me, keep my commandments."

  In the West the growth of the "me-culture" and the saturation of society with materialism through advertising has meant that the Church has also unconsciously adapted to the prevailing materialism. There is a strong strain of antinomianism at work, so that even Christians often "do their own thing". In China, the reverse is true. Strong emphasis on Christian standards and obedience to God's commands can result in an overbalance towards legalism. But where it issues from a healthy understanding of the gospel of grace a proper tension is maintained.

  Obedience also means self-sacrifice. In countless ways, Chinese Christians have followed their Lord. Some have been imprisoned or foregone opportunities for self-advancement. Others have gladly contributed their "widow's mite" towards the rebuilding of churches, the support of students at seminary, or of itinerant evangelists.

- *Prayer:* Prayer has a central place in the life of the Chinese Church, and of individual believers. I will never forget the experience of kneeling with Christians on a hard, wooden floor as they cried out to God for deliverance from persecution. The local authorities had closed down the meeting place. "Lord, we are like the children of Israel at the Red Sea, with no way forward," prayed the pastor as the little group of about a dozen wept and wrestled with God. Six months later their prayers were answered. Hundreds of Christians had returned to worship regularly, and the pastor told me, smiling, that every time they had experienced persecution over the last two decades, growth had resulted.

Prayer is usually less dramatic, but no less effective. In Henan for many years house church believers have held 24-hour prayer meetings. I have a little, crude prayer card in my hand as I write this, a precious gift from China. It consists of a poorly photocopied picture of a "Watchman on the Wall" with a text from Ezekiel 3:17 – "Son of man, I have made you a watchman for the House of Israel" – and the time for prayer, in this case 11.30 pm until midnight. Believers covenant to pray at a specific time wherever they are. One can picture a farmer planting rape-seed, which makes the fields of Henan bright yellow, turning his heart to God in prayer and singing a lilting gospel song to a traditional folk melody. Or an elderly grandmother praying as she cooks over a simple charcoal stove in a dark, poorly furnished cottage. Or a teenage high-school student, one of a privileged few, praying as he cycles into college, first wheeling his bike teetering along narrow, dusty dykes and then pedalling on through all the traffic and confusion of a market town.

An itinerant evangelist sits on the banks of the Yellow River having preached for several hours in one village, and now stops for a rest before heading for another village where eager Christians have already begun to gather in a courtyard.

The Chinese revival is saturated in prayer, and often prayer with groanings and tears. In Zhejiang a network of house churches held continuous prayer meetings in 1991 which led to a major evangelistic thrust with around 10,000 people being saved. In some areas, house church Christians have heard of the growth of the Church in South Korea and set up "prayer mountains". They go early in the morning to pray to the Lord up a nearby hill. Whatever one may think of this particular practice, it leads to a disciplined, devotional life.

Here is a description of revival in a TSPM church in a letter from a Christian in Jingdezhen, Jiangxi, renowned since imperial times for its beautiful porcelain:

> I preach in both the house churches and in the TSPM church. Within a year, the flames of the Holy Spirit were ablaze everywhere: the believers throughout the city became on fire. All the seats in the church were full by 4.00 am with people praying. People walked into town several miles to hear the Word. We had to enlarge the building, and even that could not hold the people.[4]

Prayer is central to the Chinese revival as it has been to all great movements of the Holy Spirit. The first great missionary movement of the Protestant churches began with the Moravians in the 18th century. They started a round-the-clock prayer meeting which lasted over a century, and resulted in missionaries thrust out as far as Greenland, Tibet and the West Indies, and profoundly influenced John Wesley and the subsequent Methodist revival. Today, similar evangelistic outreach flowing from prayer is taking place in China.

- *Repentance:* The Chinese revival is marked by deep repentance. Preaching in China stresses the need for turning from sin. There is little "easy believism". In some TSPM churches it is common to see people come to the front towards the close of the service to pray for forgiveness. No "altar-call" is issued – the movement appears to be quite spontaneous, with little groups praying and sometimes weeping. Some TSPM churches have held special evangelistic meetings. At one such in south-east China about 100 people committed their lives to Christ publicly. Preaching in China generally faces sin head-on with calls for repentance from idolatry and all the sins listed in the Scriptures.
  Some house church groups place such stress on repentance that they have drawn up lists of sins to be repented of and hold special "New Life" meetings. They are sometimes

called "The Weepers" because of this emphasis, and face criticism from both house church and TSPM sources for legalism and emotionalism. Their practice does lead to extremism, yet outsiders should be cautious of blanket condemnation of this movement which also shows signs of being an authentic movement of the Holy Spirit.

In no area is the Chinese revival in such sharp contrast with some recent movements in the West as this. In the West spurious revivals centred on hyped personalities with an unbiblical overemphasis on healing and phenomena have swept through some churches with devastating effect. In China the authentic gospel is being proclaimed with a strong message of the need for repentance, unashamed denunciation of sin and the realities of heaven and hell.

• *Seriousness:* This is perhaps a rather strange virtue to highlight, yet it is a mark of Chinese Christianity and a mark of all authentic revivals. The Puritans were derided for it, as were the Methodists, thus receiving these very nicknames from the unbelieving world. In China, worship in the overwhelming majority of churches and house churches is a serious matter. There are times of exuberant praise and sometimes loud, communal prayer, especially in the house churches. But the dominant note is one of reverence and awe before a mighty God, and a quietness of spirit. This again contrasts with the laid-back, chummy attitudes towards God which have become standard in many Western churches. Chinese Christians are genuinely shocked to hear of movements current in the West where evangelists encourage believers to "join the party" and refer to the Holy Spirit as the "bar-tender". This is light-years from the Spirit of holiness which is manifest in the Chinese revival. To become a Christian means becoming a disciple of Christ. In China that still may mean persecution or discrimination. New converts have seriously to "count the cost".

- *Christ and his cross:* The preaching of Christ crucified and risen is central to the Chinese revival. To a society still deeply traumatised by the Cultural Revolution, and to individuals facing unemployment as the economic boom falters in the wake of the Asian recession, the message of a gracious God who sent his Son to die strikes a deep chord. In a society where the individual under Mao was literally seen as a mere "cog in the machine" the fact that Christ died for sinners strikes home with a power and freshness largely lost in Western society. Chinese people are still struggling to emerge fully from half-a-century of unrelenting suffering. Anyone who has read Jung Chang's best-seller *Wild Swans*, the story of three generations of a Chinese family who sacrificed everything for the Party but were cruelly betrayed, will know that.[5] Christ the innocent victim was broken on the cross by a ruthless political and religious establishment. This suffering God of love speaks powerfully to helpless, broken people.

For Chinese Christians "walking the way of the cross" is not just a doctrinal truth but a way of life. At the heart of the Chinese Church is a deep devotion to the Person of Christ as I discovered again recently while attending a small meeting for young Christian workers. They sang the following song many times in a meditative spirit:

Ah, Lord! I want to be firmly established in you, so I can keep your commandments.
Ah, Lord! I desire to love you, my God, with all my heart, mind and strength.
I give all of my love to you.
Ah, Lord! You search our hearts and only you know me.
With all my heart and strength I come to love you.
As Mary knelt at your feet and broke the vase of anointing oil, may you receive my deepest love.

This is the spirit of the Chinese revival.

16

Into the 21st century

On 16 August 2005 Yuan Xiangchen, known to his foreign Christian friends as Allen Yuan, died in Beijing aged 91. 2,500 Beijing house-church Christians attended his funeral, and the police turned away another 1,000.

In many ways, the death of Allen Yuan symbolised the end of an era. It was the passing of a much-loved and much-respected patriarch. Born in 1914, Allen, like the famous Beijing preacher Wang Mingdao, who was born somewhat earlier in 1900, witnessed the turbulent events that engulfed China – and the Chinese Church – throughout the 20th century. Foreign humiliation, the Warlords, the rise of the Nationalists under Chiang Kai-shek, the atrocities and trauma of the Japanese occupation, the savage civil war between Communists and Nationalists, the triumph of Mao in 1949, the endless political purges and repression of the church throughout the 1950s, culminating in the cataclysm of the Cultural Revolution... Allen had seen it all and survived, to emerge in 1979 quietly triumphant in Christ from unjust imprisonment for over twenty years in prison and labour camp. Late in the evening of 23 December 1979 he returned to his home in a quiet "hutong" (back lane) near the White Dagoba, where his dear wife, Huizhen, had struggled to bring up his children for twenty years without their father. Her testimony of God's provision during those difficult years reads similarly to the autobiography of George Müller, who trusted in God for the care of his orphans in 19th-century Bristol. Totally different social situations, but the same faith and trust in the providence of a prayer-answering God.

There then followed twenty-five years of amazing ministry. Allen tirelessly preached and shepherded a house church of some 100 souls, squeezed into his tiny home. His influence and wise counsel extended to many other house fellowships in Beijing and throughout north China. Many Christians came for advice and for Christian books foreign friends had discreetly brought him to distribute. Over the last decade or so, the annual high point was the mass baptism of some 200–400 converts every August in a reservoir outside Beijing. When they hired a swimming pool in the city centre one year, the jittery authorities forbade him from doing so in future.

But now he has passed the torch to younger men he has carefully trained. Across China, there is a dwindling band of these elderly stalwarts who still command respect across the house-church community. Men such as Lin Xiangao (Pastor Lamb) in Guangzhou, and Li Tianen in Shanghai. But a younger generation has come to the fore. In the cities many are well educated and downloading solid theology from the Internet to prepare their own training manuals. One such manual in use in north China is called "Dengguang" (Lamp Light). Daily Bible passages are given for systematic study, with simple notes. Then the reader is encouraged to spend time in meditation as to how the passage increases his knowledge of God, and how it leads to practical outworking of the faith. This shows the house churches at their best – firmly Bible-based and with a practical spirituality.

However, as the Chinese Church continues to grow and many Christians prepare to use the opportunities presented by the Olympics in 2008 for outreach, the church faces many challenges. There are opportunities, but also clear dangers. I have selected ten key areas which I believe are vital for the continuing healthy growth of the church. They can also be a focus for our prayers.

1. URBAN MINISTRY: reaching the cities for Christ is an urgent but also long-term priority. Although available statistics are sparse, the evidence points to the sobering fact that many, if not most, Chinese cities have about 1% or fewer who are committed Christians. Paul Hattaway in his series "China's Unreached Cities" has highlighted this real-

ity. To take just one example: who has even heard of the city of Fuyu in Jilin Province in NE China? I admit I hadn't – even though I have been studying China for forty years! Yet this city has about 1.5 million people. The number of Christians is thought to be around 10,000 – or only 0.8%.

2. MINISTRY TO MIGRANTS: this is closely linked with the first area of concern. Some 200 million farmers are on the move – the largest village to city migration in human history. Some villages – and house churches – are already emptied of over 90%, even 99%, of their young people, who stream into the cities in search of work. Conditions in factories and dormitories are often poor, and there is little time to seek out Christian fellowship. Because some migrants in desperation turn to drugs, prostitution or crime, they are generally despised by the more affluent city-dwellers. Here is a marvellous opportunity for the churches (both TSPM and house-church) to provide practical help and reach out with the gospel. Some good work is going on – in Beijing in 2003 a migrant worker from Anhui in just one year had set up about a dozen new house churches for some 1,000 believers – all on the margins of society – rubbish collectors, maids, construction workers, etc. Christians in business, both Mainland and from overseas, have set up Christian-run factories where migrant believers can worship and be trained for outreach. But such ventures must be just a drop in the ocean. Much more is needed.

3. MERCY MINISTRIES TO THE POOR, THE SICK AND THE PHYSICALLY AND MENTALLY HANDICAPPED: Again, this overlaps with the above points. Hundreds of millions of people in China are still living in relative poverty. Some in minority areas and in the parched desert and semi-desert areas of Gansu, Shaanxi, etc. are living in dire poverty. Overseas Christian agencies have a real impact, bringing irrigation and simple self-help projects to poor communi-

ties. Then there are the tens of millions of blind and deaf people, as well as those suffering from HIV/AIDS, drug addiction and mental illness. How agonising it was to be approached by two Christian women in south China asking prayer for their sons, both of whom had become drug addicts. In late 2005 I visited a school for seriously mentally and physically handicapped children in west China run by house-church people. They have doubled the facility to teach seventy children – but hundreds from all across China are on the waiting list. TSPM churches in some areas have started free clinics, and a conference was held in 2005 to encourage Christians to become involved in ministry to autistic children. From overseas, OMF, MSI and many other Christian agencies are seeking to help in practical ways. The ministry of Christians in the area of adoption and fostering is well known, and government leaders and city mayors have commended it. I suspect that the needs are so enormous and can no longer be hidden as they were in the Mao days, so the government in most cases is more than ready to accept help – so long as it is given with a Christian spirit of servanthood, coming alongside, not to judge or take over, but with humility and patience.

4. CHILDREN'S AND YOUTH MINISTRIES: Although technically the "under-18-year-old" rule discouraging Christian ministry to children is still in place – and enforced in some areas – in practice, many house churches and TSPM churches can undertake children's work if they are discreet. However, they still lack trained Sunday school teachers and materials. Then there is the whole area of youth and teenage ministry. New generations have sprung up for whom the Cultural Revolution, and even the era of Deng Xiaoping, is only history. These young people are often materialistic, restless, interested in money and pop culture like their Western counterparts. How can the often rather conservative Christians in both the TSPM and the house

churches be effectively trained and motivated to reach out to this new, lost generation?

5. THE ELDERLY: Often forgotten, there are already hundreds of millions of elderly folk aged over 60 and the number will rise steeply in the near future. Pensions and health insurance have been introduced into the cities, but are almost non-existent in the countryside, where the extended family still plays a vital role in caring for the elderly. However, family bonds fray as traditional respect for parents comes under attack. China is facing a serious crisis – a greying society with fewer younger workers to provide for their care. Voices have even been raised occasionally in government circles about allowing euthanasia. Certainly, the church has a vital role to play in care for the aged, and both the TSPM and the house churches already run old people's homes. In many TSPM churches a special service is held annually to honour the elderly. This is a good example of a positive Christian adaptation of ancestor-worship which still runs deep, especially in the countryside.

6. CHINA: A MISSION FIELD IN ITSELF – THE MINORITIES: I have already looked at the challenge of the minorities in some detail in Chapter 14. Over 100 million people of nearly 500 different groups live in China. Except for some of the SW minorities – most notably the Lisu and certain Miao and Yi sub-groups – most have very few or no Christians among them. If the Chinese Church is to become a major participant in global mission later in this century then it must face the challenge of these people groups within its own borders. It makes no sense to artificially create a missions movement to the Middle East or elsewhere, if Chinese Christians have no experience of reaching out with the gospel to the Muslims who are their neighbours, and, in the case of the Hui, speak Mandarin. Here is an area for fruitful partnership – which is already

happening – with experienced Christian organisations overseas who can provide specialist cross-cultural training and materials on how to reach Muslims, Tibetan Buddhists, etc. with the gospel.

7. INTELLECTUALS AND STUDENTS: The importance of reaching the "movers and shakers" with the gospel can hardly be overemphasized. Although many Chinese universities and colleges now have small Christian fellowships, the percentage of those who have become committed Christians is still quite low. The role of Christian ministry to the hundreds of thousands of Chinese students and graduates overseas in North America, the UK, Germany, Japan, Australia, Singapore, etc. is crucial. The weak link is still often how to integrate scholars converted overseas into suitable fellowships back home. However, as religious freedom inches forward in China with house churches often bolder and a little more open to welcoming outsiders, this difficult task is perhaps becoming somewhat easier.

8. GOVERNMENT RELIGIOUS POLICY: Continued prayer is needed for a real change of heart on the part of the government towards Christianity. Recent legislation and practice at the local level remains ambiguous at best, and at worst tacitly or actively encourages persecution of those who for conscience's sake refuse to register or accept TSPM tutelage. It is highly disappointing that the entire edifice of religious control through the Party's United Front and the "patriotic" religious organs still remains intact. The operation has become sophisticated over the years, but at the heart of CCP religious policy is the claim that the Party has the ultimate authority to control all religious affairs. Religious freedom is not, as in the West, a God-given or natural right, but a boon granted by the Party, which could conceivably be withdrawn if the Party decided that the political and social situation necessitated the taking of

tough action. Politics and religion are still intertwined in an unhealthy way, with religion regarded as a department of state to be regulated, as has been the case since Imperial times. Political sensitivities over Taiwan and sometimes tense relations with America and with the Vatican further complicate the situation for both the Protestant and the Catholic Churches. It is unlikely that there will be any sudden easing of religious restrictions in the near future. However, the cause of genuine religious freedom will advance as more "civil space" is allowed in society and the Party slowly and reluctantly loosens its grip in the face of growing public dissent.

9. PERSECUTION AND PRESSURE: On my visit to six cities in late 2005 the strong impression I received was of new boldness in the house churches and a sense that many urban house-church Christians are fairly relaxed. However, this is in sharp contrast to continuing reports of large-scale arrests in certain areas. For instance, on 20 October 2005 nearly fifty house-church leaders met together in Laishui County, Hebei Province to discuss ways of helping the poor and the migrant population, and were arrested and held for twenty hours. At the end of September, Christian businessman Tong Qimiao was arrested in Kashgar and beaten so badly he was unable to walk. His "crime" was that he refused to divulge information about a local house church. Just in four towns of Henan Province alone reportedly 400–500 Christians were arrested between June and August 2005. While the number of Christians so arrested is relatively small compared to the total number of believers, one such case of unjust imprisonment or torture is one too many. There are encouraging signs that many believers are standing up for their rights under the Chinese Constitution. It is undeniable that China has moved a long way in the right direction since the days of Mao with regard to religious freedom, but unarguably there is still quite a long way to go.

10. THEOLOGY: There is healthy debate within the Chinese Church on a whole range of issues. For instance, since the Millennium many biblically-literate believers in Wenzhou have been debating the issue of perseverance and assurance of salvation. Older leaders, remembering their sufferings for Christ, and anxious to combat any drift to "easy believism", argue for the possibility of falling away if Christians disobey God and refuse to repent. Some younger leaders have eagerly imbibed Reformed Theology and argue equally strongly for the classical evangelical truth of the perseverance of the saints. Similar debates rage on eschatalogical issues and many others. Although sometimes divisions may happen unnecessarily, I regard all this as a healthy sign of a mature church wrestling seriously with God's Word. The same thing happened during the Reformation, the Puritan era and the time of Wesley and Whitefield. The simple Biblicism which is widely practiced at grass-roots level may be derided by Bishop Ding and even by some evangelical academics overseas as a relic of "missionary fundamentalism". The fact is, it was simple faith in God's Word which kept the church alive during dark days. In 2002 Thomas Harvey published his excellent study of Wang Mingdao and his stand for the persecuted church in China. The house-church emphasis on the Lordship of Christ over His church stands in the honourable tradition of the Puritans, Covenanters, Huguenots, Scottish Free Church, German Confessing Church and many others in resisting the totalitarian demands of the State. What is remarkable is that, unlike some of those I have mentioned, the Chinese house-church Christians never resorted to violence or to political means, but used purely spiritual weapons of warfare under intense persecution and provocation.

In late 2005 a Shanghai house-church leader made the very perceptive comment that the issues for which the Chinese house-church Christians have suffered – and often still suffer, such as the full authority of Scripture, the centrality of the cross, the uniqueness of Christ as the only way of salvation, and Christ as sole head of the church – are the very ones that are coming under increasing attack overseas even in supposedly "evangelical" circles.

This does not mean the Chinese Church should not develop its own authentic, evangelical theology, avoiding both the pitfalls of neo-Marxist TSPM "theological construction" on one side and a hidebound traditionalism on the other. There are encouraging signs that this is beginning to happen. As young Chinese Christians surf the Internet, the full riches of the Christian heritage – from Paul through Augustine, Luther, Calvin, Spurgeon to John Stott, as well as Wang Mingdao, Jia Yuming and many other Chinese Christian thinkers – are open to them. But so are many cults and, perhaps more subtly dangerous, extreme teachings such as "prosperity theology", which masquerade under a superficial biblical covering.

Old denominational differences rear their heads. The church unity imposed by the TSPM on its churches is fraying at the seams as foreign organisations offer money and support. Among the house churches, any wide-scale unity that was enjoyed in the 1970s and 1980s has largely fractured. (The Sinim Fellowship appears now largely moribund.) The situation is confused. There is a great need for the gulf between the academic study of Christianity at China's premier universities and the practical basic Bible training given in TSPM seminaries and house churches to be bridged. We need to pray that God will raise up a generation of Chinese evangelical theologians and thinkers nourished by the Word of God and willing to grapple with the many issues facing the Chinese church and society.

1976 saw the death of Mao. By 2006, just thirty short years later, the Chinese Church, which some saw as lying in its grave, has not only "stood up" (to quote Mao himself!) but made some giant strides forward. May many more millions in China come to know Christ. And may this church be a blessing and a challenge to the worldwide church.

APPENDIX 1

Church growth by province

Author's note: Graphs have only been provided where the data is available and sufficiently reliable.

Statistics in China are notoriously unreliable. Published official statistics of religious believers by the government or the TSPM are generally extremely conservative, including only registered, adult believers and excluding unregistered house church believers. On the other hand, Christians overseas have tended to produce exaggerated figures with little or no detailed statistical evidence. The oft-quoted figure since the early eighties of 50 million Protestant Christians in China emanated from one house church leader who, since moving to North America, has pursued a rather dubious career. This has been quoted and further extrapolated from many times over. The nature of Chinese society and of the Church is such that local pastors or house church leaders are simply not in a position to give reliable countrywide estimates for the total number of Christians.

The statistics given here are largely taken from private interviews with local TSPM/CCC leaders and are significantly higher than the "official" statistics published by the TSPM and in local government handbooks. However, they may not always include unregistered house church believers so may still be conservative. In a few cases, house church estimates for some counties have also been given. The present author readily admits that these statistics are incomplete and conservative. However, they do at least provide a baseline for further in-depth research, and, for the first time, give concrete evidence of the scale of the Christian revival in China. Speculation that there are 90 million or even over 100 million Protestant believers in China have to be firmly rejected in the absence of any hard evidence for such high figures.

For the first time graphs showing church growth for a number of provinces are published, charting the spectacular post-Cultural Revolution explosion of the Christian population compared to the very modest growth pre-1949. A clear pattern emerges showing slow growth over many decades up to 1949, and then a period (with very few exceptions) of decline during the period of persecution during the fifties and sixties. However, by the early eighties strong evidence emerges of recovery which rapidly curves upward into spectacular church growth.

The author would be most grateful for any statistical information from readers who have visited any part of China which may further throw light on the revival of the Church in China.

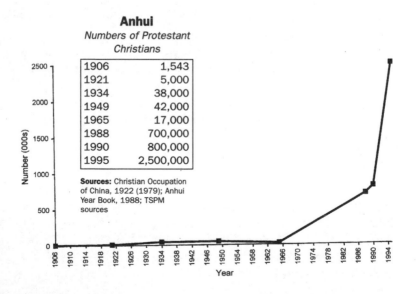

Anhui
Numbers of Protestant Christians

1906	1,543
1921	5,000
1934	38,000
1949	42,000
1965	17,000
1988	700,000
1990	800,000
1995	2,500,000

Sources: Christian Occupation of China, 1922 (1979); Anhui Year Book, 1988; TSPM sources

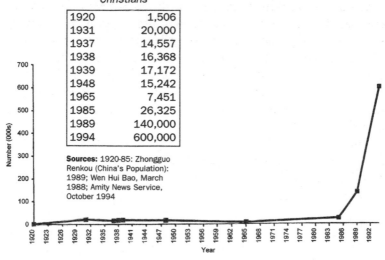

Heilongjiang
Numbers of Protestant Christians

Year	Number
1920	1,506
1931	20,000
1937	14,557
1938	16,368
1939	17,172
1948	15,242
1965	7,451
1985	26,325
1989	140,000
1994	600,000

Sources: 1920-85: Zhongguo Renkou (China's Population): 1989; Wen Hui Bao, March 1988; Amity News Service, October 1994

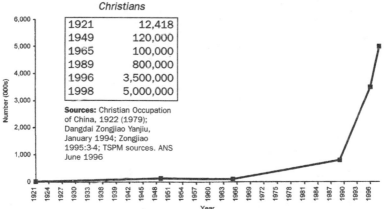

Henan
Numbers of Protestant Christians

Year	Number
1921	12,418
1949	120,000
1965	100,000
1989	800,000
1996	3,500,000
1998	5,000,000

Sources: Christian Occupation of China, 1922 (1979); Dangdai Zongjiao Yanjiu, January 1994; Zongjiao 1995:3-4; TSPM sources. ANS June 1996

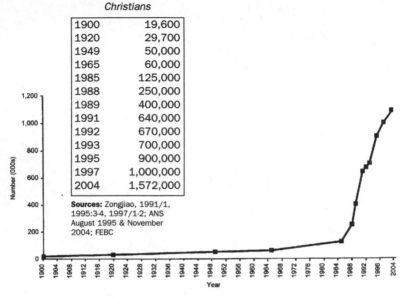

Jiangsu
Numbers of Protestant Christians

1900	19,600
1920	29,700
1949	50,000
1965	60,000
1985	125,000
1988	250,000
1989	400,000
1991	640,000
1992	670,000
1993	700,000
1995	900,000
1997	1,000,000
2004	1,572,000

Sources: Zongjiao, 1991/1, 1995:3-4, 1997/1-2; ANS August 1995 & November 2004; FEBC

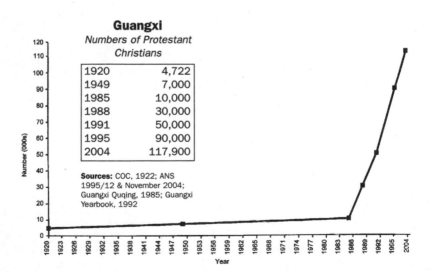

Guangxi
Numbers of Protestant Christians

1920	4,722
1949	7,000
1985	10,000
1988	30,000
1991	50,000
1995	90,000
2004	117,900

Sources: COC, 1922; ANS 1995/12 & November 2004; Guangxi Quqing, 1985; Guangxi Yearbook, 1992

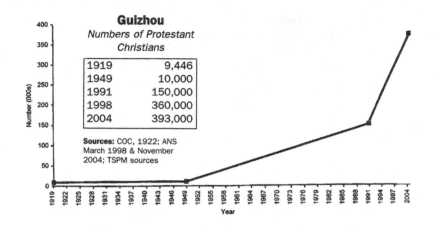

Guizhou
Numbers of Protestant Christians

1919	9,446
1949	10,000
1991	150,000
1998	360,000
2004	393,000

Sources: COC, 1922; ANS March 1998 & November 2004; TSPM sources

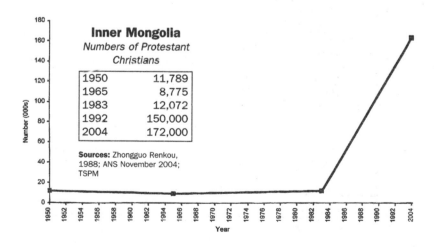

Inner Mongolia
Numbers of Protestant Christians

1950	11,789
1965	8,775
1983	12,072
1992	150,000
2004	172,000

Sources: Zhongguo Renkou, 1988; ANS November 2004; TSPM

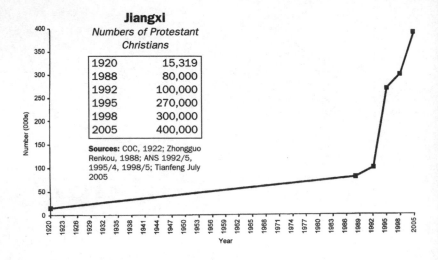

Jiangxi
Numbers of Protestant Christians

1920	15,319
1988	80,000
1992	100,000
1995	270,000
1998	300,000
2005	400,000

Sources: COC, 1922; Zhongguo Renkou, 1988; ANS 1992/5, 1995/4, 1998/5; Tianfeng July 2005

Number (000s)

Year

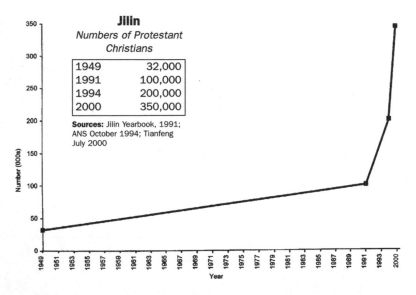

Jilin
Numbers of Protestant Christians

1949	32,000
1991	100,000
1994	200,000
2000	350,000

Sources: Jilin Yearbook, 1991; ANS October 1994; Tianfeng July 2000

Number (000s)

Year

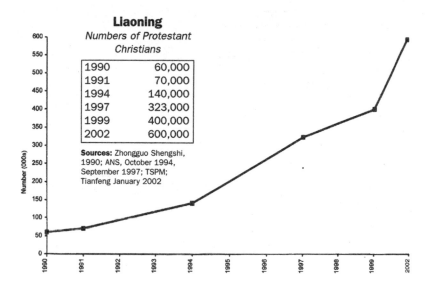

Liaoning
Numbers of Protestant Christians

1990	60,000
1991	70,000
1994	140,000
1997	323,000
1999	400,000
2002	600,000

Sources: Zhongguo Shengshi, 1990; ANS, October 1994, September 1997; TSPM; Tianfeng January 2002

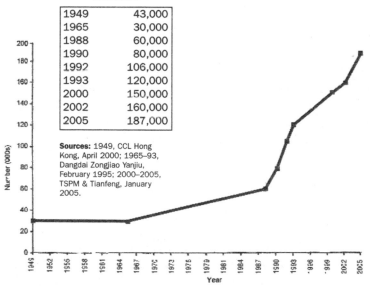

Shanghai Municipality
Numbers of Protestant Christians

1949	43,000
1965	30,000
1988	60,000
1990	80,000
1992	106,000
1993	120,000
2000	150,000
2002	160,000
2005	187,000

Sources: 1949, CCL Hong Kong, April 2000; 1965–93, Dangdai Zongjiao Yanjiu, February 1995; 2000–2005, TSPM & Tianfeng, January 2005.

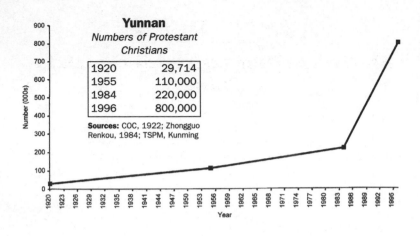

Yunnan

Numbers of Protestant Christians

1920	29,714
1955	110,000
1984	220,000
1996	800,000

Sources: COC, 1922; Zhongguo Renkou, 1984; TSPM, Kunming

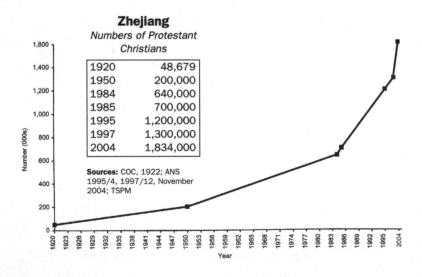

Zhejiang

Numbers of Protestant Christians

1920	48,679
1950	200,000
1984	640,000
1985	700,000
1995	1,200,000
1997	1,300,000
2004	1,834,000

Sources: COC, 1922; ANS 1995/4, 1997/12, November 2004; TSPM

APPENDIX 2

Statistics of the registered church in China

PROVINCE	No. Christians 1949–1950	No. Christians 2004	No. churches	No. registered meeting-points	Pastors
ANHUI	50,000	3,000,000	219 ('94)	1,920	30–40
BEIJING		39,300	9	300	47
FUJIAN	100,000	1,179,000	1,188	1,348	715
GANSU		262,000	103	369	20
GUANGDONG		262,000	280	199	126
GUANGXI	7–10,000	117,900	[250] *		22
GUIZHOU	10,000	400,000	197	370	60
HAINAN	7,000	39,300	21	41	9
HEBEI	70,000	400,000	163	2,600	59
HEILONGJIANG	15,000	600,000	300	"thousands"	24
HENAN	120,000	5,000,000	1,100	5,000	100
HUBEI		500,000	400		75
HUNAN		300,000	[800] *		32
INNER MONGOLIA	11,789	172,000	[1,000+] *		8
JIANGSU	50,000	1,572,000	[3,200] *		104
JIANGXI		400,000	571	1,541	130
JILIN	32,000	350,000	[1,900] *		100
LIAONING		600,000	[1,400] *		70
NINGXIA		65,500	6	9	
QINGHAI	500	39,300	5	40	5
SHAANXI	30,000	458,500	[1,300] *		49
SHANDONG	80,000	1,179,000	926	4,000	85
SHANGHAI		187,000	[162] *		47
SHANXI	26,000	200,000	99		
SICHUAN		524,000	119		100
TIANJIN	7,000	19,650	8		
TIBET		–	0	0	0
XINJIANG	Under 200	131,000	[At least 56] *		
YUNNAN	110,000	1,179,000	2,200+	1,000+	80
ZHEJIANG	200,000	1,834,000	2,600	3,500	120

NOTES: * Total figures for both churches and registered meeting-points. According to the TSPM, the registered church has grown on average by about one million believers per annum over the past two decades.

APPENDIX 3

A survey of church growth, province by province

China is a vast land, roughly equal in size to the United States, or the whole of Western Europe. Generalisations in such a huge and diverse country are difficult to make and often wide of the mark. This short provincial survey may help to illustrate that diversity, and to build up an overall picture. It should be remembered that some provinces in China have land areas and populations bigger than the United Kingdom. Sichuan, for example, has 80 million people which include sophisticated urbanites in Chengdu, and impoverished rural peasants, as well as many minority peoples such as the Tibetans, Yi and Qiang, each with their own distinctive language and culture. And this is only one province of thirty!

The Church is equally diverse, drawing in fashionable city dwellers in Shanghai and impoverished peasants living in cave-homes by the Yellow River. In some regions such as Wenzhou, Christianity is flourishing and there is a higher percentage of active evangelicals than anywhere in Western Europe; in other areas, including many cities as well as rural areas, Christians are scattered in tiny groups, or even exist as lone individuals reliant on gospel radio for spiritual sustenance.

The following provincial survey is meant to give insight into the widely varying situation of the Chinese Church. It also, for the first time, provides detailed statistics of church growth over the last twenty years, and in some cases, since the beginning of the century. A word of caution: most of the post-Cultural Revolution statistics are based on estimates given by local TSPM pastors. They may not include unregistered Christians and are therefore likely to be conservative in most instances.

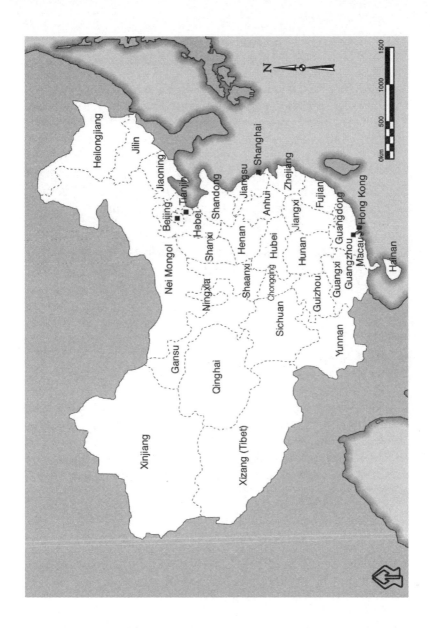

ANHUI PROVINCE
Population: 60 million (2002)

This province has traditionally been backward and impoverished but has seen marked economic improvement in recent years. Church growth has been nothing short of explosive from about 50,000 in 1949 to some three million at present. This figure was given by a TSPM spokesman to a visiting British delegation in 1995. Growth has been particularly spectacular in the northern part of the province. There are many house church meetings and networks, but also a growth of sects and cults.

District	No. of Christians	No. of Churches	No. of meeting-points
HEFEI	10,000+ (1994)		
CHANGFENG COUNTY	10,000+		[20+ reg. churches and meeting-points]
HUAINAN CITY	11,000+ (1997)		[100 reg. churches and meeting-points]
HUAIBEI DISTRICT	80,000 (1989)	4	67 reg.+ 170 unreg.m/ps
HUAIYUAN COUNTY	25,000 (1989)		
SUXIAN REGION	200,000 (1994)	600	
CHUZHOU CITY	20,000 (1994)	1	19
LAIAN COUNTY	989 (1987)		
QUANJIAO COUNTY	48,000 (1994)		["At least" 10 reg. churches & m/ps]
FUYANG REGION	273,187 (1998)		
Inc. TAIHE COUNTY	40,000		
JIESHOU COUNTY	20,000		
YINGSHANG C'NTY	60,000 (2003)		[64 churches/meeting-points]
BOZHOU CITY	50,000		
FUNAN COUNTY	80,000		
LIXIN COUNTY	10,000+	4	100 house churches
MENGCHENG C'NTY	30,000 (1995)		
HUOQIU COUNTY	25,000	65	200 house churches
WUWEI COUNTY	30,000		
SHOU COUNTY	20,000		
HE COUNTY	10,000 (1993)		
FENGYANG COUNTY	50,000 (1994)		48
HAOZHOU CITY	20,000 (1990)		

See Chapter 6 for a detailed treatment of church growth in Anhui.

BEIJING MUNICIPALITY
Population: 14 million

As the capital, Beijing is tightly controlled. The people are conservative and the gospel has not spread as rapidly as in some cities, such as Shanghai or Wenzhou. According to the TSPM magazine *Tianfeng*, in December 2002 there were 30,000 Protestants meeting in nine churches and over 300 registered meeting-points. About 2,000 people are baptised in TSPM churches annually. In 2004, Amity, reporting TSPM sources, gave an updated figure for the registered church of 39,300.

Many university students from China's top universities, such as "Beida" and Qinghua, attend the open churches. Many also attend house churches. There is a very large foreign fellowship allowed to meet in a hotel, but local Chinese are strictly forbidden. The government has become concerned about the proliferation of house-churches especially among Beijing's educated classes. According to reliable house-church sources, they conducted a discreet survey through TSPM channels in 2003. They discovered there were at least 3,000 unregistered fellowships in the city! Most of these are quite small, with perhaps twenty to fifty members, although some in the suburbs and country have over 100 members. If a conservative estimate is made of thirty people per meeting then this would place the house-church community at about 90,000 – or three times the number meeting in registered churches. If one allows for the facts that there is some duplication (i.e. Christians attending both registered and unregistered meetings) and doubtless that the authorities did not discover every meeting or were not too bothered with very small meetings of under a dozen people, then this estimate is probably a fairly good pointer to the actual number of believers. If so, it is a sobering thought that only some 130,000 people (40,000 TSPM + c. 90,000 house-church) meet as Protestant Christians in China's capital – or just under 1 per cent.

CHONGQING MUNICIPALITY
Population: 31 million

Chongqing, formerly in eastern Sichuan Province, is China's newest municipality having only been created in 1997. It now ranks alongside Beijing, Shanghai and Tianjin, having this privileged status. In Chongqing's case this was granted to open up the vast hinterland of China to economic development, particularly the teeming province of Sichuan.

Claims have been made that Chongqing, with 30 million inhabitants, is now the largest city in China, if not in the world. However, the actual urban area of Chongqing is much smaller than either Beijing or Shanghai, having a population in 2001 of 5.4 million. The vast majority of the new "municipality" which in area is nearly the size of the UK, is comprised of rural counties and other large cities such as Wanxian.

In January 1998 representatives from the twenty-seven districts within the new municipality met for the first time together to establish a new Chongqing TSPM and Christian Council.[1] According to TSPM sources in 2005 there were at least 300,000 Christians in the new municipality, about equally divided between the urban and rural areas. They meet in sixty-six registered churches and over 400 meeting-points but are served by only sixty-two pastoral workers.[2] The Roman Catholics number 170,000.

Chongqing, like Sichuan, is very needy spiritually. The city is experiencing rapid economic development and the gap between rich and poor is particularly marked. The church finds itself strategically placed to minister to a region in the throes of rapid social change.

TABLE OF CHRISTIANS IN CHONGQING BY DISTRICT

	Protestants (TSPM)	Catholics (CPA)
Jiangbei District	10,000+	2,200
Shapingbei District	7,500	7,800
Jiulongpo District	7,000	4,000
Nanan District	7,000	2,000
Dadukou District	2,500	3,000+
Beibei District	15,000	20,000
Yubei District	8,000	100+
Wansheng District	3,000	200
Shuangqiao District	30	–
Jiangjin City	4 churches	3 churches
Yongchuan City	1,200+	1,500+
Qijiang County	30,000	2,000+
Changshou County	2,800	2,200
Dazu County	?	6,000
Tongnan County	Some	Nearly 2,000
Tongliang County	5,000	4,000
Rongchang County	200+	3,300+
Bishan County	3,200	4,300
Fuling District	Nearly 2,000	1,700
Nanchuan City	?	1,289
Dianjiang County	6,000 (3,000 True Jesus)	3,000+
Fengdu County	4,600	2,500
Wulong County	?	300
Liangping County	3,000	31,000
Wanzhou District	8,000	30,000
Zhong County	3,980 (mainly True Jesus)	1,044
Fengjie County	2,000+	3,000+
Kai County	5,000	5,000
Yunyang County	300+	320
Wushan County	?	4,600+
Qianjiang County	300	700
Pengshui Miao/Tujia County	0	800+
Youyang Tujia/ Miao County	446 (146 baptised)	120?
Xiushan Tujia/ Miao County	117	–

TABLE OF THE MAIN TSPM CHURCHES IN CHONGQING

No. of believers

Shejiao Church	1,200	"3,000+ baptised 1979–2000"
Liberation West Rd	700	
Jiangbei Gospel Hall	1,000+	
Beipei Gospel Hall	2,000+	
Maanshan Church	1,000+	(baptised since reopening in 1982)
Nanquan Church	900	
Tianxingqiao Church	2,000	
Dadukou Church	1,500	
Liangping Gospel Hall	3,000+	(including "seekers")
Dianjiang Church	5,500	(inc. "3,000 seekers")
Wanzhou churches	8,000+	(in one main church + 3 m/points)
Youyanglongtan Hall	1,000+	
Qianjiang Gospel Hall	500	
Kai County Saviour	5,000	(inc. seekers)
Fengjie Gospel Hall	1,000+	(inc. 2 rural m/points)

(Statistics taken from Chongqing Zongjiao [Chongqing's Religions], Chongqing Publishing House, 2000.)

FUJIAN PROVINCE
Population: 35 million

Fujian has a thriving and rapidly-growing Christian community. As a coastal province in the south-east, it was one of the
first to be evangelised from the early 19th century. By 1949
there were about 100,000 Protestants. Official estimates of
Protestant Christians in 2004 were 1,179,000 – a twelve-fold
growth after fifty-five years of Communism. In early 1999 a
TSPM spokesman stated there were 4,000 registered churches
and meeting-points. In 2000 the TSPM magazine *Tianfeng*
revealed there were over 1,200 pastoral workers in Fujian.

Fuzhou, the capital, with its six surrounding rural counties
and two smaller municipalities had at least 350,000 Protestants
in 2002, meeting in 300 registered churches and 2,000 meeting-points.[3] In 2004, Fuqing City had 350,000 believers meeting in 520 churches, according to a Hong Kong pastor. After
Wenzhou, it is the area with the second greatest number of
churches in the whole country, and has been dubbed "China's
Second Jerusalem". About 26 per cent of the population are

Christian. Pingtan, a large island off the coast, has also seen incredible growth, from under 5,000 Christians in 1959 to 60,000 today, divided equally between registered and unregistered congregations. At least 15 per cent of the island's population are Christians.

The "Little Flock" or "Assemblies" were started by Watchman Nee in the 1930s and are still very strong in Fujian, especially in the Fuzhou and Fuqing areas where they number many thousands. Many of them prefer to have no links with the TSPM. In Xiamen at least one-third of the believers meet in over 100 independent house churches, according to a knowledgeable Hong Kong Christian. The "True Jesus Church", another indigenous church, is also strong in the province with some 70,000 members in total. They are very strong in Putian County, numbering about 20,000 there. There are about 210,000 Roman Catholics in Fujian. In general, the official religious policy has been applied relatively liberally in Fujian, although there have been occasional crackdowns on house churches and "underground" Catholics.

TABLE OF CHURCH GROWTH IN FUJIAN PROVINCE

	No. of Christians	Churches	Meeting points
FUZHOU MUNICIPALITY	200,000	300	2,000
Inc. LIANJIANG COUNTY	20,000	27	3
QUANZHOU			
(Inc. 6 rural counties)	90,000	91	100 +
FUQING CITY	350,000	520	Many
PUTIAN MUNICIPALITY	90,000	79	141
			(41 reg.)
Inc. XIANYOU COUNTY	30,000		
NINGDE REGION	60,000		
Inc. XIAPU COUNTY	25,000	76	52
SHOUNING COUNTY	3,500	40	
ZHANGZHOU CITY	20,000	[– 60 –]	
	(baptised)		
PINGTAN COUNTY	60,000		
XIAMEN CITY	5,000	15	10
NANPING REGION			
(10 counties)	40,000 (2002)	148	
ZHOUNING COUNTY	800		

GANSU PROVINCE
Population: 26 million

Arid Gansu Province is a "panhandle" stretching out along the length of the Great Wall beyond which was traditionally desert, the nomads, and barbarism. Today it is one of China's poorest provinces. Lanzhou, the capital, is a bleak, polluted city ringed by petro-chemical plants. There is a large Muslim population.

Information on the church in Gansu is not easy to find. In 1997 the TSPM issued the very low figure of 67,000 registered Protestants. In 2004 Amity News Service estimated 262,000 which seems more realistic. This is huge growth since 1947 before the Communist victory when there were only 6,551 Protestants. Lanzhou has over 20,000 Christians meeting in at least eight churches and thirty-eight registered meeting-points. In 1989 there were an equal number of unregistered meeting-points known to the TSPM in the city.

Min County has about 10,000 Christians meeting in fourteen meeting-points. One report in 1990 stated that every Sunday four or five people were converted at the main church. Lintan County has about 2,000 believers out of a total population of 130,000. There are three churches in the area. According to one unconfirmed report there may be as many as 90,000 Christians in the Tianshui region. There are also many Christians in the Pingliang district according to a report published in *Bridge* in October 1996. Huating County has two churches and two meeting-points with a baptised membership of 250. In nearby Jingchuan there were about 250 believers in 1950. The church was closed down in 1958 and not reopened until 1980. Today there are over 1,000 Christians. The Qingyang District has seen even greater growth: in 1949 there were only 200 Christians, but today there are over 10,000 of whom about 5,000 live in Zhengning County. In Jinchang City according to the local gazette there were 1,112 Protestants in 1994 and three churches or meeting-points.

In 1989 I had the joy of witnessing 250 people being

baptised in the main TSPM church in Lanzhou. The elderly pastors stood up to their waists in the old China Inland Mission baptistry and carried out the baptisms by full immersion for several hours. It was exhausting, but happy work.

GUANGDONG PROVINCE
Population: 86.4 million (2001)

Although Guangdong was the first province to be evangelised by Western Protestant missionaries as early as 1807, it is not in the forefront of church growth today. There were about 80,000 Protestants by 1949. In 2004, TSPM sources put the total number of Protestants at only 262,000, which seems very low and does not take into account many house churches. Nevertheless, the Cantonese-speaking southerners may be more resistant to the gospel than other Chinese, partly because of the infamous association of Christianity in their minds with the opium trade as a hated "foreign religion". Guangzhou itself may have 50,000 Christians.

Apart from several large TSPM churches in the city, Pastor Samuel Lamb has run a thriving unregistered house church over the last twenty years, at which thousands have come to faith and been baptised. The church appears to be strongest in the eastern part of the province. Shantou (Swatow) has at least 10,000 believers in eleven churches in the city itself, and 142 meeting-points in the surrounding countryside.[4] The Hakka-speaking area of Meizhou Municipality had 60,000 Christians in 1997.

Another area which has seen spectacular growth is the Xuwen peninsula where there are over 10,000 believers. One meeting-point with only forty members in July 1993 had grown to 650 by September 1994. In 1991 there were reportedly twenty-three churches and four home meetings in the area.

GUANGXI ZHUANG AUTONOMOUS REGION
Population: 45 million

In steamy, sub-tropical south-west China, Guangxi is home to 16 million Zhuang people. Related to the Thai, they are China's largest "national minority". In 1949 the Protestant Church only numbered 7,000–10,000. In 2004 Amity News Service, based on local TSPM statistics, estimated there to be 262,000 Protestants in Guangxi. There were about 250 registered churches and meeting-points in 1991 and these have doubtless increased somewhat. However, there are only twenty-two formally ordained pastors. About half of the Christians may be Zhuang, the other half, Han Chinese. Nanning has two main churches. All the other major cities such as Wuzhou, Liuzhou, Beihai, Guilin and Yulin have churches. In Liuzhou 1,300 people attend the main TSPM church but there are also over forty meeting-points each with fifty to one hundred members. Throughout the province, there are many meeting-points, both registered and unregistered. City house churches are small, and run their own short-term training sessions. There is little evidence of children's work in the area.

GUIZHOU PROVINCE
Population: 35.25 million

Situated in mountainous southwest China, Guizhou is one of China's poorest provinces. An old proverb summed up the situation succinctly: "Not an inch of level ground, and not a penny in my pocket!" Pre-1949 the China Inland Mission planted vigorous churches among the Miao tribal peoples in the north-west of the province. There were probably about 10,000 or more Protestants then. In 1993 when I spoke to a leading TSPM pastor in Guiyang, the capital, he estimated there to be 300–400,000 believers – a thirty to forty fold increase! Hezhang, a Miao area has seen growth from 4,000 believers to over 26,000, meeting in sixty churches and meeting-points.

LUPANSHUI	30,000	(in 140 churches and meeting points.)
ANSHUN REGION	20,000	
Inc. ANSHUN CITY	800	
BIJIE REGION	100,000	
Inc. HEZHANG COUNTY	26,000	(meeting in 60 churches and meeting-points.)
WEINING COUNTY	20,000	(Inc. 9,000 Miao and 7,000 Yi, in 43 meetings.)

In Lupanshui, 60 per cent of the Christians are Miao, 20 per cent Yi or Bouyei, and 20 per cent Han Chinese. In Weining 9,000 are Miao, 7,000 are Yi and the remainder mainly Han.

In north-west Guizhou the concentration of Christians among the minorities is sometimes very high. For instance, Geda village in Hezhang has sixty-five Yi families, of which fifty-seven are Christian. Some villages in Puding and Zhijin Counties inhabited by Big Flowery Miao are 95 per cent Christian.[5]

In the Wumeng Mountains there are over 10,000 tribal believers meeting in several dozen churches. However, south-east Guizhou, in contrast, which is a huge area, has only 1,000 believers, I was reliably informed.

Guizhou has large numbers of Christians but the church has a chronic shortage of educated leaders. In Hezhang, for example, 80 per cent of the preachers have had only a primary school education. Miao villagers I visited in relatively prosperous south-east Guizhou reported an annual income of only RMB1,000. But in the mountains of the north-west incomes as low as RMB100 per annum are not uncommon. A new Bible school has opened in Guiyang to train pastors and teachers.

HAINAN PROVINCE
Population: 7.87 million (2001)

This sub-tropical island basks in the heat most of the year round. Traditionally, a place of exile for political dissidents,

Hainan still maintains a raffish air and independent spirit from the Mainland. This was shown some years ago in a major car "scam" in which hundreds of luxury cars were smuggled in illegally. More recently, hotels have opened along its coral beaches attracting top cadres from the frozen north during the winter. They also attract prostitutes who openly tout their trade to Chinese and foreign tourists alike. With the collapse of Hainan's economic boom, the sex-trade has become a major industry, sadly.

Hainan has at least 39,000 Christians. Reports by some overseas sources that there are over 200,000 have yet to be verified. House-church leaders from several places across the island have given estimates reaching as high as 50,000. Idolatry and folk religion are rife and very strongly rooted.

In 1992 there were twenty-one registered TSPM churches and forty-one meeting-points.[6] But the TSPM infrastructure is rather weak and house churches flourish. In some places they do so quite openly. In others, there has been pressure. Educated house church Christians met in Haikou in small groups but were threatened by the authorities in 1997 not to meet. One group of poor peasants in the interior had their mud-walled church torn down by the authorities in October 1997 because they had failed to register. Now they meet in groups of fifty people in three farmhouses. Wanning County on the east coast may have 10,000 believers, 90 per cent of whom meet in independent house churches. In the interior some of the Miao and Li people have been converted. House churches on Hainan are numerous, but appear to be split with rivalries between leaders.

HEBEI PROVINCE
Population: 68 million

Hebei, in north China, has the grim reputation of being a "black-spot" in terms of religious persecution. There are hundreds of thousands of Catholics, mostly loyal to the Vatican, and they have been persecuted severely over the last two decades. Baoding is the nervecentre of the "underground" Catholic Church in China. In 1994 there were reportedly 55,000 "underground" Catholics in Baoding, but only 10,000 meeting legally under the auspices of the government-controlled Catholic Patriotic Association. Protestants are less numerous but also face pressures. They numbered over 400,000 in 2001, meeting in 163 registered churches and 2,600 meeting-points. However, in 2001 there were only fifty-nine TSPM pastors in the entire province. This means the church has grown nearly six-fold since 1949, when there were only about 70,000 Protestants. Detailed statistics are hard to glean – a sure sign of an endemic "leftist" mentality by provincial authorities who cling to Maoist views that religion is the "opium of the people".

Protestants are numerous in the Handan Region and may total 200,000 according to a letter written by a local Christian in 2004. Yongnian County in Handan has 10,000 Christians meeting in three churches and 130 meeting-points. Cheng'an County, also in Handan, also has about 10,000 Christians in 108 meeting-points.[7] There has been major growth in Xinglong County near Chengde in the far north. In 1983 there were only half-a-dozen believers meeting. But by the end of 1994 the church had grown to 5–6,000 believers in five registered meeting-points – growth of 1,000 per cent in the space of a decade![8]

HEILONGJIANG PROVINCE
Population: 37 million

Heilongjiang Province is situated in China's remote far northeast corner. Temperatures here can fall during winter to minus 40 degrees Celsius. Harbin, the capital, is famous for its ice-festival where local artists create sculptures and palaces from the ice.

Church growth in Heilongjiang has been nothing short of breathtaking since the mid-1980s. However, many believers are still isolated and lack fellowship, and the response to gospel radio is high compared with many other provinces. Detailed statistics of church growth exist dating back to 1920 (see the graph on p. 197). This shows that by 1931, 20,000 people had been converted. But then there was an actual decrease in numbers, due to the chaos and persecution resulting from the Japanese occupation. On the eve of the Communist victory in 1949, numbers had fallen to about 15,000. The pressure of the Mao days reduced the church even further to only 7,000 brave souls who were prepared publicly to admit their allegiance to the gospel on the eve of the Cultural Revolution.

However, the recovery and growth since the Mao years has been astonishing. In 1985 official TSPM statistics gave a figure of over 26,000 Protestants. In 1989 numbers had climbed to 140,000 according to a Communist newspaper report, and by 1996 TSPM sources had them at a staggering 600,000 (300,000 baptised and 300,000 serious enquirers).[9]

In 1999 there were 1,200 churches open and thousands of unregistered house churches. However, there are fewer than fifty officially ordained pastors and elders in the province. A TSPM spokesman in February 1999 said that the ratio of pastors to believers was 1:10,000! Some ten of the pastors work in Harbin, which has fifteen large churches officially open and about 400 meeting-points to serve a Protestant population estimated in 2001 at 180,000.

House-church growth has been rapid. A former house-church leader reported that in Wuchang County there were just three meetings in 1987. The following year it had grown to twenty. By 1991 there were over 200 churches. In 2003, "Asia Harvest" estimated there could be as many as 1.6–2.5 million house-church believers in Heilongjiang. Christian Communications in Hong Kong is more cautious and estimated the total number of believers in 2001 (both TSPM and house-church) as probably over one million. The Fangcheng-based house church network claims about 100,000–200,000 members in Heilongjiang. In 2003 "Asia Harvest" reported there were "at least 200,000 believers in 2,500 house churches" in Daqing City, which has a total population of 1.6 million.

In 2003 TSPM sources reported that Qitaihe City had 150,000 believers (about 17% of the total population of 860,000). Three years earlier a local believer wrote to FEBC saying there were 100,000, but only three elders to pastor them. This is extraordinary growth from the 30,000 officially reported in 2002 in the Nanjing Seminary Bulletin.

In 1986 there were 35,000 Roman Catholics in the province according to an official handbook and there is also a very small community of Russian Orthodox numbering about 400 – a remnant from the earlier part of the century when Harbin was the centre of a vigorous émigré White Russian community of over 30,000.

HENAN PROVINCE
Population: 93 million

Henan is a centre of Christian revival and powerhouse of evangelism. The unregistered house church movement is very strong in this province, but so, sadly, are a number of sects and cults. Henan has seen astronomic church growth since the Cultural Revolution. In 1949 there were about 100,000 Protestants. On the eve of the Cultural Revolution in 1965 that number had decreased to 78,000. However, in 1990 a local government handbook estimated the number of Christians had risen to 800,000!

In 1996 TSPM sources in Henan estimated the church had grown to a staggering 3.5 million of whom only 1.5 million had been formally baptised – the remaining 2 million were classified as "seekers".[10] This was probably a way of admitting the existence of large numbers of unregistered house church believers who had not been baptised in registered TSPM churches or meeting-points. In October 1998 a TSPM pastor in Henan told a Western visitor that there were "between 3 and 5 million" Protestants in Henan. In 2004 Amity News Service, based on

TSPM sources, estimated 4,585,000. This must be very conservative. A house-church estimate in the late 1980s put the figure at 10 million. However, even if we accept a figure of only 5 million then this is evidence that the church in Henan has grown fiftyfold over the last thirty years!

In October 2001 the TSPM magazine *Tianfeng* stated there were 1,100 registered churches and 5,000 registered meeting-points in Henan. This is a massive increase over only five years from 600 churches and 3,400 meeting-points in 1996. There is a grave shortage of pastors, as in late 2001 there were only 100 in the entire province (one to every 50,000 believers!) They are aided by 394 elders and some 3,000 registered evangelists. These figures do not include the very large number of unregistered house-church preachers in Henan. In late 1988 an internal government news report stated there were at least 2,200 unregistered house churches in the province. The huge "Born Again", Fangcheng and Tanghe networks all started, and are based, in Henan. The Tanghe network (also known as the China Gospel Fellowship) had 2.3 million members nationally in 2004, according to its leaders. The Fangcheng network is reputed to be bigger, and in 2005 may have 5 million members nationally, according to a Hong Kong organisation in close contact. The "Born Again" has fractured into five to seven smaller factions, has come under severe government pressure, and is widely regarded as extreme, or even heretical, by mainstream house churches.

Henan is a centre both for house-church growth, and also for heretical sects, which feed upon the poverty and ignorance of many of the peasants.

Statistics of church growth in Henan

City/County	No of Christians	
ZHENGZHOU REGION	100,000	(TSPM: 1993)
Inc. DENGFENG COUNTY	30,000	(TSPM)
LUOYANG PREFECTURE	140,000	150,000 (1993 TSPM estimate)
	500,000	(house church estimate)

Inc: YICHUAN COUNTY	20,000	(house church estimate 1993)
YIYANG COUNTY	16,000	(TSPM)
LUSHAN COUNTY	100,000	(house church estimate)
YE COUNTY	55,000	(house church estimate)
JIAOZUO PREFECTURE	87,500	(TSPM 1996)
PUYANG COUNTY	20,000	(house church estimate)
LINGBAO COUNTY	40,000	(house church estimate)
MIANCHI COUNTY	50,000	(house church estimate 1989)
WUYANG COUNTY	15,000	(TSPM)
YANLING COUNTY	10,000	(TSPM)
SHANGQIU PREFECTURE	100,000	(TSPM 1983)
Inc. YUCHENG COUNTY	10,000	(TSPM)
ZHOUKOU PREFECTURE	160,000	(TSPM registered only, Dec 1997)
Inc. LUYI COUNTY	30,000	(house church estimate 1987)
DANCHENG COUNTY	50,000	(house church estimate)
ZHUMADIAN PREFECTURE	200,000	(TSPM)
Inc. ZHUMADIAN CITY	30,000	(house church estimate)
PINGYU COUNTY	10,000	(TSPM)
XINYANG PREFECTURE	150,000	(TSPM 1996)
Inc. GUSHI COUNTY	50,000	(TSPM 1996)
HUAIBIN COUNTY	15,600	(Official source 1995) 41 reg. chs & m/points.
NANYANG PREFECTURE	130,000	(TSPM 1997) 530 churches and m/points.
Inc. TANGHE COUNTY	200,000	(house church estimate 1989)
FANGCHENG COUNTY	160,000 –300,000	(house church estimate, 1985, etc.)
Inc. DENG COUNTY	50,000	(1999)
ZHENPING COUNTY	9,000	(c. 2000)

For further details of church growth in Henan please see
Chapter 6.

HUBEI PROVINCE
Population: 60.3 million

Hubei strategically straddles the Yangtze River in central China.
Its capital is the great city of Wuhan, which was the centre for
the labours of Griffith John who pioneered the gospel here for
more than fifty years at the end of the 19th century. In 2002 a

leading TSPM pastor in the province estimated that there were about 500,000 Protestants. In early 2003 there were about 400 registered churches open as well as many meeting-points. Also in 2003 the TSPM reported that Wuhan itself had 60,000 Protestants meeting in six large churches. As early as 1986 Wuhan was reported to have about 200 house churches each with between 200–300 people.

There is evidence of church growth in other areas. Wuchang County just south of Wuhan had only 100 Christians in 1981. By 1990 numbers had risen to over 3,000, meeting in thirty-two meeting-points.[12] Xiangfan City in the north had about 1,200 Protestants in 1949; by 1985 the number had grown, according to a government handbook, to over 3,000. Mention is made of evangelism by True Jesus Church preachers (an indigenous church) from neighbouring Henan and there is other evidence that Henan house churches have been active in the northern part of Hubei.

In the far south-east, Chongyang County had over 5,000 Christians by 1992 meeting in twelve "spontaneous meeting-points" (i.e. house churches) according to the TSPM.[13] Also in the south, the State Farm at Zongkou has seen growth: in 1973 fifteen believers began to meet in a house church. By 1990 they had increased to 480 in four meetings.[14] Ezhou City, east of Wuhan had a few believers meeting in a home in 1987. Now they have grown to over 1,200. They purchased an old ware-house to use as a church, but more than half the congregation have to stand outside.

Many rural house churches have sprung up and have grown to a size where they want to have their own building, but are hampered by lack of funds. Christians in Xianning in the far south have been meeting since 1980 and now number over 1,000 but are still without a building. They hope to build a church to hold 1,500 people, at a cost of RMB250,000. Gong'an County has over 3,000 Christians who hope to build a church in the county town to hold 700 people. In Shishou City a meeting-point was set up in 1980. By 1997 the church had grown to over 7,000 people meeting in forty-one meeting-points. The old church was demolished during the Cultural Revolution and now they wish to rebuild at a cost of RMB80,000. In Jingshan County, central Hubei, Christians began meeting in a house church in 1985. Now they number more than 2,000.

HUNAN PROVINCE
Population: 64.4 million

Hunan Province is renowned for its red chilli peppers and the fact that it was Chairman Mao's home province. Spiritually, it was the last major province to be entered at the close of the 19th century as the people were fiercely anti-foreign. By 1918 there were only 18,000 Protestant communicants belonging mainly to the Lutheran, Presbyterian and China Inland Mission churches. Today remnant Maoism leads to a tight control of the church.

By 2000, according to TSPM sources, Hunan had 300,000 Protestant Christians. They meet in some 800 registered churches and meeting points.[15] There are also many house churches. In 1996, local house-church people estimated the total number of Protestants in Hunan as about 500,000, when the TSPM were giving a figure of 200,000. This would mean a rather larger proportion of house-church Christians to registered believers in the province.

The indigenous True Jesus Church is strong in parts of the province. Apart from orthodox evangelical house churches the "Shouters" and other sects are active. There were only about seventy registered pastors and seminary graduates in 1998 – far too few to cope, although they were aided by about 1,000 voluntary church workers.

Changsha, the capital, is a modern city of 6 million people. When I visited in 1993 I was told by a pastor that there were fewer than 10,000 Protestants. Seven years later in 2000 the TSPM was still issuing a figure of 10,000, but stating that 700–900 were baptised every year! These figures do not add up, and reveal the hazards of taking even the "official" statistics too seriously!

Two former China Inland Mission churches have been re-opened and are filled to overflowing on Sundays. I was able to attend a baptismal class for new converts. There were about ninety people in all and the teaching by the young lady pastor was excellent. It focused on the new birth – why one must be born again, how one can be born again and how one can be sure that one has been born again! Basic biblical truth of a high calibre was being imparted to the new believers, which helps explain why the Church in China is so vibrant and expanding.

Some areas of Hunan have experienced rapid church growth. In 1984 there were thirty believers meeting in the city of Yueyang in northern Hunan. By 1995 they had grown to over 1,000. Today in the entire Yueyang area, which includes six rural counties, there are over 10,000 Christians. They meet in some sixty registered churches and meeting points. In addition there are fifty other still-unregistered meeting points.[16]

In nearby Yuanjiang there were just thirty Christians in 1980, but by 1994 they had increased to more than 3,000. There are now seven churches and seven meeting points in the city.[17] The Zhangjiajie region has over 20,000 believers (2,000 in the city itself) and the church is growing at the rate of 300 new baptised believers annually![18] Xiangtan had over 1,300 Christians in 1988 and in 1990 120 new converts were baptised. In Chenzhou in the far south, there were over 10,000 Christians in 1991, 80 per cent of whom were meeting in house churches independent of the TSPM. Nearby Yizhang has over 2,000 Christians – the fruit of a revival in the early 1980s. In Yizhang in 1982 Little Flock Christians were very active in evangelism. Two Communist Party members were converted, who then used their position to evangelise openly in the schools (which, of course, is strictly forbidden by the State). They even arranged children's meetings which sang hymns well into the night. In a very short period, more than 2,000 people were converted to Christ. Unsurprisingly the pair were forced to resign their Party membership.[19] There is a thriving house church movement in Hunan. Some young men and women have responded to the call to full-time ministry and resigned from their jobs to live by faith.

Many Hunan rural believers still live in dire poverty: on one Sunday in September 1997 over 100 believers at the Shadi meeting point were only able to contribute 12RMB to the church collection – or just under £1. Hunan has nearly 50,000 hearing-impaired children under the age of seven. So there is great material and spiritual need in this province.

INNER MONGOLIA (AUTONOMOUS REGION)
Population: 24 million

Inner Mongolia is a windswept frontier region in north China, whose population is now overwhelmingly Han Chinese through immigration. However, there are still about 3.5 million Mongols in this "Autonomous Region", a minority of whom carry on the ancient nomadic traditions.

Statistics on Christians are distinctly lacking in this area, which is tightly controlled and has seen persecution of unregistered believers. According to the TSPM in the November 2001 issue of *Tianfeng*, there were 172,000 registered Protestants in over 1,000 registered churches and meeting-points. An earlier TSPM report in March 2000 gave 160,000 believers in 962 meetings. This suggests steady, if unspectacular growth – at least in the registered churches. There are many house churches, but statistics are unavailable.

As there were only 11,789 Protestants in 1950 it is safe to state the Church has grown about fifteen-fold under Communist control! The Catholic Church has about 200,000 members, many of whom belong to the "underground" church loyal to the Vatican. There are four large TSPM churches in Hohhot, the capital, which in 1996 had at least 10,000 believers. When I visited the main church there it was packed out with some 2,000 worshippers for the funeral service of an elderly pastor. This church has been baptising 700–800 people annually!

Baotou, a major industrial centre, has seen amazing growth. In just the six years from 1982 to 1988 Protestants multiplied from 2,400 to 40,000. In one part of Baotou in 1980 a dozen Christians were meeting in a small house church. By 1989 they had built a church to hold 500. By 1990 the number of people who had been converted was nearly 1,000. Over the same period, 1982–88, according to TSPM sources, Christians increased in Bayannuur from 3,000 to 10,000; in Wuhai from 250 to 1,000; in Zerim from 110 to 2,500; in Xingan from 100 to 300, and in Zhaouud from 61 to 400. Unfortunately, later statistics are unavailable. However, in 2003 TSPM sources stated there were 5,000 church members in the eastern city of Ulanhot. Tight control seems to be placed on the number of church workers. In 1996 there were only eight ordained pastors, although a year later a letter was written to FEBC claiming 120 pastoral workers – far too few for this vast area.

Inner Mongolia runs a tight and repressive religious policy. Liu Qinglin began preaching salvation through the cross in Moguqi in eastern Inner Mongolia in 1984, and led more than fifty people to Christ. Liu seems to have been given a genuine gift of healing (see Chapter 8) and by the end of 1988 twenty house churches had been set up in Moguqi with a baptised membership of nearly 3,000. In August 1987 Liu was jailed by the police for fifteen days. In 1988 he was rearrested and on his release wrote to Bishop Ting, head of the China Christian Council, to ask if a Christian who lacked theological training could legally be allowed to preach without breaking the law. Ting reportedly replied that self-taught Christians are also allowed to preach, and encouraged Liu to remain firm in the faith. In mid-July 1988 Liu was arrested for the third time and sentenced to three years of "re-education through labour". He appears to have died in captivity.

The Director of Religious Affairs of Inner Mongolia stated in a speech on 31 December 1988 that "the number of Christians in our region has doubled in the last five years and in some districts this increase has been five-fold. This has created confusion in the church and harmful effects in society."[20] Such a statement confirms both the rapid growth of the Church in Inner Mongolia, but also the hard-line "leftist" attitudes of leading officials. In 1993 I was reliably informed that in 1991 authorities in Baotou pulled down a house church with a distinguished history. In 1970 while the Cultural Revolution was still raging, a brother quietly built a house for worship where fifty Christians met secretly. Much later, the local TSPM leader insisted that they join his newly reopened church. When they refused, he called in the police who completely demolished the building. Two other similar incidents reportedly took place about the same time in Inner Mongolia.

Not many Mongols appear to have been converted. Those who have, largely attend Han Chinese fellowships. Requests for Bibles in Mongolian traditional script have been received. But evangelism to the Mongols in Inner Mongolia, who far outnumber their compatriots in independent (Outer) Mongolia across the border, is conspicuously lacking.

JIANGSU PROVINCE
Population: 74.4 million

Known as the "province of fish and rice", Jiangsu is a fertile area near Shanghai on the east coast. It is one of the most prosperous areas in the country.

The Christian faith has made rapid progress over the last two decades, particularly in the north. Detailed statistics exist showing modest growth from about 20,000 in 1900 to 50,000 in 1949. Since the early 1980s there had been an explosive rise in the number of Christians (see graph on p. 198). By 2004 there were 1,572,000 Protestants meeting in over 3,200 registered churches and meeting points as well as numerous unregistered house churches. To take one example only: Yancheng Prefecture had about 7,000 believers in 1949. By 1985 this had increased to 50,000 and by 1995 to 120,000.[21] The greater Nanjing Municipality (which includes two counties) was reported in 2003 by the TSPM to have over 100,000 believers.

CHURCH GROWTH IN JIANGSU

	1982	1986	1988	1991	1993	1995	1998
Northern Jiangsu							
HUAIYIN MUNICIP.	37,000					370,000	
XUZHOU CITY			80,000	120,000		170,000	
SHUYANG COUNTY	780	16,000		22,800	31,000	48,000	
SIYANG COUNTY		13,000				33,000	
YANCHENG MUNICIP.		50,000				120,000	
BINHAI COUNTY		1,800				35,800	
GUANNAN COUNTY	6,080	12,700		27,200		41,400	
SUINING COUNTY	1,000	5,000		13,500	18,000	53,000	70,000
Southern Jiangsu							
SUZHOU CITY			29,000	37,000		40,000	
LIYANG CITY	690	1,493		5,274		5,596	
XISHAN CITY	1,400	4,024		6,673		7,775	
CHANGSHU CITY	3,450	4,386		4,820	5,200	5,376	
QIDONG CITY	1,210	2,238			3,182		
JIANGDU COUNTY	96				3,500		
JIANGPU COUNTY	3,000	4,500		8,000	8,500		

From this table we see that the number of Christians in Huayin has increased ten-fold in just thirteen years (1982–95)! This area was evangelised by the father of Ruth Graham, wife of Billy Graham. She had the joy of returning to China a few years ago and saw first-hand the great revival now taking place where her father had laboured sixty years ago.

JIANGXI PROVINCE
Population: 41.4 million

Jiangxi was the base area from which Mao set off on the Long March. Today, it is still backward and religious affairs are often run by the local cadres very strictly. In July 2005 the TSPM reported 400,000 believers in the province which is a massive increase over the last two decades. They meet in 571 churches and 2,290 registered meeting-points (compared to 317 churches and 1,541 meeting-points in 1998). In 2000 the provincial capital had 50,000 Protestants meeting in 150 churches and meeting-points – mainly in the outlying suburbs and rural areas.

Other areas have seen rapid church growth. For example, Duchang County in the north has seen ten-fold growth in a decade:

1987:	617
1989:	1,360
1991:	3,100
1994:	4,530
1996:	6,787

(Figures published in *Shijie Zongjiao Wenhua* [World Religion & Culture], December 1997)

In Ganzhou city, in the south of the province, there were about 200 Christians in 1949. The old CIM church was re-opened in 1983 after being closed for many years during the Cultural Revolution. In 1990 alone, 400 people were baptised and there was a total then of 1,200 Christians in a thriving congregation.[22] Yichun City has about 10,000 believers according to a report in 1998. Jiujiang City has 15,000 meeting in four churches and 168 meeting-points "in and around the city". The country folk are so poor that they are unable to build proper churches.[23] The Yushui District of Xinyu City had 25,000 believers in 2002, meeting in 162 registered churches and meeting-points.

Shangrao County had 10,000 believers in ninety meeting-points in 1990, according to the TSPM. Jinxian County has 3,600 believers in thirty-two "activity points". There are also large numbers of unregistered house churches. In Ruijin in 1990, 1,000 Christians were attending the large former China Inland Mission church, but 3,000 were attending an independent house church run by a Brother Zeng. All the new converts are the fruits of house church evangelists who have come from other areas to preach.[24] In 1992 authorities cracked down on an "illegal Bible study" in Yichun, and a dozen Christians were forced to attend political indoctrination studies.[25]

JILIN PROVINCE
Population: 27.3 million

Jilin is in the former Manchuria in north-east China. According to a government handbook, it had about 30,000 Protestants in the early 1950s. In 2000 there were 350,000 Protestants meeting in 1,900 registered churches and meeting-points. There are over 100 pastors and elders and 1,134 voluntary church workers.

The main denominations active before 1949 in the capital, Changchun, were: Presbyterian, Baptist, Lutheran, Little Flock, True Jesus Church and Seventh Day Adventist. The former Presbyterian church was reopened for worship at Christmas 1979. Between 1981-84 300 converts were baptised there on three occasions.

There are 1.2 million Koreans living in Jilin, many in the Yanbian Autonomous Region by the North Korean border. At least 35,000 Korean Christians meet in Yanbian in forty-five churches and over 200 registered meeting-points.[26] An earlier independent report in 1988 from house church sources estimated 70,000 Korean Protestant Christians in Jilin. There are also about 80,000 Roman Catholics in the province. Some Koreans in Jilin are able to visit relatives in famine-stricken North Korea and have brought back harrowing tales of the suffering of the people and the continuing repression of the Church there, which apart from one or two show-churches in Pyongyang is deeply underground. In recent years tens of thousands of North Koreans have fled their country to escape famine and oppression. Many are being looked after by Korean Christians in Jilin. Those discovered face deportation back to unimaginable torment in labour camps for daring to escape the "People's Paradise" created by Kim Jong-Il. The Chinese Korean church is already playing a strategic role for the re-evangelisation of North Korea which a century ago experienced genuine spiritual revival.

LIAONING PROVINCE
Population: 42.4 million

Liaoning is also in the north-east. Its capital, Shenyang, is the largest city in the area and a centre of industry. In recent years the decay of State-controlled heavy industry has led to massive unemployment, as workers have been laid off. In 2002 the TSPM stated there were 600,000 Protestants meeting in over 1,400 registered churches and meeting-points. There are also many unregistered house churches. As there were only 60,000 believers in 1965, on the eve of the Cultural Revolution, the registered church has seen explosive ten-fold growth in under forty years.

I was told in 2000 that the total number of registered believers in Shenyang was 200,000 – compared to only 70,000 in 1996. In 2003 Kangping county reportedly had 10,000 Protestants.[27] The city of Fushun, just east of Shenyang, has seen growth from about eighty people meeting when the first church was reopened in about 1980 to 8,000 Christians meeting in seventy churches and meeting points. However, they have only one authorised pastor.[28] In the area of northern Liaoning there were only about 1,000 believers in 1948. By 1994 they had grown ten-fold to 10,000 still mostly worshipping in the Presbyterian tradition which was strong in the north-east.

Dandong is a strategic city on the North Korean border; in 1991 a Christian living there estimated there were 10,000 believers, mostly in the house churches, as well as many Roman Catholics. According to the TSPM in 1993 there were at least 10,000 Korean Christians in Liaoning meeting in sixteen churches and over 100 registered meeting-points. A year later, another TSPM report estimated 20 per cent of all the Christians in the province (then estimated at 140,000) were Koreans – or about 28,000. In 1993 there were twenty-three Korean students at the North East Theological Seminary in Shenyang, of whom eleven were from Liaoning. The province also has about 80,000 Roman Catholics.

NINGXIA HUI AUTONOMOUS REGION
Population: 5.6 million

Tiny Ningxia is sandwiched inside the great loop of the Yellow River in the arid north-west. It is home to over 1.8 million Hui (Chinese Muslims) who speak Chinese, but cling tenaciously to their Islamic faith. Their stronghold is in the south. In the north the Church has made rapid progress among the Han Chinese immigrants. In Pingluo Christians met openly again for the first time in 1979. Just ten attended. By May 1986 400–500 were meeting. By 1989 600 new converts had been baptised. By 1994 the Church had grown to over 1,800, according to TSPM sources![29]

They have set up about a dozen churches and over thirty small meeting-points, but in 1992 had only one ordained pastor, helped by a few theological students and a band of volunteer lay workers. The church in Shizuishan City (also called Dawukou) is the fastest-growing in Ningxia. It began with just eight believers in 1982. By the spring of the next year the congregation had increased to seventy with forty asking to be baptised. Nearly all are new converts including many coal miners. By 1989 there were over 900 baptised believers in the area. By 1994 there were 2,000 in several dozen meeting points, most with twenty to thirty believers, but four had over fifty.

Shitanjing is a relatively new mining area. In 1982 there were only three believers. By 1985 they had grown to over 300 and by 1990 to over 600![30]

In 2004 TSPM sources estimated a total of 65,500 Protestants in Ningxia. It is doubtful whether there would have been even 500 believers before 1949 in the days of missionaries. There are also at least 5,500 Roman Catholics.

QINGHAI PROVINCE
Population: 5.2 million

Qinghai is a huge, desolate area traditionally inhabited largely by Tibetans with a substantial Hui Muslim population in Xining, the capital. It has the dubious reputation of having a large number of labour camps scattered throughout its barren plateaux. In the 1940s there were about 400 Christians in Xining and a few other centres, pioneered by the China Inland Mission. By 2004 there were 39,300 believers according to official TSPM estimates, which had previously stated 30,000 in 1997.[31] This means there must have been a hundred-fold growth since the Cultural Revolution! When the main Xining church was re-opened (rather late) in 1981 there were only forty in attendance. Numbers grew by 1984 to 300 but by 1997 there were 6,780 baptised believers![32] There are five registered churches and over forty meeting-points scattered throughout the province at places such as Huangyuan, Ledu, Guide and Qinghai Lake Farm. Qinghai's believers are poor but fervent in outreach.

SHAANXI PROVINCE
Population: 36.1 million

During the Tang dynasty over 1,000 years ago the capital of this province, Xi'an, then known as Changan, was the capital of China and the largest, most opulent city on earth rivalled only by Byzantium. Today many tourists come to see the tomb of the Emperor of Qin who first unified China, built the Great Wall, and was buried here with an army of terracotta warriors.

On the eve of the Communist victory in 1949 there were about 30,000 Protestants in Shaanxi. Over fifty years later, in 2004, the number had increased to 458,500, according to TSPM statistics. They meet in 517 registered churches and 1,142 registered meeting-points. However, in 2003 there were only forty-nine ordained pastors, although they are helped by thirty-six teachers, 167 elders, 475 evangelists and 2,136 voluntary church workers.

In 1981 a Hong Kong magazine reported there were 30,000 registered Christians in Xi'an and "many more unregistered".[34] In 1983 an internal report from the Religious Affairs Bureau estimated that 98 per cent of all the Christians converted in the Xi'an area between 1977 and 1982 had been converted by unregistered house church evangelists, and only 2 per cent through the "proper" channels of the TSPM-controlled churches. This gives a rare glimpse of the reality of the situation in many areas of China where the extensive network of visible, authorised Christianity is paralleled by a vast, more hidden network of house church activity.

There is other evidence of rapid growth in this province. Tongchuan, a mining area, was first evangelised in 1913 by the British Baptists. By 1949 there were still only thirty converts. Numbers grew by 1956 to 150. Then came the time of great persecution. In 1977 a house church was formed again. Between 1977–80 the house churches expanded rapidly in Tongchuan, baptising 2,700 people, seeing an annual growth of 900 converts. By 1986 Tongchuan had twenty meeting-points with

5,000 Christians. One coal pit where nearly 2,000 people live had 500 believers. In 1993 the Tongchuan churches had grown to more than 10,000, meeting in over ten churches and dozens of meeting-points.[35] By 1999 they had grown to 15,000.

Baoji city in 1950 had only about 300 Christians; by 1995 they had increased to 26,000 (twenty-one-fold growth!) according to an official report.[36] Yongshou County to the north-west of Xi'an has also seen growth: from 1,200 Christians in just one church in 1992 to over 4,000 baptised believers in thirteen churches in 1996.

House churches in Shaanxi have come under pressure. In 1996 a house church leader reported that his church had been able to build a 1,000-seater church in the countryside. There was no TSPM in the area and local cadres turned a blind eye. He knew of eight other smaller towns where house church believers had done the same thing. However, in January 1996 the Religious Affairs Bureau insisted the church be registered. In principle, the church was opposed to registration, fearing it would mean atheist control of their internal affairs, and also because they were unwilling to hand over a list of names and addresses of all members and church workers, especially the young people. Eventually, after much prayer, they did register, but only gave a list of elderly members, hoping to keep their building and avoid future harassment.

There are also about 200,000 Roman Catholics in Shaanxi. In July 2005 Agenzia Fides reported that 20,000 of these live in Xi'an. The Xi'an Catholic diocese runs ten health centres and fifty clinics.

SHANDONG PROVINCE
Population: 91 million

Shandong, the home of Confucius, has seen rapid church growth in recent years. From the 1920s it saw the growth of indigenous churches which threw off control by Western denominations and mission boards. There were revival movements, and early forms of charismatic and Pentecostal worship which sometimes veered into extremism frowned on by orthodox, evangelical missionaries. The Jesus Family practised a form of Christian Communism, sending out evangelists all over north China and setting up self-supporting communes of believers. They still have house churches today and have had a great, but largely unacknowledged, influence on the development of indigenous Christianity enabling it to survive and multiply under Communism.

The church in 1949 had 50–80,000 members and on the eve of the Cultural Revolution in 1965 some 70,000 members. In 2004 the TSPM-based figure was 1,179,000 – seventeen-fold growth in forty years! This is probably very far short of the reality because of the widespread existence of house churches. In 1996 there were 926 churches and 4,000 registered meeting-points in the province. In the one year of 1994 alone, 50,000 people were baptised in Shandong (probably including both new converts and older believers who had not been able to be baptised earlier because of the lack of ordained pastors).[37]

The poor area of Linyi Prefecture in the south has seen great growth with some 200–250,000 believers by 1998. Fei County in this district had 20,000 believers out of a population of 743,000 in 1992 according to a local Christian who wrote to FEBC in November that year. The Weifang District, covering eight cities and three districts, has 30–50,000 believers.

There is much pressure, even persecution, of unregistered house church Christians in Shandong. In 1995, 10,000 Christians in Zibo City left the TSPM-controlled churches preferring to meet in their own unregistered house churches.[38] In 1998 a Christian house church leader in Qingdao reported how Party officials had come to his home three times to interrogate him and warn him against holding "illegal" meetings. He related how a house church leader was still in prison in a nearby rural area. Local believers, although very poor, contributed a large sum of money to give to his family so that his children could continue their education.

In 2005 the Fangcheng house-church network based in Henan was claiming some 100,000 members in Shandong.

REGISTERED PROTESTANTS IN SHANDONG

Jinan	11,805	Qingdao	8,217
Zaozhuang City	33,125	Yantai	8,698
Weifang (2000)	40,000	Jining	25,757
Weihai	1,200	Dezhou Region	15,223
Huimin Region	4,259	Linyi Region	200–250,000
Heze Region (1985)	16,161	Liaocheng Region	19,969
Zibo City (1991)	17,000	Dan County (2003)	50,000
Shen County (1998)	30,000	Cao County (1993)	20,000

All statistics except those for Zibo, Weifang, Linyi, Dan, Shen and Cao Counties are taken from *Shandong Shengzhi* (Shandong Provincial Handbook), 1998. They give figures for the situation in 1990 except where noted. This official handbook states "Christians unconnected with TSPM not included".

SHANGHAI MUNICIPALITY
Population: 17 million

Shanghai is China's largest city. Glittering glass office buildings and hotels are dwarfed by the giant TV tower. Well-dressed crowds walk along the waterfront "Bund" and Nanjing Road, which is lined with huge department stores and elegant boutiques. Since the 19th century, Shanghai had become an international port city, controlled by foreigners as a centre of commerce. Then in the early 1950s the Western traders and missionaries were expelled, businesses expropriated and prostitutes and opium-addicts reformed. Today, the city is again booming and has recaptured some of its old atmosphere and self-confidence.

Shanghai had been the base for numerous churches, denominations and missions, both Catholic and Protestant, and before 1950 there were more than 200 church buildings. By 1961 however, 235 churches had been closed down or amalgamated under TSPM political control, reducing the number to only twenty-one, and in 1966 even these last few were closed. As Red Guards vandalised the last few sanctuaries, desecrating altars with busts of Chairman Mao, burning Christian literature and parading clergy through the streets, a Hong Kong reporter who was a witness stated: "The final page of the history of the Christian religion in Shanghai was written on August 14."[39]

How wrong he was! Yet he could be forgiven the error. When I visited Shanghai in 1973 I came across one large church, empty and shuttered, festooned with red banners. There was no overt sign of Christian witness anywhere. Yet some Christians continued to meet quietly in their homes and the house churches grew in secret. After the death of Mao in 1976 meetings became more open and were even held in parks.

When the first few large cathedrals were reopened in 1979–80, the authorities were shocked by the large number of people who streamed in to attend worship, including many young people. In 2005 there were 165 registered churches and meeting-points open in the city, according to the TSPM magazine *Tianfeng*. These are far too few to serve a vastly larger Christian community, which the same source stated to number 187,000 in 2005. A TSPM pastor who also has close connections with the house churches estimated in 2004 that the total number of Christians in Shanghai including the house-church believers could be as high as 300-400,000. This seems a reasonable estimate and means the city's Protestant community may have gown about ten-fold since 1949, when it was only 43,000.

There are many house churches in the city, catering for every sector of society: the elderly, workers, youth and students and intellectuals. As early as 1980, a Hong Kong magazine estimated there were 3,000 such gatherings.[41] One leader has been ministering to university students and graduates for many years, and in 2005 estimated that two-thirds of the sixty universities in the Shanghai/East China region now have Christian fellowships for both students and faculty, meeting discreetly on or off campus.

SHANXI PROVINCE
Population: 33 million

This northern province was extensively evangelised by the China Inland Mission. It was the scene of the labours of the indefatigable Pastor Xi (Hsi) who preached the gospel and successfully healed many opium-addicts in the late 19th century. In 1950 there were 26,256 Protestants in Shanxi. By 1996 numbers had risen according to TSPM estimates to 200,000 believers meeting in ninety-nine churches. As early as 1987 Hong Kong visitors were told by the TSPM that every one of Shanxi's eighty-five counties has "an active church group".

There are many more meeting-points and unregistered house churches, but the local authorities operate a repressive religious policy. The TSPM church in Taiyuan is filled to overflowing on Sundays with over 1,200 people. The church had a flourishing network of fifty-six registered home meetings, but in 1998 these were all closed down by the authorities.

The church in the area of Datong, a grim industrial city in a coal-mining area, has seen explosive revival as well as arbitrary persecution. Between 1992–98 the number of believers grew from about 200–300 associated with the TSPM church to 70,000 meeting in house churches throughout the city and surrounding countryside. In September 1991 some 300 police surrounded the registered church at No. 9 colliery near Datong, and ordered the building to be vacated although a service was going on at the time. The authorities then ordered it to be flattened by bulldozers. One elderly woman suffered a heart attack and reportedly died the following day. One official told Christians that the church was too prominent, built too close to the road and the cross could be seen by too many people. Officials dismissed the fact that church leaders had already obtained official permission to build it.

The leaders of the church took their case to the Religious Affairs Bureau, the Party's United Front Work Department and the China Christian Council. All were sympathetic and seemed to agree this was a flagrant case of disregard for freedom of religious belief (NB this was *not* an unregistered house church). However, a year later the church still lay in a pile of rubble, and a photograph smuggled out shows a wooden cross re-erected defiantly in the midst of the ruins. It is not known if the church has since been rebuilt.

SICHUAN PROVINCE
Population: 84 million

Sichuan used to be China's most populous province with 114,300,000 people in 1996 until in 1997 the new municipality of Chongqing was carved from its territory which has 30 million inhabitants. The capital, Chengdu, has nearly 5 million people. Sichuan with its huge rice-growing basin, secure behind mountain barriers, often became an independent kingdom when the central dynasty was weak.

Griffith John of the London Missionary Society first preached the gospel in Sichuan in 1868 but it was only in 1881 that Clarke of the CIM was able to rent permanent property in Chengdu. By 1922 there were 13,000 baptised Christians in the province of whom nearly half were Methodists.

In 2004, Amity News Service based on TSPM sources gave 524,000 Protestants, although in 2001 they had given a figure of only 250,000. There are only about 100 pastors for this huge province. In 1996 (before Chongqing split off to become a separate municipality) there were only 119 churches officially reopened. The "official" TSPM/CCC presence of the church is thus spread very thinly compared with many other provinces. There is no doubt from my personal observation that Sichuan operates a tight policy of religious control on Christians, especially in more remote areas and in cities off the tourist track. It is the only province where I recall being refused entry into a TSPM church when visiting the city of Nanchong. This tight policy is reflected in the relative dearth of information.

Until recent years there was little sign of church growth on the scale of Henan or the coastal provinces. However, large numbers of country people have been converted through itinerant evangelists from Henan and elsewhere. In 2005 the Fangcheng church based in Henan claimed some 100,000 members in Sichuan. The authorities have cracked down on sects such as the Mentuhui (Disciples), and it seems that genuine Christians have suffered as a result.

In Chengdu, the capital, there are two large TSPM churches. Officially, there are only about 3,000 Christians in this city of nearly five million. A house-church report in 1999 claimed there may be 50,000 house-church believers in the city. Even if this is accepted, it means only 1 per cent of the population are Christians which is well below the average in many other parts of China. Mianyang City north of Chengdu reportedly has over 1,000 Christians meeting in 1989. Four hundred new converts were baptised in the space of four years soon after the church was reopened in 1985.

There is evidence of growth, particularly in country areas in the north of the province. In 1995 or 1996 the old Anglican cathedral was reopened in Langzhong (formerly Baoning which was the centre of the former CIM Anglican diocese of East Sichuan). About 1,000 people attend the church and there have been about 200 baptisms. Several thousand house-church Christians were reported to be meeting in the same county in 1992–93. In March 1993, 3,000 PLA soldiers raided a village and beat and fined forty-seven Christians in Langzhong, including women and children. A house church report dated 1993 stated: "Over the past several years the growth of the church here has been fantastic. It is not unusual for us to have meetings during which more than 1,000 believers gather to worship." A year later, a Christian in another city reported: "Family-meetings are relentlessly being suppressed."

In Guangan County (Deng Xiaoping's birthplace), numbers of Christians grew from a handful in 1982 to 2,000 by 1995 meeting in three churches and one registered meeting-point. However, as Guangan has over one million inhabitants only

0.2 per cent are Christians by this official estimate. This low percentage is reflected in similar statistics for Santai County where about 2,000 believers meet at Lingxing church out of a total population of 1.3 million. In 1990 200 enquirers were baptised when the church was officially opened. In 1989 the number of Roman Catholics in the province was officially estimated at 300,000 meeting in 142 churches.

TIANJIN MUNICIPALITY
Population: 10 million

Details of the Church in this large northern port city are difficult to obtain. It is tightly controlled, and does not appear to have seen any great church growth. House churches exist but are small and operate underground. In the early 1950s there were about 7,000 Protestants and in 1986 a government handbook listed the number to have risen slightly to 8,000 (doubtless associated with the three large TSPM churches reopened in the city). In 1997 the TSPM issued a figure of 15,000 Protestants – a tiny number for such a large metropolis. In late 2003 Christian Communications in Hong Kong estimated there were between 25,000-40,000 believers (both registered and unregistered) in the city. There are now five large TSPM churches open and over 160meeting points. The "official" church has only ten pastors, five evangelists and about 130 part-time volunteer workers.

In 1989 the *Tianjin Daily* reported that the main TSPM church in Binjiang Road had seen its congregation grow from 200 to over 900 in the decade 1979–89. There is another church which has been officially reopened at Tanggu, the port on the Bohai Gulf, which falls within the jurisdiction of the Tianjin municipality.

The Roman Catholic population is much stronger, and reported as 90,000 in 1989 and as 100,000 in 1991, half of them young people (i.e. 18–35).

TIBET (XIZANG AUTONOMOUS REGION)
Population: 2.6 million

In July 2005 the New China News Agency reported that there are 1,700 Buddhist temples open in Tibet and 46,000 Tibetan Buddhist lamas and nuns. There are also 3,000 Muslims.

For centuries the Dalai Lamas ruled Tibet with absolute theocratic power. Paradoxically, it is Chinese Communism which has opened a chink of gospel light into the darkness of the "Roof of the World". Many Han Chinese have come to work in Tibet and some have been Christians. In more recent years, house churches have sent workers to Lhasa to establish churches. There are no registered Protestant churches in the entire country, but there is at least one small house church fellowship functioning in Lhasa, attended mostly by Han with a few Tibetan converts or enquirers. It is possible two others exist, and more uncertainly one or two other groups in other towns. There are certainly scattered Christians who listen to gospel radio.

Tibet is impoverished materially and is also the most needy area of China spiritually. The number of committed Tibetan Protestant Christians outside of China in India, Nepal and elsewhere is probably no more than 100–200. There is strong evidence of a Tibetan fellowship in southern Gansu Province which has survived in the face of strong opposition from local Tibetan lamas and cadres. The only functioning church building in Tibet is in Yanjin in the extreme south-east of the region where there are about 600 Tibetan Roman Catholics. This church was repaired and reconsecrated in 1988.

XINJIANG (UYGUR AUTONOMOUS REGION)
Population: 19.3 million

Xinjiang has traditionally been a Muslim region inhabited by Uygurs and Kazaks. However, in recent years there has been a large influx of Han Chinese so that the Muslims are now in danger of becoming a minority in their own territory. Because of this, riots and bombings have been not uncommon occurrences as the more radical Muslims have called for independence from Beijing,

The church in Xinjiang has enjoyed rapid growth. There were probably only about 200 Christians in 1949. In 2004, TSPM sources estimated 131,000. There are at least fifty-six registered churches and meeting-points in this huge region, and many house churches.

In 1995 the TSPM reported that thirty out of sixty counties in Xinjiang had churches. Urumqi may have 40,000 believers – in 1949 there were fewer than 100. The largest TSPM church has 3,000 people meeting every Sunday. However, a strict ban on local Muslims entering the registered churches was in force when I visited in 2005. The church (both TSPM and house churches) is overwhelmingly Han Chinese, with a tiny handful of Uygur and Kazakh converts.

Hami, in the east, has over 1,000 Christians and had the largest church in Xinjiang until the new one planned in Urumqi. There are altogether three churches in Hami, home of the famous Hami melon, known throughout China for its luscious sweetness.

The Church in Xinjiang has enjoyed growth and spiritual revival. However, it is overwhelmingly Han Chinese. The number of known Uygur or Kazak converts is very small. Overseas Christians have a strategic part to play in outreach to the Muslims and in Bible translation, but the great need is for the resident Han Chinese Church to catch a vision for outreach to their Muslim neighbours.

In 2005, one of the elderly "Back to Jerusalem" evangelists who went out to Xinjiang in the late 1940s was still alive in Kashgar, seeking by low-key, lifestyle evangelism to witness to a small number of Uygur workers on her smallholding. However, informed sources from neighbouring Kazakhstan report there is more evidence of Gospel outreach *from* Kazakhstan into Xinjiang than the other way round. There is no evidence in Xinjiang of large numbers of house-church evangelists poised to take the gospel across Central Asia back to Jerusalem. Some house-church evangelists have moved into Xinjiang to witness to Muslims, but outreach is small-scale, and those few Muslims won for Christ have been won through personal contact and friendship.The cultural, linguistic and religious barriers between the Han Chinese community and the local Muslims are formidable.

YUNNAN PROVINCE
Population: 43 million

Yunnan in the far south-west is a subtropical paradise, home to over forty different national minorities. The Church was firmly planted by the China Inland Mission and other groups pre-1949 (see Chapter 8). Today those seeds have taken root and multiplied.

In 2004 there were 1,179,000 Protestants, according to TSPM sources. Confusingly, in 2005, Anglican visitors were told only 800,000, but as I had been given this lower figure as far back as 1996, it seems that the figure of over one million is credible. Amity had been given a similar figure in 1996 of 750,000 of whom only 50 per cent had been baptised.[43] In 2003 there were 2,200 registered churches and over 1,000 registered meeting-points (*Tianfeng*, July 2003). However, in 2005 there were still only eighty registered pastors in the entire province. This is far too few, even though they are helped by over 640 elders and a small army of over 1,300 voluntary church workers. Some 73 per cent of the Christians belong to national minority tribal groups; only 27 per cent are Han Chinese.

PROTESTANT CHRISTIANS IN YUNNAN BY ETHNIC GROUP

Han Chinese	216,000
Lisu	200,000
Eastern Lisu	20,000
Miao (Hmong)	150,000
Yi	150,000
Jingpo	40,000
Wa	25,000
Hani	5,000
Bai	30,000
Lahu	60,000
Drong (Dulong)	2,000 (Figures for c. 1996)

NUMBERS OF PROTESTANT CHURCHES IN YUNNAN

1882:	1 (Built by China Inland Mission at Dali)
1900:	10
1920:	156
1948:	900
1954:	901
1966:	370
1982:	800
1986:	1,000+
1997:	1,296 + 705 "activity centres" (registered meeting-points) = 2,001
2001:	2,500+ churches and registered meeting-points = 2,500
2003:	2,200 churches + 1,000 registered meeting points = 3,200

ZHEJIANG PROVINCE
Population: 47 million

Zhejiang is one of China's smallest provinces, but one of its richest. Situated on the eastern seaboard it was one of the first to be penetrated by the gospel and today has one of China's largest Christian communities. Church growth has been rapid, especially in Wenzhou, Xiaoshan and Ningbo areas. In 1949 there were less than 200,000 Protestants in Zhejiang. In 2004 there were 1,834,000 according to official TSPM statistics. In 2000 there were at least 2,600 registered churches and about 3,500 registered meeting-points. This may be a very conservative figure as in the same year, TSPM sources revealed there were 2,000 registered churches and 2,000 meeting-points in the Greater Wenzhou region (the "Jerusalem of China") alone. There are, however, only 120 registered pastors in the province, helped by a massive force of over 7,000 voluntary church workers and 970 elders. The church growth in many parts of Zhejiang is staggering. For example, Ruian had only 8,170 Christians in 1950 but 90,000 by 2000!

Protestant Christians in Zheijiang		No. of registered churches/ meeting-points
GREATER HANGZHOU	200,000 (2000)	
Inc. Hangzhou city	30,000	18 churches
Xiaoshan	110,000 (2002) [House-church sources claim 400,000]	
Lin'an City	4,500 (1992)	
GREATER WENZHOU	750,000 (2004)	4,000
Inc. Ruian City	90,000	203
Yueqing County	70,000	
Pingyang County	30,000 (1988)	100
Cangnan County	70,000 (1995)	126
Yongjia County	130,000	
NINGBO MUNICIPALITY	90,000 (1994)	271
Inc. Cixi City	60,000 (2000)	42
Xiangshan County	13,000 (2001)	38
TAIZHOU MUNICIPALITY	140,000 (1992)	300 +
Inc. Wenling City	72,000 (1998)	101
Jiaojiang City	20,000	12
Dongyang City	20,000	
YIWU CITY	20,000	
KAIHUA COUNTY	6,000 (1997)	60 +
QINGTIAN COUNTY	60–70,000 (2002)	
JINHUA COUNTY	24,633 (1981)	308

APPENDIX 4

A bibliography on the Chinese Church

This bibliography has been drawn up for the general Christian reader who would like to know more about the recent history of the Church in China. Some books are out of print but all are available through libraries.

Pre-1949

BROOMHALL, J *Hudson Taylor and China's Open Century.* (Hodder & Stoughton, 1981–85 in seven volumes)

COVELL, Ralph, *Confucius, the Buddha & Christ: A History of the Gospel in Chinese.* (Orbis, 1986)

CROSSMAN, Eileen, *Mountain Rain: A New Biography of James O Fraser.* (OMF, 1984) This tells the exciting story of the earlier Lisu revival.

FAIRBANK, John K., *The Missionary Enterprise in China and America.* (Harvard University Press, 1974)

KINNEAR, Angus, *Against the Tide: The Story of Watchman Nee.* (Victory Press, 1976)

LATOURETTE, Kenneth Scott, *A History of Christian Missions in China.* (SPCK, 1929; reprinted Ch'eng-Wen Publishing Co., Taipei, Taiwan,1975) This is a classic work of nearly 1,000 pages, but unfortunately only covers up to 1928.

LUTZ, Jessie (Ed.), *Christian Missions in China – Evangelists of What?* (D.C. Heath, 1965) This is an important compendium of differing views.

LYALL, Leslie, *Flame for God: The Story of John Sung.* (OMF, 1960) John Sung was China's greatest evangelist.

LYALL, leslie, *Three of China's Mighty Men : David Yang, Watchman Nee & Wang Mingdao.* (OMF, 1974)

MOFFETT, Samuel, *A History of Christianity in Asia Vol. I: Beginnings to 1500.* (Harper Collins, 1992) Excellent coverage of the Nestorians in China.

NAKAMURA, Hajime. *Ways of thinking of Eastern Peoples: India, China, Tibet, Japan.* (Kegan Paul, 1997) A profound treatment of this vital subject for all Western Christians seeking to understand the Chinese people.

SPENCE, Jonathan, *God's Chinese Son – The Taiping Heavenly Kingdom of Hong Xiuquan.* (Harper Collins, 1996) A MUST-READ! Puts all present-day pseudo-Christian sects in China in clear perspective.

STEER, Roger, *J Hudson Taylor: A Man in Christ.* (OMF, 1990)

WONG Ming-Dao, *A Stone Made Smooth.* (Mayflower, 1981) This is his autobiography up to 1950.

Post-1949 until the Cultural Revolution

BUSH, Richard, *Religion in Communist China.* (Abingdon Press, 1970) The best documented source for pre-Cultural Revolution Christianity.

CLIFF, Norman, *Fierce the Conflict* (Ontario: Joshua Press, 2001) A moving account of eight Chinese Christian leaders who suffered during the 1950s–60s.

HARVEY, Thomas A., *Acquainted with Grief: Wang Mingdao's Stand for the Persecuted Church in China.* (Brazos Press, 2002) A very important book, showing how Wang Mingdao's stand for the Lordship of Christ over the church places him firmly in the heroic tradition of the Puritans, Covenanters, German Confessing Church, etc., and how the TSPM collaborates with the totalitarian State.

JONES, Francis Price, *Documents of the Three Self Movement*. (New York: National Council of the Churches of Christ in the USA, 1963)

CHANG, Jung & HALLIDAY, Jon *Mao: The Unknown Story*. (Jonathan Cape, 2005) A bombshell! Demolishing many long-accepted myths about Mao, who was responsible for the deaths of some 70 million Chinese. Essential reading to see the church in context.

LEE, Lydia, *A Living Sacrifice: The Life Story of Allen Yuan*. (Sovereign World, 2001.) Moving biography of the Beijing house-church patriarch who died in 2005.

LYALL, Leslie, *Come Wind, Come Weather*. (London: Hodder & Stoughton, 1960)

LYALL, Leslie, *Red Sky At Night*. (London: Hodder & Stoughton, 1970)

(Lyall's books contain important material on the experience of evangelicals under persecution, and the early history of the TSPM.)

McINNIS, D.E., *Religious Policy & Practice in Communist China*. (Macmillan, 1972) Valuable academic sourcebook with many documents translated.

PATTERSON, George N., *Christianity in Communist China*. (Waco & London: Word Books, 1969) Valuable source giving details of the subversion of the church in the fifties by the CCP and TSPM.

REES, Vaughan, *The Jesus Family in Communist China*. (Paternoster Press, 1959) Rare glimpses of an indigenous, communal Chinese church.

TOW, Timothy, *Wang Ming Tao and Charismatism*. (Christian Life Publishers, Singapore, 1989.)

WANG, Stephen, *The Long Road to Freedom: The Story of Wang Mingdao*. (Sovereign Word, 2001) The definitive biography by a close friend. Vital reading.

WILLIS, Helen, *Through Encouragement of the Scriptures*. (Hong Kong: Christian Bookroom, 1961) Author's experience as the last evangelical missionary to cling on in Shanghai from 1949 to 1959.

Post-Cultural Revolution (1979–2006)

ADENEY, David, *The Church's Long March*. (Regal Books, 1985)

AIKMAN, David, *Jesus in Beijing*. (Regnery, 2003) An important book on the growth of Chinese house-church Christianity with fascinating information, but marred by the author's very Western, pro-American and overly charismatic bias.

ANDERSON, Ken, *Bold as a Lamb*. (Zondervan, 1991) Biography of Samuel Lamb, house-church pastor in Guangzhou.

CHAO, Jonathan, *The China Mission Handbook: A Portrait of China and Its Church*. (Hong Kong: Chinese Church Research Centre, 1989)

COVELL, Ralph, *The Liberating Gospel in China: Christian Faith among China's Minority Peoples*. (Grand Rapids: Baker Books, 1995)

DANYUN, *Lilies Among Thorns: Chinese Christians Tell Their Stories Through Blood & Tears*. (Tonbridge: Sovereign World, 1991) Heartbreaking & inspiring.

FUNG, Raymond, *Households of God on China's Soil*. (Geneva: WCC, 1982)

HUNTER, Alan & CHAN, Kim-Kwong, *Protestantism in Contemporary China*. (Cambridge: Cambridge University Press, 1993) Balanced overview.

LAMBERT, Tony, *The Resurrection of the Chinese Church*. (London/Sydney: Hodder & Stoughton, 1991. Revised edition: Wheaton: Shaw /OMF, 1994) Author's M. Phil thesis on the church giving much original documentation. .

LYALL, Leslie, *New Spring in China*. (Hodder & Stoughton, 1979)

LYALL, Leslie, *God Reigns in China*. (Hodder & Stoughton, 1985)

LYALL, Leslie (Ed.), *The Phoenix Rises: The Phenomenal Growth of Eight Chinese Churches*. (OMF, 1992)

MCINNIS, D.E., *Religion in China Today: Policy & Practice*. (New York: Orbis, 1989) Many documents covering all religions.

PATTERSON, Ross, *China: The Hidden Miracle*. (Sovereign World, 1993)

WHYTE, Bob, *Unfinished Encounter: China & Christianity*. (Collins,1988)

Those wishing to obtain information on a regular basis and to pray for China are invited to subscribe to *CHINA PRAYER NEWS* (monthly) and *CHINA INSIGHT* (bi-monthly). You may also be interested in obtaining up-to-date information about opportunities to teach English, study Chinese or work in other capacities in China. The Chinese government welcomes qualified professionals in many fields. Please write to the OMF office in your country. See addresses on page 6.

NOTES

Chapter 4: Renewal in the Three-Self churches

1   Letter to the Religious Affairs Bureau, 26 November 1988
2   "Document 19", 31 March 1982
3   *Shaxun*, December 1996

Chapter 5: The house church movement

1   Court document from Huainan City dated 26 June 1984
2   There are several biographies available now. The most popular are: *Taylor: Biography of James Hudson Taylor* (Hodder and Stoughton – many impressions) or the fuller version on which it is based: *The growth of a soul / The growth of a work of God* (two volumes: OMF International). For a readable modern biography see Roger Steer, *J Hudson Taylor: A Man in Christ* (OMF International, 1990 and later impressions)
3   *Bridge*, March 1986
4   Document dated 10 December 1997 published in *China News and Church Report*, 17 August 1998
5   CNCR, 21 December 1998
6   Translation taken and very slightly abridged from CNCR, 21 December 1998
7   Compass Direct, 18 December 1998
8   South China Morning Post, 3 December 1998
9   Compass Direct, 19 February 1999
10   Compass Direct, 19 February 1999

Chapter 6: "The Jesus Nest" : Revival in Henan

1   *Jidujiao Luntan*, 21 February 1982
2   *China & the Church Today*, Sept–Oct 1984
3   Letter dated 3 January 1994
4   This was easily one month's wages for peasants at this time.

Chapter 7: Church growth in Anhui

1   South China Morning Post, 2 June 1996

[2] *Anhui Daily*, late November 1995

Chapter 8: Revival among the tribes

[1] 1990 census
[2] 63 per cent of adult Lisu above the age of fifteen, according to the State Statistical Bureau in 1990
[3] See Brill, 1993 *Peaks of Faith: Protestant Mission in Revolutionary China*, T'ien Ju-K'ang
[4] Shimenkan – the great Methodist revival centre started by Samuel Pollard in 1904
[5] *The Stone Threshold*, by Zhang Dan, Yunnan Educational Press, 1992
[6] ANS December 1996

Chapter 9: Signs and wonders

[1] *Areopagus*, Advent, 1993
[2] See Chapter 9 for details
[3] *Bridge*, Jan–Feb 1985
[4] *Bridge*, August 1994
[5] *Bridge*, July 1989
[5] See *Wang Ming Tao and Charismatism* by Timothy Tow, Christian Life Publishers, Singapore 1989.
[6] See *A Living Sacrifice – The Life Story of Allen Yuan* by Lydia Lee, Sovereign World, 2001, especially pages 247–48.

Chapter 10: Ravening wolves

[1] *Ruhe Shibie Yiduan [How to Detect Heresies]*, Weng Yage, TSPM/CCC, 2005
[2] *Changchun Evening News*, 22 October 1992
[3] These include : Zongjiao, *Jiaopai Yu Xiejiao [Religions, Sects and Cults]*, Guangxi People's Publishing House, 2004. ISBN 7-219-04966-8/B. This is a collection of papers delivered at an international forum on cults held in Beijing in November 2002 and attended by scholars from South Korea, the United States, Russia and China. Also: *Xiejiao de Mimi [The Secrets of Cults]*, Wu Dongsheng, Social Sciences Academic Press, 2004. ISBN 7-80190-457-5. See also "How to Detect Heresies", [Note 1, above.]

Chapter 11: Suffer the little children

1   Report of 7 May 1982, David Adeney
2   Christian Communications Ltd, Hong Kong, report, November 1998
3   There is a *Children's Story Book of the New Testament* published by Amity, but it cost £10. Hardly something that the average family could afford.

Chapter 12: Party members find Christ

1   *Zhengming Monthly*, No. 4 1990
    Alongside the spiritual awakening which has affected party membership is the recent phenomenon of people moving into more lucrative jobs which provide the opportunity for social mobility.

Chapter 13: Intellectuals find Christ

1   *Baokan Wenzhai*, 7 February 1989
2   Cheng Ming, Hong Kong, August 1994

Chapter 14: Evangelism explosion!

1   11 December 1997
2   *Tianfeng*, January 1998

Chapter 15: Lessons from the church in China

1   *Zongjiao*, February 1988
2   Summarised from Hunter and Chan, *Protestantism in Contemporary China* (Cambridge University Press, 1993)
3   See E. Lowe *China's House Churches: the Sociological and Sovereign Work of God*. (Unpublished thesis, 1996)
4   Letter from Jiangxi, 26 October 1995
5   Jung Chang, *Wild Swans* (HarperCollins, 1991)

Appendix 3: A survey of church growth province by province

1   ANS, May 1998

2   *Tianfeng*, November 1997
3   Amity Newsletter, March 1997
4   Shantou TSPM leaflet dated October 1991
5   *Tianfeng*, October 1995
6   *Bridge*, June 1992
7   *Tianfeng*, August 1998
8   *Tianfeng*, August 1995
9   ANS, October 1994
10 ANS, June 1996
11 *The Tablet* 8, June 1996
12 *Tianfeng*, March 1990
13 *Tianfeng*, June 1997
14 *Zongjiao*, No. 2, 1990
15 ANS, June 1998
16 *Tianfeng*, August 1998
17 ANS, April 1994
18 ANS, May 1998
19 *Mowang Shenzhou*, January 1994 and *Bridge*, March 1985
20 *Bridge*, October 1988
21 ANS, April 1995
22 *Bridge*, August 1990
23 *Tianfeng*, July 1994
24 *Bridge*, September 1990
25 Yichun People's Government Document of 3 June 1992
26 ANS, October 1994
27 ANS, June 1996
28 *Tianfeng*, November 1997
29 ANS, January 1994
30 *Tianfeng*, May 1990
31 *Tianfeng*, February 1997
32 ANS, August 1998
33 ANS, April 1997
34 *Bai Shing*, No 17. 1981
35 *Bridge*, May 1993
36 *Zongjiao*, 1–2, 1995
37 *Bridge*, August 1996
38 CNCR, February 1997
39 *South China Morning Post*, 16 August 1966
40 *Tianfeng*, September 1998
41 *Bai Shing*, No. 17 1981
42 ANS, September 1997
43 ANS, December 1996

TIMELINE OF MODERN CHINESE HISTORY
1900–2008

1900 Boxer Rebellion and Siege of Beijing Legations. Massacre of many Chinese Christians & missionaries.

1911 Fall of the Qing Empire and establishment of the Republic.

1914–18 First World War. China allied with UK and US against Germany.

1916–26 Ascendancy of the Warlords who fight for domination in a divided China.

1919 May 4th student protest: beginnings of political and cultural reform movement.

1921 Chinese Communist Party (CCP) founded in Shanghai.

1931 Japanese move into Manchuria.

1932 Japanese set up puppet state of Manchukuo with Puyi as "Last Emperor".

1934–35 Mao Zedong's epic Long March which saved the Communists from encirclement.

1936 Chiang Kai-shek forced to agree to a united front with the CCP against the Japanese invaders.

1937 Marco Polo Bridge incident near Beijing: Japanese invade north China.

1937–45 "Free China" led by Chiang Kai-shek moves west to Chungking; Mao builds base at Yan'an.

1945 Defeat of the Japanese and end of World War II

1946–49 Civil War between the Nationalists (Chiang Kai-shek) and CCP (Mao Zedong).

1949 October 1st: Establishment of the People's Republic of China by Mao.

1950 Beginnings of Three-Self Patriotic Movement to control the Church.

1952 Withdrawal of all foreign missionaries from China completed.

1955 Wang Mingdao, noted evangelical leader, arrested; later sentenced to twenty-three years in prison for his faith.

1956 Brief period of liberalisation known as "The Hundred Flowers".

1958 CCP launches the "Great Leap Forward"; TSPM unites and closes most churches.

1958–62 Failure of the communes and Mao's extreme economic policies: 20 million people starve to death.

1959 USSR withdraws technicians from China. End of Sino-Russian alliance.

1966–76 The Cultural Revolution launched by Mao who encourages the Red Guards: it devastates China.

1966 Red Guards close few remaining churches. Church goes underground for thirteen years.

1972 Nixon visits China. First reports emerge from south China of secret house church activities.

1976 Death of Mao; fall of the leftist "Gang of Four". House churches operate more freely.

1978–97 The Era of Deng Xiaoping and the "Four Modernisations" and economic open-door policy.

1978 Rise to power of Deng Xiaoping; rehabilitation of intellectuals and religious people. US recognises PRC as sole government of China.

1979 First churches reopened; TSPM re-established by CCP under the Religious Affairs Bureau.

1980 Formation of the China Christian Council to reopen churches and seminaries.

1983 "Anti-spiritual Pollution Campaign" unleashed by CCP: many Christians persecuted and jailed.

1987 "Anti-bourgeois Liberalisation Campaign" by CCP; period of pressure on the Church begins.

1989 4 June: Democracy Movement suppressed in Beijing and throughout China. CCP liberals fall from power.

1992 Deng "goes south" to Canton giving a boost to the economic "Open-Door" policy.

1997 Death of Deng (February): Jiang Zemin peacefully takes power. Return of Hong Kong to Chinese control (July).

1997–99 Period of tightening control of the house churches with enforced registration and arrests.

1999 Celebration in Nanjing as the 20 millionth copy of the Bible is printed within China. NATO bombing of Chinese Embassy in Belgrade; Sino-Western relations become tense.

2002 Hu Jintao takes over leadership of the CCP.

2003 March: Hu Jintao becomes President of China.
December: Gas disaster in Chongqing kills 191.

2004 Over 70,000 riots and demonstrations in China as the gap between rich and poor grows.

2005 June: Nearly 600 house-church leaders including students and professors arrested in Jilin. Most soon released.
August 16: Death of Beijing house-church leader Allen Yuan, aged 91.
November: Beijing decides to vaccinate 14 billion poultry to stop avian flu.
Visit of President Bush to China.

2008 Beijing due to host the Olympic Games and welcome the world.